UNIVERSITIES AND LIFELONG LEARNING SERIES

University engagement and environmental sustainability

I0099689

MANCHESTER
1824

Manchester University Press

UNIVERSITIES AND LIFELONG LEARNING SERIES

Series editor:
Professor Michael Osborne (University of Glasgow)

Universities and lifelong learning analyses the external engagement activities of universities and third- level institutions and is concerned with the range of activity that lies beyond the traditional mission of teaching and research. This is an area that until now has seldom been explored in depth and has rarely if ever been treated in a holistic manner.

Lifelong learning, the arts and community cultural engagement in the contemporary university: International perspectives
Edited by Darlene Clover and Kathy Sanford

Knowledge, democracy and action: Community-university research partnerships in global perspectives Edited by Budd Hall, Edward Jackson, Rajesh Tandon, Jean-Marc Fontan and Nirmala Lall

A new imperative: Regions and higher education in difficult times
Michael Osborne, Chris Duke and Bruce Wilson

University engagement and environmental sustainability

Edited by
Patricia Inman and Diana L. Robinson

Manchester University Press

Copyright © Manchester University Press 2014

While copyright in the volume as a whole is vested in Manchester University Press, copyright in individual chapters belongs to their respective authors, and no chapter may be reproduced wholly or in part without the express permission in writing of both author and publisher.

Published by Manchester University Press
Altrincham Street, Manchester M1 7JA, UK
www.manchesteruniversitypress.co.uk

British Library Cataloguing-in-Publication Data is available

Library of Congress Cataloging-in-Publication Data is available

ISBN 978 1 5261 0720 6 *paperback*

First published by Manchester University Press in hardback 2014

This edition first published 2016

The publisher has no responsibility for the persistence or accuracy of URLs for any external or third-party internet websites referred to in this book, and does not guarantee that any content on such websites is, or will remain, accurate or appropriate.

Printed by Lightning Source

This book is dedicated to the memory of
Sandra Streed, a passionate advocate for the environment

Contents

CONTENTS

Figures and tables

Figures

Tables

List of contributors

IDOWU BIAO is professor of Lifelong Learning at the Department of Adult Education, University of Botswana. He was previously Deputy Director and Ag. Director at the Institute of Extra-Mural Studies, National University of Lesotho and Professor of Adult Education at the Department of Adult and Continuing Education, University of Calabar, Nigeria.

MORGAN CHAWAWA is the director of a community engagement project in Ghanzi District, Botswana, funded by the Kellogg Foundation Project, in partnership with Ba Isago University, Gaborone, Botswana. He is a graduate of Georgia State University and Immanuel Theological Seminary, both in Georgia, USA. He taught political science at DeKalb College, USA, for six years. Dr. Chawawa has worked as a district administrator and town clerk in Zimbabwe. He was a lecturer at the University of Zimbabwe and Chair of the Department of Educational Management, Zimbabwe Open University.

STEVE GARLICK has professorial positions at the University of Newcastle and the University of Technology, Sydney, Australia. He is a spatial economist and an applied ethicist. He is an academic, advocate, activist and political party leader. His publication record focuses on knowledge systems, human capital, innovation, environmental sustainability, wildlife emotion and behaviour, and trans-species learning. He has undertaken many international reviews of higher education and regional development and is an inaugural fellow of the Australian Universities Community Engagement Alliance. With wife Rosemary, Dr. Garlick operates a self-funded wildlife recovery and research centre for traumatised and severely injured native mammals. He is the founder and president of the newly formed Animal Justice Party of Australia – Australia's only political party devoted to animal well-being.

PATRICIA INMAN is a Senior Research Associate for International Engagement for the Center for Governmental Studies at Northern Illinois University. Dr. Inman's research interests include asset-based community development, engaging educational institutions, and sustainable regional policy, particularly as it relates to the development of local food systems.

ROBERTA LAMMERS-CAMPBELL is a Senior Lecturer at Loyola University of Chicago, where she regularly teaches general biology, plant biology, and wetland ecology. She is also the Special Assistant to the Vice Provost for Ecological Restoration and is in charge of carrying out wetland and oak-hickory woodland restoration at Loyola's Retreat and Ecology Campus. Dr. Lammers earned her Ph.D. from the University of Minnesota, where she studied plant and insect communities in a wetland.

JULIE MATTHEWS is an interdisciplinary researcher with a background in education, sociology, and cultural studies. Her work brings socio-cultural perspectives to bear on a broad range of contemporary issues and problems. She has expertise in postcolonial, Foucauldian, and feminist theory and an interest in visual research methods. As Director of Research in the Faculty of Arts and Business she is responsible for mentoring staff and students. She is also Associate Director of the sustainability research centre Transforming Regions.

CHRISTOPHER D. MERRETT is Director of the Illinois Institute for Rural Affairs (IIRA) and Professor of Geography at Western Illinois University. He earned a Ph.D. from the University of Iowa with a focus on regional development and international trade. Before he became director, Merrett's duties at the IIRA included research, community outreach, and teaching. His current research focuses on cooperatives and community development. Merrett co-edited (with Norman Walzer) two books on this topic: *A Cooperative Approach to Local Economic Development* (2001) and *Cooperatives and Local Development: Theory and Applications for the 21st Century* (2003). He has also published in a range of journals on topics such as community development, value-added agriculture, cooperatives, and rural development.

BRIONY PENN is a geographer who leads an active career in environmental education, community action, and design, and has won awards for her books and articles. She works to combine research and advocacy in temperate ecosystems. More information can be found at www.thewildside.ca/bio.html.

WAPULA NELLY RADITLOANENG serves as an Associate Professor in the Department of Adult Education, University of Botswana, Gaborone. She is an interdisciplinary sociologist and an adult and health educator with more than thirty years of professional experience. Her areas of research, publications and activism include the social context of adult and continuing education with particular emphasis on gender issues (education and empowerment of women and men, gender-based violence, gender disaggregated impacts of HIV/AIDs), poverty (multi-dimensional definitions, community service and engagement, educational and entrepreneurship interventions), and lifelong learning (knowledge economy, non-formal education, and post literacy).

HOWARD RICHARDS holds the title Professor Emeritus of Philosophy and Peace and Global Studies at Earlham College, Richmond, Indiana, USA, a Quaker college where he taught for thirty-five years. He was the founder of the Peace and Global Studies Program there and co-founder of the Business and Nonprofit Management Program. Now he divides his time between the private practice of law and continuing his research and teaching.

DIANA ROBINSON is the Director of the Center for Governmental Studies at Northern Illinois University. She has extensive experience in workforce development and has served the state of Illinois as the Deputy Director of Adult Education.

JESUS GRANADOS SÁNCHEZ holds a Ph.D. in education from the Universitat Autònoma de Barcelona (UAB). A graduate in Geography, he holds a master's degree in social sciences education and a master's degree in environmental education and communication.

LINDA SILKA, PHD, directs UMaine's Margaret Chase Smith Policy Center and is a Professor in the School of Economics. Prior to moving to the University of Maine, she was a faculty member for three decades at the University of Massachusetts Lowell where she directed the Center for Family, Work, Community and served as the Special Assistant to the UML Provost for Community Outreach and Partnerships. Recent research partnerships she has facilitated include the NIEHS-funded *Southeast Asian Environmental Justice Partnership* and the *New Ventures Partnership,* the HUD-funded *Community Outreach Partnership Center* and *Diverse Healthy Homes Initiative,* and the *Center for Immigrant and Refugee Community Leadership and Empowerment.* Silka has written extensively on the challenges and opportunities of building research partnerships with diverse groups and has consulted internationally on how to build community-university research partnerships.

SANDRA STREED was a senior research associate for the Center for Governmental Studies at Northern Illinois University. She possessed an extensive background in business and organizational development for commercial, academic, and non-profit entities with a focus on food, agriculture, education, and sustainability. She served as a strategic advisor for a number of private, public, and academic entities, developing partnerships and providing input into the formation of the Illinois local food system.

MARGARET SUTHERLAND lectures at the University of Glasgow. She is the Director of the Scottish Network for Able Pupils and Deputy Director of the Centre for Research and Development in Adult and Lifelong Learning. She has written in the field of gifted education and is the author of two books. She is on the editorial board of the *Korean Journal of Educational Policy.* A regular speaker at conferences, she has worked across the UK and has been invited to work with staff and students in Tanzania, Malawi, Korea, and Denmark.

ROSELINE TAWO is Associate Professor at the Department of Adult and Continuing Education at the University of Calabar, where she has served as the Coordinator of the B.Ed. Consultancy Programme, Course Adviser, Examination Officer and

Industrial Attachment Coordinator. She also served as the Head of the Department of Research and Statistics in the Local Government Education Authority,

NORMAN WALZER earned a Ph.D. in Economics from the University of Illinois (Urbana). He was directly involved in creating the Governor's Rural Affairs Council and started the IIRA as part of a rural initiative in Illinois during the late 1980s. He is a senior research scholar for the Center for Governmental Studies at Northern Illinois University, where he researches local economic development practices, entrepreneurship factors associated with microenterprise starts and closures in the Midwest, and innovative community development measurement approaches.

Preface

This book is part of a series sponsored by the PASCAL International Observatory. PASCAL is a not-for-profit, non-governmental organization dedicated to transforming universities through meaningful engagement in regional issues and generating collaborative knowledge to address those issues. PASCAL draws on cross-disciplinary and trans-national ideas to enhance place management, social capital, and lifelong learning. Transcending political boundaries and the associated funding streams requires innovative policy development and implementation.

This book is a collection of international case studies representing the four PASCAL centres. Four continents are represented: RMIT University in Australia, the University of South Africa in Africa, the University of Glasgow in Europe, and Northern Illinois University in North America.

Universities are well positioned to not only influence but participate in social change. This book is a product of an organization whose mission is to transform universities so that they can better serve in this way. By honouring place in the context of bioregions, listening to communities as they identify their issues, and generating knowledge with these communities, we develop healthier spaces.

Special thanks to Janiece Bollie and Sandra Petit for providing technical support for this publication.

Introduction

Patricia Inman and Diana L. Robinson

Universities have historically generated knowledge outside specific local contexts. These pure research methodologies produce knowledge that is carefully partitioned from the practical realities of a phenomenon. This book suggests that a world in peril requires us to question this approach, particularly in the field of environmental sustainability. Environmental health affects everyone and requires integrated and interdisciplinary answers to complex issues. This requires bold action and a radical take on the world. The term 'radical' is derived from the Latin *radix* or 'root'; a radical spirit is one that searches for meaning and affirms community. The community, in this case, is an environment that supports diverse life.

An institution looking at issues within this ecological context must consider diverse perspectives and assets. Universities traditionally are more comfortable with standardized curriculum and bounded knowledge generation. It takes a courageous institution to honour difference and incorporate another's take on the world, but honouring the indigenous is what a radical university is about. How else will we come to truly know the natural world and find our place within it?

Institutions that seek diversity must accept a certain loss of control and inability to predict what they will encounter. The chapters in this volume will provide new perspectives and frames of reference for transforming universities by engaging in the development of resilient communities. According to the American Planning Association, resilience describes the capacity of a city or town to thrive in the face of social, economic, or environmental challenges. A resilient city reduces its dependence on natural resources (land, water, materials, and energy) while simultaneously improving its quality of life (ecological environment, public health, housing, employment, and community) so that it can better fit within local, regional, and global ecosystems.

The environment has become the victim of an economic system that assumes endless growth. The increasing tension between those who use more than their share and those who stand powerless as they do leads us to the concept of 'right relationship'. This suggests the current economic model cannot be 'fixed'. Instead, we must unleash the power of imagination to build a new sustainable foundation in providing basic essentials for all as we nurture the earth's community. What better to do this than our institutions of higher education? However, as our opening chapter suggests, we must rethink thinking. This book strives to integrate scientific understanding with an ethical stance. The theme that runs through each chapter is that of the tension that accompanies such an endeavour and the need for innovation as we challenge the assumption of unbridled growth. The discussion presented in this publication focuses on research agendas rather than what exists in our universities as 'service learning' for students. While programmes such as these are vitally important in connecting to our regions, this publication looks more broadly at providing a path towards engaging our institutions of higher education in environmental sustainability.

The Global University Network for Innovation (GUNi) has written extensively on the topic of higher education's commitment to sustainability. One of the latest reports describes opportunities open to academics, university leaders, policy makers, members of civil society, and the business community to promote healthy regional development. While many institutions of higher education are comfortable with 'greening' themselves, GUNi suggests that true sustainability will require a much stronger commitment to institutional change in culture and design. The chapters in this book address this need for a deeper commitment, which includes developing a vision or mission on sustainable development, changing incentive systems to promote interdisciplinary work, engaging the local community, providing ownership and participation in sustainability initiatives, and monitoring the implementation of sustainable development contents in curricula.

The book is organized into two parts. Part I, 'Laying the foundation', offers a broad view of what an engaged university should look like as it relates to environmental sustainability. Part II, 'Studies of environmental sustainability', provides specific examples of various university projects in environmental sustainability. Common themes heard throughout the publication include:

- The complexity of dealing with environmental issues;
- The need for interdisciplinary research;
- The need for new methodologies and data analysis in addressing issues of environmental sustainability;
- The need for universities to listen to community stakeholders rather than consult;
- The need for connected knowledge production;
- The need for research that honors place rather than abstract knowledge generation;
- The need to respect indigenous knowledge; and
- The importance of relationships.

It is clear that we need to look at methodologies that establish common ground between universities and situated regions. Our opening chapter contends that education has failed to provide leadership in caring for our environment. Institutions advocate plundering resources to promote 'human' development, ignoring all else that supports our human lives. This chapter advocates a 'third way' of knowing about nature in universities, predicated on an ethic of care and 'being-for' relationism that connects the energy of each element in the environment with its broader context. It is not enough to 'know': we must 'know for' the sustainability of our natural world. Garlick and Matthews promote a concept of 'ecoversity' to be used by institutions of higher education as a framework for their own sustainability transformation and engagement with our natural world. The knowledge and human capital of the university must contribute to a greater good that embraces all forms of life.

Chapter 2 takes this argument one step further. Richards makes the point that 'ecology' extends itself well beyond a study of projects of conservation. The study of environmental sustainability requires us to come to terms with the more complex and ethically sound and ecologically constituted ways of thinking that characterize many indigenous and non-Western ways of thinking. Major changes in the relationships of humans to the earth require universities to play significant roles in this transformation of thought. Dr. Richards makes the controversial point that universities must rethink what they do. Indigenous knowledge systems (IKS) in the curriculum of higher education posit philosophical, ethical, moral, and metaphysical challenges to all areas of current academic systems of thought as well as the practices that result. This chapter recounts the history of how universities have arrived at such ungrounded practice. This chapter, which advocates for the transformation of the university, invokes traditional African wisdom and combines it with other insights from different parts of the world. It builds on the concept of human development as creative capacity building and the ethical construction of life. The content criticizes modernity not to destroy it but to transform it by enlarging it to include the moral authority of 'community'.

Education, the area to which we usually first turn for human transformation, has failed us when it comes to environmental matters. Much of the environmental mismanagement we see around us today has come from the decisions and actions of 'educated' people, and all the talk of an 'education revolution' by governments seems unwilling to address the real question of 'what kind of education?' Chapter 2 explores this question.

The discussion of the value of place-based knowledge continues in Chapter 3. Western knowledge is often linked to universality and spatial transferability, while indigenous knowledge is considered to be part of a traditional and outdated way of life. Development agencies such as the World Bank and institutions of higher education have sought to reconcile these two apparently discrete forms of knowledge. In recent times the value of indigenous knowledge has come to be recognized in various fields including medicine, agriculture, science, and education. Alongside this has been growing recognition that if communities and universities are to engage as co-workers in finding solutions to transnational issues then there has to be meaningful dialogue between the epistemologically different knowledge systems. Using the work of Wenger (1998), Chapter 3 explores the role of universities within such dialogic opportunities and considers how an apparent range of contending and contested knowledge systems can be brought together to create a communities of practice.

The abandonment of regional geography in the mid-twentiethth century through pressures of globalization, urbanization, and corporatization lost two generations of local knowledge and engagement. The studying of place, finding the genius of loci and helping communities to articulate the uniqueness and relevance of place, has been left to poets, activists, and guerrilla geographers. Chapter 4 looks at the role and tasks of guerrilla geography in the renaissance of place, community mapping, and naming of place, and ultimately the protection and restoration of place through the word and illustrations of one practitioner from Canada's rarest ecosystem – the Garry oak meadows overlooking the Salish Sea. Up until 1991, this drought-adapted ecosystem, now the focus of research on ecosystem resilience in climate change, had no name, no map, no cultural identity beyond Little England, no recognition from academia, and no protection.

With the return to localism and demand for regional solutions, what is the role for young guerrilla geographers in their respective places across Canada? The stories and maps that make sense of our relationship to the land will be important in creating resilient communities. This discussion will help university students chart a course of meaningful work as they pick up the lost stories of their place and weave them with the new. It suggests ways for the academic community to support, educate, and legitimize the next generation of guerrilla geographers.

The final chapter of this section explores the challenges posed by the unsustainability of higher education institutions and discusses the barriers preventing them from overcoming these difficulties. Higher education has contributed to the generation of knowledge and actions that have led to the crisis situation we are currently experiencing. We must start to reconceptualize our understanding of higher education institutions in a way that will bring about sustainable development in society – in short, to stop being part of the problem and become part of the solution. The need to give sustainable development meaning in a specific context involving multiple stakeholders makes these concepts attractive from an educational perspective as they require joint meaning-making, co-creation of new knowledge, collaborative learning, and, indeed, critiquing. GUNi developed a study to establish what barriers and possible solutions higher education institutions encounter when trying to implement changes in their performance for achieving sustainability. The chapter presents findings.

Part II presents specific examples of successful programmes that have addressed the issues discussed in the first part of the book. The first three chapters focus on food production as a vehicle for environmental sustainability. Chapter 6 discusses opportunities within the development of local food systems and presents an example of an 'enlightened' institution of higher education that has been a leader in embedding environmental issues in their curriculum as well as their everyday operations. Northland College in beautiful Ashland, Wisconsin, was founded in 1892 by community members who 'wanted to provide a unique educational opportunity for residents of the region'. Ashland's curriculum emphasizes environmental stewardship in an amazing array of programmes described in this chapter.

Soil erosion is a major ecological problem in Nigeria in general, but particularly in south-eastern Nigeria. In addition to being a major issue, the incidence of soil erosion in Nigeria is a long-standing problem as it has been a subject for numerous high level discussions since the beginning of the twentieth century.

Agricultural practice is one of the suspected causes of soil erosion in the country, yet concerted efforts seem to be lacking in effectively tackling this menace. One weakness in the process of tackling soil erosion in Nigeria is linked to the supply of fertilizers for purposes of agricultural practice. Chapter 7 examines the triple relationship existing among erosion, agricultural practice, and access to fertilizers in Nigeria. It analyses the nature of the relationship that should exist among these three phenomena. Finally, it calls attention to the role that higher education should play in helping to solve this hydra-headed monster.

The discussion of environmental challenges in African agriculture is continued in Chapter 8. The San community in D'kar and surrounding villages has developed a community based planning programme focused on a community farm. The San are a population who has a history of marginalization and poverty within Botswana. The farm serves as a community organizer as well as a food source and is administered by the San women. The programme highlighted in this case study was developed to build leadership systems and capabilities for the women of the village while developing sustainable business opportunities for economic transformation. The tension between addressing issues of sustainability and business development are discussed.

Chapter 9 discusses alternative research paradigms to address the 'wicked' problems presented by the complexity of environmental issues. Higher education has splintered into disciplinary enclaves in which the goal often becomes one of doing research to address disciplinary concerns and little else. On topics such as sustainability, there is an urgent need to become interdisciplinary and solutions focused. Maine's Sustainability Solutions Initiative (SSI) offers an exemplar for addressing complex environmental problems. This chapter presents a model for universities as they address a range of issues that interlink social and environmental concerns.

Chapter 10 continues the discussion of complex measures as it suggests the need for strategizing environmental engagement within our institutions of higher education. A model is presented and an example of its use in Chiapas, Mexico, is highlighted. While this publication advocates for institutions of higher education that adhere to a value-laden curriculum, it also advocates fresponsible strategic planning.

The book concludes with the narrative of caring. Loyola University of Chicago is a Jesuit institution of higher education whose main campus is located in a crowded urban setting. The university has organized a satellite campus for both undergraduate and graduate students that focuses on restoration of the environmentally sensitive wetlands that surround the property as well as supporting life off the grid with organic farming practices supporting a healthy food system. This takes place in a context of moral and ethical focus, unusual in most universities. Chapter 11 highlights the challenges of listening to community and establishing relationships as they integrate sustainable practices in an innovative and unconventional curriculum.

The reader will note the diverse voices in this publication. These are intentional. The authors in this publication are passionate about their work. We have structured each chapter so that this intensity illuminates the narrative.

Reference

Global Network for Innovation (GUNi) (2011). *Higher Education's Commitment to Sustainability: From Understanding to Action*. London: Palgrave Macmillan.

PART I

Laying the foundation

1

University responsibility in a world of environmental catastrophe: cognitive justice, engagement and an ethic of care in learning

Steve Garlick and Julie Matthews

Introduction

Education, the area to which we usually first turn for human transformation, has failed us when it comes to environmental matters (Orr, 1992). Much of the environmental mismanagement we see around us today comes from the decisions and actions of 'educated' people and, despite talk of the need for an 'education revolution', governments are unwilling to address the real question of 'what kind of education – what kind of learning?' (Orr, 2010).

Education has provided little leadership and few conceptual tools to assist us to better understand our environment and how we can lead the world towards a more sustainable future. We continue to educate society in ways oblivious to the mounting crisis of unsustainability and catastrophe (Orr, 1992). By reinforcing human exceptionalism … education can equip people merely to be more effective vandals of the earth (Orr, 1992, p. 4). Human exceptionalism has contributed greatly to our current environmental mess, but can it help us clean it up? We say this will require other kinds of learning and sources of knowledge and other kinds of relations and understandings.

It is unfortunate that university solutions to the significant environmental issues of the day are, it seems, predicated on a diet of managerialism, funding demands, competitive ratings, institutional instrumentalism, and path-dependent curricula based on a 'knowing about' pedagogy rather than one that enhances human capability in a 'being-for' sense (Bauman, 1995). The 'knowing about' approach to learning and knowledge acquisition has proved spectacularly disastrous in dealing with critical concerns for our planet.

As publicly funded institutions of learning, it is not enough for universities to argue their role as being simply to generate human capital and knowledge to meet the vague market requirements and functions of society, economy, culture, and the environment. Universities must surely have a 'larger purpose, a larger sense of mission, a larger clarity of direction in the national life' (Boyer, 1996, p. 20). Elsewhere, we have argued that this larger role of universities involves instructing a 'being-for' moral value of connectivity that recognizes in our learning a close connection with and responsiveness to all the diverse locations, beings and conditions of the natural world (Garlick and Palmer, 2008; Garlick and Matthews, 2009).

It is argued in this chapter that there is a need for a 'third way' of knowing about nature in universities, predicated on an ethic of care (Noddings, 1984; Kheel, 2008) and 'being-for' (Bauman, 1995) relationism that connects the energy of each element in the environment with its broader context. This relational ethic of care is a different and much deeper knowing than a mere 'knowing about' the environment and its inhabitants. It suggests that educated humans through their knowledge should not simply apply 'a good at' approach to the environment, but should instead involve themselves in 'a good for' way, which engages with the broader environment and all those who depend on it. It sees the scholar not only as erudite, but as activist and advocate, as politician, as carer, as rehabilitator, as listener. The knowledge and human capital of the university must contribute to a greater good that embraces all forms of life.

In a sense such an approach to learning parallels the notion of cognitive justice in knowledge acquisition and usage. It challenges the epistemological foundation of northern science (Santos, 2007).

The term 'cognitive justice' was coined by Visvanathan (1997) to represent the need for a plurality of knowledge sources and processes to offset the straight-jacket disciplinary culture of traditional human science analysis. It is an ethical principle that equally values diverse sources of knowledge (knowers) without drawing conclusions about relative knowledge superiority. Such diverse and new knowledge sources could even extend beyond indigenous peoples and indigenous knowledge systems (IKS) (Odora-Hoppers, 2009; SARCHi Retreat, 2012) and include wild animal or animal knowledge systems (AKS) when considering questions of environmental sustainability (Garlick, forthcoming; Garlick and Austen, 2013).

The 'ecoversity' concept has at its heart the notion of the university leading by example, taking responsibility, ensuring that daily activities engage students and communities in understanding and active participation in what it means to address the 'unsustainable core characteristics of our time' (Jucker, 2002, p. 10). The concept of the ecoversity offers universities a useful framework for their own sustainability transformation and engagement with human and non-human capability in other education sectors and contexts. Formal and informal education sectors have an important role in contributing to learning about environmental sustainability, and universities have a responsibility to engage with them in contexts such as regions, landscapes, seascapes, and habitats to ensure a relational approach. They can work with regional communities to tackle global sustainability matters in practical ways of knowledge production and distribution.

The ecoversity notion thus offers a framework for relational learning underpinned by an ethic of care, or 'being-for' the environment and its inhabitants. It connects the 'green campus' with curricular development, while extending into external partnerships and community and non-human relationships built around location and place (Matthews, Garlick, and Smith, 2009), and inspires all universities to engage with and transform their regional communities on sustainability matters.

What kind of education?

Modern higher education was founded on ideas about a world that no longer exists. We have created a different planet, a different human nature, and a different global culture. These are the result of an industrial economic system, which now threatens living planetary ecosystems and the survival of all life. The problem as Orr (2010) sees it is not simply how to arrest current environmental deterioration, but how to conceive and build a durable and civilized society.

Education has failed to prepare people to live in an environmentally sustainable way, and many environmental problems are an effect of the decisions and actions of 'educated' people (Orr, 1992), but education at its best is able to create the conditions in which people refuse to participate in injustice and work to eliminate it (Giroux, 2004). The conviction that education is our best resource for achieving a just and ecological world has been reiterated in international reports such as the Brundtland report (WCED, 1987), which argued that teachers were critical to the achievement of social change, and the Talloires Declaration (1990), which commits signatories to environmental sustainability in higher education.

The Talloires Report (1990) underlined the fact that universities bear the responsibility to increase awareness of necessary knowledge and technology among future leaders of society. The report also noted that universities were microcosms of society and should therefore model environmentally responsible behaviour by practising what they preached. Wright's study of international reports into sustainability education (2002) noted that they all underline the significance of a moral and ethical rationale underlying university approaches to sustainability:

> Perhaps the most unifying theme among all declarations and policies is the ethical and moral responsibility of universities to be leaders in promoting sustainability. (Wright, 2002, p. 218)

We argue below that this is what universities can and should do. They can also do more than deliver environmental knowledge and establish green campuses. As Fien (1997) argues, environmental knowledge ('knowing about') is no longer enough. Narrow approaches to environmental education need to be connected to broader political, economic, social, cultural, and ethical matters.

Many people know that ostensibly simple human actions and choices such as how we obtain our food, how we heat and cool our houses, our technology, how we get around, and how we dispose of our waste can have catastrophic consequences for planetary survival and sustainability. As Bauman (2001, p. 4) puts it: 'what we do (or abstain from doing) may influence the conditions of life (or death) of people in places we will never visit and of generations we will never know'. It is important, therefore, that we evaluate the unique possibilities opened up by industrial technology and how they prompt actions that have untold consequences for the future of human and non-human others. For instance, producing food for animals causes soil degradation and decreases water supplies. The breadth of this sector's impact on the environment and global warming is not fully appreciated.

According to the Food and Agriculture Organization (FAO) of the United Nations (UN), the animal agriculture sector is responsible for approximately 18 per cent, or nearly one-fifth, of human-induced greenhouse gas (GHG) emissions. In nearly every step of meat, egg, and milk production, climate-changing gases are released into the atmosphere, potentially disrupting weather, temperature, and ecosystem health. Mitigating this serious problem requires immediate and far-reaching changes in current animal agriculture practices and consumption patterns (HSUS, 2011).

We need to understand the consequences and sheer magnitude of the escalating brutality our actions inflict on both humans and non-human species. In *Education after Auschwitz*, Theodor Adorno (1966) argued that the premier purpose of education was to ensure that the monstrosities of genocide and fascism would not happen again. For Adorno all education should be directed towards ensuring that the barbarism that made Auschwitz possible would never recur. In failing to educate the next generation in the ethics necessary to live sustainably and justly, we allow the rise of new forms of barbarism:

> Everybody knows what a terrifying and intolerable picture a realist painting could give to the industrial mechanical, chemical, hormonal, and genetic violence to which man has been submitting animal life for the past two centuries. Everybody knows what the production, breeding, transport, and slaughter of these animals has become. (Derrida, 2004, p. 120, cited in Matthews, 2012)

While everybody knows that species are exploited and annihilated in 'a dissimulated globalisation of cruelty, a genocide of monstrous proportions' (Matthews, 2012) – an unprecedented escalation of brutality and violence against life and nature – universities have become increasingly distracted by economic imperatives, markets, and auditing, thereby diminishing their capacity to promote an environmentally just and sustainable society. Universities rarely play a role in challenging and opposing current forms of economic rationalism and the large-scale systematic abuse of animals and nature by facilitating alternative research and engagement.

Indeed, in many cases, it is universities, for the sake of grant monies, 'good' performance assessment, public recognition, and credentialism, that embark on knowledge generation that is ethically grotesque in its abuse of farm, wild, companion, and introduced animals. On the other hand, there are many opportunities for potential alliances with rural production workers on factory farming conditions; with consumers on health questions such as antibiotics, salmonella, and bovine spongiform encephalopathy (BSE or 'mad cow disease'); with environmental movements on water pollution and other community consequences; with local farmers and growers on the destruction of small-scale producers and industries; with activists on neoliberal and global trade practices; and with other groups concerned with questions of compassion and animal ethics (Plumwood, 2000).

Learning in the modern university has been reduced to providing work certification and finding a job (Arthur, 2004). How can we form 'ethical and active citizens with capabilities in capacity-building, community development, entrepreneurship, and public activism' when the political purpose of education is overshadowed by economic agendas? (Seddon, 2004, p. 172). How can universities equip future generations to live lives relevant to the 'larger topography of their time' (Orr, 2010)? Education and the knowledge it legitimizes are not unequivocally beneficial. Education can be used for liberation but it can also be used for domination. It can be shared to the greater good or it can be restricted to generate profit and foster exclusion and elitism (Giri, 2011). It is precisely because the political, economic, and ethical purposes of education are neither self-evident nor automatically given, precisely because education has as yet offered little guidance towards environmental sustainability, biodiversity preservation, and planetary survival, that it is necessary to subject education and its institutions to critical deliberation. Education is unconnected to global environmental causes.

An ethic of care

The 'environmental crisis' is, above all, a crisis of perception. It is a crisis not only by virtue of what our culture sees, but by virtue of what it does not see (Kheel, 1993, p. 256).

The violence perpetrated against the natural world tends to be out of sight, making it difficult for many people to comprehend the negative impact of their individual behaviour. The first task of the educator is thus to make apparent the whole story, to put together the fragmented pieces and stretch the imagination to see the interrelated connectivity of life. For instance, the story of using animals as food must include an account of their brutal treatment in factory farms and slaughterhouses, the environmental impact of animal agriculture, and the impact of meat production on world hunger and human health. Only when we have all the details, and connect all the issues, will we be able to act holistically with our bodies, minds, and souls (i.e., a 'being good for' lifestyle).

Interestingly, much of the work of feminist moral theory is concerned with the development of an ethic of care, and calls into question ethical approaches concerned with the identification of particular obligations and rights. An ethic of care is based on the idea that people should care for and become actively engaged in a 'local manifestation of a particular problem', as well as understanding its environmental, economic, social, and political contexts. Dominant forms of rights-based ethics are founded on a concept of separate self that assumes individuals are in competition with one another for scarce resources (Kheel, 1993). In contrast, a feminist conception of morality based on an ethic of care anticipates that problems arise from conflicting responsibilities rather than competing rights. The resolution of problems requires decisions based on case-by-case contextual understandings and an understanding of responsibilities and relationships (Kheel, 1993).

For Plumwood (2007) the idea of human exceptionalism not only conceptualizes the world and relationships as entirely distinct and separate, but posits human superiority and moral worth over all other life forms. It is the basis of Western metaphysics and philosophy and serves as a key ideological tool of the West. Importantly, the view inferiorizes animals and environments and has allowed, and continues to allow, Western culture to ruthlessly exploit the natural, animal, and human world. Ecological theory continues to abstract animals in mass general terms as mutually replaceable, interchangeable, and disposable, while identifying humanity with a 'glorified predatory ecological role, which is only too readily given the lineaments of mastery and managerialism' (Plumwood, 2000, p. 286). However, while ecological feminism has offered valuable critiques of various anthropocentrisms and dualisms, it has yet to develop a relational ethic (Jenson, 2002).

Zygmunt Bauman's account (1995) of forms of togetherness provides a valuable tool for getting to the heart of an engaged ethic of care able to stimulate trans-formational learning. 'Being-for-the-other' is essentially located in an encounter with the other. This moment establishes a fundamental and unconditional respon-sibility to decide what would enable and enhance the other's freedom, preserva-tion, and autonomy. It involves transformational learning of the kind that Derrida spoke about with regard to a relational encounter with an animal. At the heart of Bauman's being-for ethic is consideration of the future and how the world ought to be – not simply how it is. Bauman challenges the idea that society makes us moral beings; rather he argues that societies construct what it means to be moral beings through socialization. Implicit in the way we learn morality and ethics is the idea that the only obligations we have to others are those defined by society. Care, responsibilities, relationships, circumstances, and contingencies are all subsumed to externally detailed rights and obligations.

A relational ethic of care based on 'being-for-the-other' has the capacity to generate holistic and large-scale systemic solutions to environmental matters. It goes beyond the idea of learning from fragmentary, episodic encounters with humans, non-humans, and environments to engage learners in the contexts and conditions of relations and co-presence with human and non-human others. This focus on reciprocal relations, responsibilities, and how the world must be organized to secure survival challenges consumerist social relations. The inces-sant search for unattainable happiness fostered by consumerist society, with its promotion of dissatisfaction, is for Bauman (2008) the enemy of civic education and political citizenship. Such a society promotes education based on professional learning and the values of competition, efficiency, and individualism. Practical engagement undertaken with a 'being-for-the-other' ethic of care requires the expression of compassion, kindness, trust, and mutuality. It generates knowledge through the quality of the engagement rather than in a remote assessable quantita-tive manner. Ecology without a 'being-for' ethic of care cannot have transforma-tional learning engagement with nature.

According to Noddings (1984 and 2002), a caring encounter will have three elements: First, A is consciously motivated to care for B. Second, A performs some act of care that accords with the consciousness and motivation revealed in the first element. Third, and significantly, B recognizes that A cares for B. According to Noddings, there is no contractual requirement in this last element for B to exhibit any mutuality or reciprocity.

The ecoversity and engaged learning

The goal of the ecoversity, following Sacks (2008), is to teach us that we are part of the world and intimately connected to all its other entities. It seeks to share knowledge, identify local or global problems and solutions, stimulate ethical debates, and challenge unsustainable development and the excesses of transnational capitalism (Matthews, Garlick, and Smith, 2009). Rather than integrating environmental education and education for sustainability into universities, the idea of ecoversity suggests that universities need to transform themselves into the integrated holistic communities implied by sustainability perspectives (Sterling, 2004).

The concept of ecoversity is intended to remind us of the importance of imagining ourselves into the future; into just relationships with other beings and with nature; into understandings of the unjust treatment of other beings and nature; into understanding inequities in resource access; and into exploring the ethics of our existence. To walk the walk and talk the talk, the ecoversity requires (a) faculties and administrators who provide role models of integrity, care, and thoughtfulness and (b) institutions capable of embodying ideals wholly and completely in their operations (Orr, 2010, p. 14).

The green campus movement aims to redesign campuses by making them more water- and energy-efficient (Orr, 2010, p. 70). Beyond this idea of green campuses and environmental education, the ecoversity concept seeks to provide a holistic framework for engaged and relational learning. It seeks to lead sustainability transformation by building eco-literate and enterprising human capacity through engagement with regional communities to tackle sustainability issues. The ecoversity also provides a framework for the practical implementation and development of ecological values and relational ethics. It has at its heart the idea of leading by example to engage the daily activities of students and communities with understanding of and active participation in what it means to address the unsustainable core characteristics of our time (Jucker, 2002, p. 10).

The ecoversity approach models practical and local applications in community engagement in a whole-of-institution approach to teaching, scholarship and research for local, regional, national, and global ecological sustainability through:

- Campus operations, estates and buildings, wildlife, energy, water, recycling (i.e., a green campus);
- Curriculum and pedagogy (ecoliteracy and sustainability literacy);
- Research, innovation, policy, and planning for the common good;
- Community, businesses, schools, local, and international partners (Garlick and Matthews, 2012).

As shown in Figure 1.1, the ecoversity 'reaches in' to encompass estates, the natural, and built environments (flora and fauna, energy and water saving, recycling, fair trade purchasing), teaching and learning, curricula and pedagogy, research, innovation and policy; and it 'reaches out' to involve partnerships with community, schools, and businesses.

15

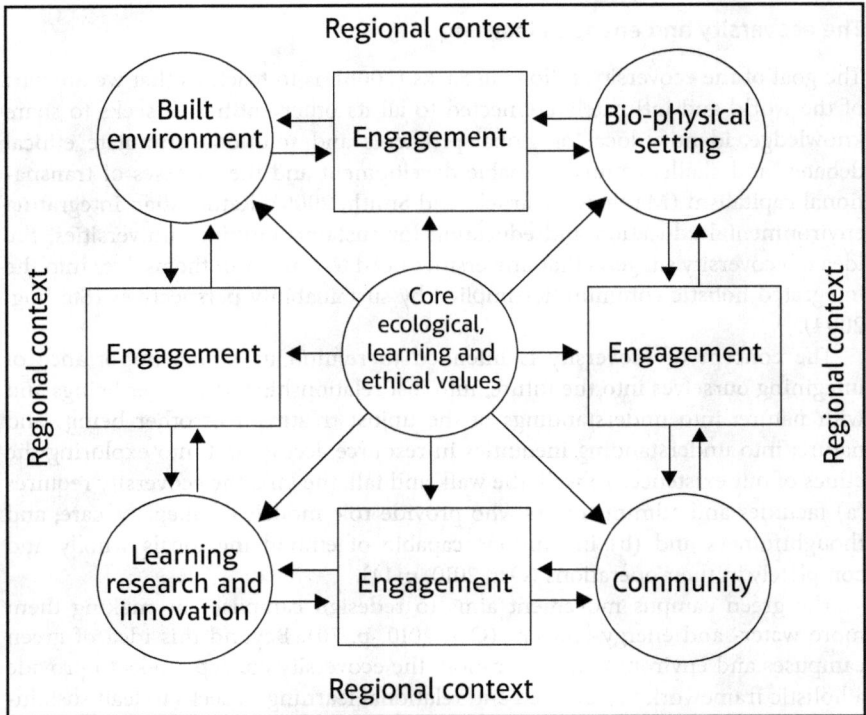

Figure 1.1 Model of the ecoversity
Source: Garlick and Matthews, 2009

At its core the ecoversity approach encompasses a commitment to a relational ethic of care and being-for-the-other, and to adopting an ethical stance towards the generation of knowledge and critique. The ecoversity approach locates universities as agents of social change and transformative learning.

Cognitive justice and the 'commons'

We see parallels between the concept of the ecoversity and the concept of the 'commons' used in conjunction with cognitive justice. In this sense the 'commons' reflects a place-based notion of connectivity with what 'has been', 'what is', and 'what could be' – a connection between humans and nature, and a connection between dreaming and fact (SARCHi Retreat, 2012).

The notion of cognitive justice and the democratization of knowledge (Visvanathan, 1997 and 2002; Santos, 2007; Odora-Hoppers, 2009) is a humanist concept that we can use to emphasize the importance of using the innate and experiential knowledge of others (first peoples, wildlife, etc.), in order to help us understand questions of environmental sustainability. 'Cognitive justice' was coined by Visvanathan to represent the need for a plurality of knowledge sources and processes to offset the straightjacket disciplinary culture of traditional human science analysis and knowledge. It is an ethical principle that values diverse sources of knowledge (knowers) equally, without drawing conclusions about relative knowledge superiority. We see this notion as balancing current episodic ecological views about the environment with knowledge from in-situ inhabitants.

As Visvanathan notes, 'cognitive justice recognises the right of different forms of knowledge to coexist', but he adds that this plurality needs to go beyond tolerance or liberalism to an active recognition of the need for diversity. It demands recognition of knowledge, not only as method but as a way of life. This presupposes that knowledge is embedded in ecology where it has its place, its claim to a cosmology, its sense as a form of life. In this sense knowledge is not something to be abstracted from a culture as a life form; it is connected to livelihood, a life cycle, a lifestyle; it determines life chances (Visvanathan, 2009).

Conclusion

Maintaining an anthropomorphic approach to environmental sustainability will continue the crisis of environmental unsustainability: 'a crisis of the ways modern capitalist societies combine with nature and a crisis of understanding whereby the citizens of those societies fail to understand their relations with nature' (Huckle, 2004, p. 34). Communities require a knowledge base that is able to inform them about the complex natural systems of the earth so that they can make responsible choices. Importantly, this knowledge base and values require an ethic that is able to recognize and value the relationship of all beings with one another and an understanding of the dangers of human exceptionalism and other dualistic forms of thought that regard people as distinct from, superior to, and separate from animals, and nature as the adversary of culture (see Plumwood, 1993). It recognizes the importance of cognitive justice connected to a 'commons' – a plurality of knowledge sources linked with and derived from place.

Universities have a moral purpose; they are not and should not become utilitarian training grounds for 'a career'. The role of a university is not fundamentally and solely concerned with developing the technical and vocational skills necessary to sustain the economy. Economic goals require shared values, and the discussion and articulation of these is precisely the role that universities can and should undertake. In addition, universities have the capacity to stimulate the imagination and innovative capacity of students by making accessible a wide range of cultural, artistic, scientific, and local resources. As publicly funded institutions, universities should be concerned with the public good; they have a 'larger purpose, a larger sense of mission, a larger clarity of direction in the national life' (Boyer, 1996, p. 20).

We have argued here that the ecoversity provides a location, a place, a 'commons' where students and residents can live a 'mutually engaged' existence with local communities, ecosystems, and wildlife. This fits well with the community engagement role to which universities are increasingly committed, where teaching, research, and core business activities connect to the communities in which they are located. Community engagement necessarily involves mutuality and reciprocity both within and outside the university. An ethic of care and being-for-the-other brings genuine engagement and mutual benefits because it takes account of all standpoints, interests, responsibilities, and relationships – a cognitive justice. Connecting academic scholarship to the public sphere to produce life-enhancing knowledge is for Boyer (1996) an ethical imperative. It requires universities to find new ways of teaching and researching, ways that cross disciplinary boundaries and become a locus for social engagement, action, and change. This approach to engaged scholarship creates new forms of learning and enterprise that more adequately address the big-picture global questions.

References

Adorno, T. (1966). Education after Auschwitz. http://ada.evergreen.edu/~arunc/texts/frankfurt/auschwitz/AdornoEducation.pdf (last accessed 19 June 2013).

Arthur, C. (2004). What are Universities For? *Contemporary Review* 285: 146–149.

Bauman, Z. (1995). *Life in Fragments: Essays in Postmodern Morality.* Oxford: Blackwell.

Bauman, Z. (2001). The Ethical Challenge of Globalization. *New Perspectives Quarterly* 11 (4): 4–9.

Bauman, Z. (2008). *Does Ethics Have a Chance in a World of Consumers?* Cambridge, MA: Harvard University Press.

Boyer, E. (1996). The Scholarship of Engagement. *Journal of Public Service & Outreach* 1 (1): 11–20.

Derrida, J. (2004). Violence against Animals. In J. Derrida and E. Roudinesco (eds), *For What Tomorrow: A Dialogue.* Stanford, CA: Stanford University Press.

Derrida, J. (2008). *The Animal that Therefore I Am.* Trans. D. Wills. Perspectives in Continental Philosophy. New York: Fordham University Press.

Fien, J. (1997). Understanding the Macro-Context of Teaching Environmental Education: A Case Study of Queensland, 1989–91. *Australian Journal of Environmental Education* 8: 77–114.

Garlick, S. (forthcoming). Learning from Wildlife Emotion: A Lacuna in our Knowledge of Environmental Sustainability. In Barbara Budrich (ed.), *Sustainability Frontiers: Critical and Transformative Voices from the Borderlands of Sustainability Education.* Leverkusen Opladen, Germany: Barbara Budrich Publishers.

Garlick, S., and Austen, R. (2012). Learning about the Emotional Lives of Kangaroos and Environmental Sustainability. Paper, Second Minding Animals Conference, Utrecht, Netherlands.

Garlick, S., and Matthews, J. (2009). Engaged Learning and Enterprise through the 'Ecoversity': Implementing an Engagement Theory to Meet Sustainability Concerns. Paper, AUCEA National Conference, Whyalla, South Australia. *Australasian Journal of University–Community Engagement* 3 (2).

Garlick, S., and Palmer, V. (2008). Toward an Ideal Relational Ethic: Re-Thinking University–Community Engagement. *Gateways: International Journal of Community Research and Engagement* 1: 73–89.

Giri, A. K. (2011). Gift of Knowledge: Knowing Together in Compassion and Confrontation. *Sociological Bulletin* 60: 1–26.

Giroux, H. (2004). Education after Abu Ghraib: Revisiting Adorno's Politics of Education. *Cultural Studies* 18: 779–815.

HSUS (2011). *An HSUS Report: The Impact of Animal Agriculture on Global Warming and Climate Change.* www.humanesociety.org/assets/pdfs/farm/animal-agriculture-and-climate.pdf (last accessed 19 June 2013).

Huckle, J. (2004). Critical Realism: A Philosophical Framework for Higher Education for Sustainability. In P. B. Corcoran and A. E. J. Wals (eds), *Higher Education and the Challenge of Sustainability: Problematics, Promise and Practice.* Dordrecht, Netherlands: Kluwer Academic Publishers.

Jensen, M. (2002). Fleshing out a Relational Ethics: Maurice Merleau-Ponty's Contribution to Ecological Feminism. Doctoral thesis, Vanderbilt University, Nashville, TN.

Jucker, R. (2002). Sustainability? Never Heard of It! Some Basics we Shouldn't Ignore when Engaging in Education for Sustainability. *International Journal of Sustainability in Higher Education* 3 (10): 8–19.

Kheel, M. (1993). Nature Ethics: An Ecofeminist Perspective. In G. Gaard (ed.), *Studies in Social, Political, and Legal Philosophy.* Lanham: Rowman & Littlefield.

Kheel, M. (2008). *Nature Ethics: An Ecofeminist Perspective.* New York: Rowman and Littlefield.

Matthews J. (2012). Compassion, Geography and the Question of the Animal. *Environmental Values* 21: 125–142.

Matthews, J., Garlick, S., and Smith, T. (2009). 'Ecoversity': Towards a Sustainable Future. *Journal of the World Universities Forum* 2 (3): 113–124.

Noddings, N. (1984). *Caring: A Feminine Approach to Ethics and Moral Education.* Berkeley: University of California Press.

Noddings, N. (2002). *Starting at Home: Caring and Social Policy.* Berkeley: University of California Press.

Odora-Hoppers, C. (2009). Education, Culture and Society in a Globalizing World: Implications for Comparative and International Education. *Compare: A Journal of Comparative and International Education* 39 (5): 601–614.

Orr, D. (1992). Ecological Literacy: Education and the Transition to a Postmodern World. Albany, NY: SUNY Press.

Orr, D. (2010). What is Education for Now? In Worldwatch Institute (ed.), *State of the World: Transforming Cultures from Consumerism to Sustainability.* New York: W. W. Norton.

Plumwood, V. (1993). *Feminism and the Mastery of Nature.* New York: Routledge.

Plumwood, V. (2000). Integrating Ethical Frameworks for Animals, Humans, and Nature: A Critical Feminist Eco-Socialist Analysis. *Ethics & the Environment* 5: 285–322.

Plumwood, V. (2007). Human Exceptionalism and the Limitations of Animals: A Review of Raymond Gaitor's *The Philosopher's Dog. Australian Humanities Review* 42. www.australianhumanitiesreview.org/archive/Issue-August-2007/EcoHumanities/Plumwood.html (last accessed 14 January 2014).

Sacks, A. B. (2008). The University and Sustainability: New Directions in Science, Technology and Culture. *Journal of the World Universities Forum* 1 (2): 93–100.

Santos, B. de S. (ed.) (2007). Cognitive Justice in a Global World: Prudent Knowledges for a Decent Life. Plymouth: Lexington Books.

Seddon, T. (2004). Remaking Civic Formation: Towards a Learning Citizen? *London Review of Education* 2: 171–186.

South African Research Chairs Initiative (SARCHi) Retreat (2012). *Cognitive Justice and the African and Global Commons.* Pretoria: University of South Africa.

Sterling, S. (2004). Higher Education, Sustainability, and the Role of Systemic Learning. In P. B. Corcoran and A. E. J. Wals (eds), *Higher Education and the Challenge of*

Sustainability: Problematics, Promise and Practice. Dordrecht, Netherlands: Kluwer Academic Publishers.

Talloires (1990). Report and Declaration of the Presidents Conference. Convention of University Presidents, Rectors, and Vice Chancellors. Talloires: Tufts European Center.

United Nations, World Commission on Environment and Development (WCED) (1987). *Our Common Future*. www.un-documents.net/our-common-future.pdf (last accessed 14 January 2014).

Visvanathan, S. (1997). *A Carnival for Science: Essays on Science, Technology and Development*. London: Oxford University Press.

Visvanathan, S. (2002). The Future of Science Studies. *Futures* 34: 91–101.

Visvanathan, S. (2009). The Search for Cognitive Justice. *India Seminar*. www.indiaseminar.com/2009/597/597_shiv_visvanathan.htm (last accessed 14 January 2014).

Wright, T. (2002). Definitions and Frameworks for Environmental Sustainability in Higher Education. *International Journal of Sustainability in Higher Education* 3: 203–221.

2

Unbounded organization and the unbounded university curriculum

Howard Richards

I want to make some basic points about the human species, about the world today, and about the role of the university in it. My title is meant to suggest a need to broaden our thinking, to place ourselves in wider context, and thus to open the way to innovative solutions that cannot be conceived or implemented while our thinking is confined within a narrower 'bounded' context.

My points will take the form of answers to three questions:

- Who are we?
- Where are we going?
- How will we get there?

Here are very brief summaries of my answers:

- We are the species whose ecological niche is the creation of culture.
- We are going to a global mosaic of green and open societies.
- We will get there by transforming capitalism.

I will do my best to explain these answers clearly. Most of what I have to say is an exercise in articulating facts that are likely to be acknowledged as true if they were only clearly depicted. The challenge is more in formulating the concepts in a useful way than in marshalling the evidence. But some of what I say falls in the zone of controversial facts – not so much controversial simple brute facts as controversial interpretations of the causes at work driving the social and natural worlds we live in. I will try to be brief and clear, so that even those who may not be persuaded will see my reasoning.

I fear I have already said something confusing. I am making a double use of the pronoun 'we'. On the one hand, I am using the pronoun 'we' to refer generally to all human beings. But on the other hand the pronoun 'we' names specifically all professors. 'We' are the academics, and when I ask 'What are some next steps in getting there?' I mean how 'we' (we who work in universities) can contribute to moving 'us' (all human beings) from where 'we' (all human beings) are to where we (all human beings) need to be.

There is a connection between using we' both to name all humans and using 'we' to name all professors. The connection is the suggestion that universities in principle work for human development.

One of the world's largest universities, the University of South Africa, aspires in its vision to be 'the African university in the service of humanity'. I suggest that in principle all universities are in the service of all humanity. The very word 'university' in its etymology refers to something universal. An original and central purpose of the university is to prepare people to practice professions, and the word 'profession' in its etymology implies commitment to an ideal of service.

And let me now ask a question about my first question: 'What am I seeking when I ask the question "who are we?"?'

Here is the answer to my question about my question: 'I am seeking an inclusive and believable metanarrative.'

I take the word 'metanarrative' from the book *The Postmodern Condition* by Jean-François Lyotard. A metanarrative is a big story. It is a comprehensive story about our world and who we are in our world. Examples are Christianity, Marxism, and liberal economics. If we go out to non-Western societies and back to pre-modern societies we find that metanarratives have invariably played an organizing role wherever large numbers of humans have lived together. Sometimes human beings have organized themselves telling stories about gods, sometimes they use stories about ancestors, and sometimes they use stories about military heroes. What Lyotard calls a metanarrative is sometimes called a cosmology or a founding myth or a worldview. Unfortunately, metanarratives have often been exclusive. They have often established a first-person plural by casting our people as a chosen people distinct from (and often superior to) other people.

The need for a metanarrative to organize human life led the cultural historian Thomas Berry to say there is no community without a community story. In *The Postmodern Condition* Lyotard says that people do not believe metanarratives any more. He says that our post-modern age is an age of incredulity towards metanarratives. Putting Berry and Lyotard together, it would follow that since today we have no metanarrative today, we have no community. There exists no 'we' to be the collective subject of 'our' efforts to save the biosphere and reweave the social fabric.

No doubt Lyotard is partly right to say we live in a time of incredulity towards metannaratives. There is indeed a growing trend among intellectuals, among young people, and among depressed people of all ages to believe in nothing. This bald and threatening use of the word 'nothing' deliberately suggests that lack of belief in big stories goes with lack of belief in little stories, for example lack of belief in one's spouse, one's parents, one's children. Nevertheless, Lyotard exaggerates. Today there are still many people who believe in a metanarrative. Indeed, one of the motivations of the post-modernist trend that Lyotard represents has been to combat the continuing influence of what I shall call the 'bounded' university, the Humboldtian and Kantian university dedicated to ideals of the European Enlightenment. A more recent variant of bounded modernizing is the Bologna process embedding the university in the metanarrative of liberal economics. It is not an exaggeration to say that one of the consequences of the deconstruction of Marxism, of onto-theology, of humanism,[1] and other main targets of postmodernist criticism, has been to abandon the university to the last metanarrative standing, that of liberal economics. At a more popular level, the discrediting of modernity has favoured the rise of fundamentalisms openly hostile to the Enlightenment.

So we have a problem: nothing authorizes us to believe that humanity today is so different from humanity in the past that today we can get our act together and work in concert to solve our problems without sharing a metanarrative that tells us who we are and what our role is in the great scheme of things. But liberal economics is a toxic brew. It shreds community more than it builds it. It smothers diversity and imposes the crudest and most violent forms of cognitive injustice. Its growth imperative and its systematic demand to create conditions for capital accumulation and ever more capital accumulation are killing the biosphere very rapidly, so rapidly that if we think in a perspective of geological time the end of life on this planet is the equivalent of only a few seconds away.[2]

Sometimes we seem to face a cruel choice: either no metanarrative or a toxic metanarrative. Either civil wars between mutually incompatible ethnic fundamentalisms which in principle can share no common ground, or else a secular state imposing certain death by liberal economics on one and all. Samuel Huntington´s cruel choice accepts that the clash of civilizations is what Lewis Coser would call an absolute conflict, that is, one where dialogue in pursuit of rational consensus is impossible because the parties in conflict share no common rationality. Huntington goes on to advocate that the modern West stand its ground, defending its own characteristic norms, that is, those of property, contract, the individual juridical subject. He defends the cultural and legal foundations of liberal economics.

In this context, which is our context today, some of us are proposing a comprehensive metanarrative that honours diversity, includes everyone, and makes sense of rational progress. It has the simple virtue of being true. We, humanity, are creators of cultures. We have always been creators of cultures. We are biologically coded to be culturally coded. We have the capacity to invent cultural codes that can be passed on to the next generation by upbringing and education. This capacity has given us an evolutionary advantage over species that can adapt to changing environments only by genetic mutation and natural selection.

The intellectuals of today are called on to make rational progress as cultural creatives have been doing ever since our common matrilineal ancestor the Mitochondrial Eve was giving birth to children and bringing them up to be humans somewhere in Africa some 200,000 years ago. Namely, in the words of Antonio Gramsci, we are adjusting culture to its physical functions.

Who are we? We are creators of cultures. I offer this as a simple answer to a simple question. This simple answer already begins to fill in the meaning of the phrase 'unbounded curriculum'. It is a curriculum open to the wisdom and to the knowledge systems of the many cultures humanity has created and is continuing to create.

My second simple question is: 'Where are we going?' The beginning of a simple answer is: 'We are going to a green future.' The simple reason why we are going to a green future is that we cannot possibly go to any other future. Failing to maintain the delicate equilibriums of the biosphere is not an option. Human cultures whose constitutive rules and basic norms are incompatible with the laws of physics, the laws of chemistry, and the facts of biology are not sustainable.

This is the simple proof that we are going to a green future if we are going anywhere at all. It defines a mission for the university that is legitimate because it is necessary. Given that a university is (among other things that it is) what Cardinal Newman said it was, a place where specialists in diverse specialties talk to each other, we (the professors) must all be aware in general terms of what those of our number who are natural scientists are learning about the conditions that must be satisfied in order for the human species to continue to exist. Of course there is no unanimity among the natural scientists, but even the optimists do not believe that the status quo can continue. What the optimists believe is that human ingenuity will succeed in making us green enough soon enough. Once we are aware of the danger, loyalty to our species and concern for other species imply a duty to act.

But my simple answer to the question 'Where are we going?' includes another key word. The key word is 'open'. Where are we going? We are going green and we are going open. There is no place else to go.

What do I mean by 'open' and why do I say an 'open society' is our only possible future? The phrase 'open society' was coined by the philosopher Karl Popper. Popper endorsed several things with it. Three of them I endorse: democracy, science, and unbounded organization.

- Democracy. In an open society the people have the power to choose the leaders and the institutions that work best for them. The principle that where the people have power they shape society to serve the people´s interests is more a tautology than an empirical finding. Amartya Sen gives it empirical content in several of his works, for example in his finding that in democracies there are no famines.
- Science. In an open society the results achieved by the leaders and the institutions are constantly studied and evaluated by independent scholars responsible in principle only to participate sincerely in the search for truth. 'In principle' scholars are accountable only to truth-seeking, but since truth-seeking has no email or postal address and no telephone number, in practice it is represented by such surrogates as peer reviewers, dissertation examiners, and accreditation panels. Popper himself might well have wanted scholars to be required to accept his version of the scientific method, and to agree with him that although truth is always sought it is strictly speaking never found. The very diverse and controversial field of philosophy of science assumes central importance in an open society because the legitimacy of social institutions comes to depend on claiming that the essentially contested entity 'science', if properly conducted, will make essential contributions to solving social and ecological problems.
- Unbounded organization. In an open society there are no limits constraining science or social innovation. Society, like science in Popper's philosophy of science, is never perfected. Both science and society consist of hypotheses

that so far have withstood the tests of experience. By using the concept 'democracy' I mean (and I think Popper means) to import into the open society concept the many safeguards against the tyranny of the majority that democratic theorists have built into the democratic concept. 'Unbounded' is not intended to mean 'anything can happen' in the sense Hannah Arendt employs when she uses the phrase 'anything can happen' to describe the totalitarian abolition of the rule of law. 'Unbounded organization' is not a phrase Popper uses. I take his railing against Plato, Hegel, Marx, and others whom he calls enemies of the open society to be railing against bounded thought, and his praise of an open-minded and fallibilist scientific method to be an endorsement of unbounded thought.

If we lived in an open society, its leaders and its institutions would be working for the benefit of all of us. If we lived in an open society, we would be constantly improving our institutions to make them work better for all of us. If we lived in an open society, science would be monitoring our successes and our failures. We do not live in an open society. Popper suggests at one point that an open society will be thwarted if economic power dominates political power, and recommends that in such a case people struggle to achieve the supremacy of (democratic) political power over economic power. Richards and Swanger show why this recommendation is not feasible without a culture shift.

Still I say that where we are going is both green and open because there is no place else to go. My argument has two parts:

- Part 1: We are necessarily going for a green society, because if we are not going there we are not going anywhere.
- Part 2: We are necessarily going for an open society, because without it we cannot make the necessary transition to a green society.

Part 1 I think I have already proved. If you will grant me a premise, I will offer you a proof of Part 2.

The premise: an open society *just is* a society organized to pursue rationally the best interests of all. It can be argued that a command society, say the former Soviet Union or China, could go green because its rulers could command it to go green. I do not believe this, so I have to beg you to grant that democratic rationality can make the green transition while authoritarian power cannot. As Amartya Sen has argued in several works, even if both were capable of making the green transition, there are reasons why the democratic route would be preferable.

The offer of proof: if we can govern ourselves in ways that rationally pursue the best interests of all, then we can make the necessary transition to a green society. And if not, I omit some premises that are in strict logic required, but which should be non-controversial, for example the premise that if we can reach our goals at all we can do so by pursuing them rationally, but we cannot reach them either by pursuing them irrationally or by not pursuing them at all.

So if we are going anywhere we are going open. It may not be obvious that I am claiming that protracted violence such as that in Sudan, Somalia, and Palestine could be overcome if the societies involved and the international system were open in my modified Popperian sense. It may not be obvious but I find this pro-peace claim to be implicit in saying that an open society is a set of procedures and an institutional setup designed to act rationally for the good of all.

My next simple question is: 'How will we get there? How will we get to a green and open society?'

My simple answer is: we will get there (that is to say we will satisfy a necessary although not sufficient condition for it) by liberating ourselves from domination by capitalism. There are of course other obstacles to achieving an open society. Making capitalism governable is key, and it is a necessary giant step forward that deserves priority attention. Some people may disagree with me even if they understand me, since they may believe that some other key problem, for example patriarchy, deserves higher priority in efforts to make capitalism governable, or, some would say, to abolish capitalism altogether.

A short definition of capitalism is that it is the production of goods and services for profit. A slightly longer definition is that capitalism is the production of goods for sale, where the sale in turn is for the sake of profit. This definition traces closely the meaning given to the term by the man who coined it, Karl Marx. One needs the definition to avoid the meaning given to the term by anti-socialists like Ludwig von Mises, Friedrich von Hayek, and Francis Fukayama. They define capitalism as competitive pricing and socialism as central planning. It follows from their definitions, both by logic and by historical experience, that socialism is unworkable. Fukayama holds that socialism was an option for basic industrialization, but that in today's knowledge society, where flexible response to constant change is the name of the game, socialism is a non-starter. One also needs to follow roughly its coiner's definition to avoid the meaning given to the term by writers like Peter Drucker and David Korten, who define it in such a way that capitalism is already over. From their viewpoint it is a waste of time to discuss the role of capitalism in a mixed economy because we already live in a post-capitalist society. Drucker and Korten are right. Capitalism no longer exists (for example, in the knowledge society, capital is no longer the key factor for production that it once was), but their being right does not eliminate the question of what role to assign to production for profit, that is, to capitalism as (roughly speaking) Marx defined it. I say 'roughly speaking' partly because Marx can also be read as making the exploitation of 'free' labour part of the definition of 'production of commodities' (*Waren*) and therefore part of the definition of capitalism is defined as 'production of commodities'.

Let me say why we are dominated by capitalism: because when production is for profit, if there is no profit there is no production. Therefore, simply put, everything about society, including wage rates, labour supply, education, taxes, government, culture, science, and so on, must be geared to complying with a single imperative: there must be profit. There must be accumulation of capital. Without profit, nothing moves.

Here we see a key reason why we do not have an open society. Democracy is truncated because the first thing governments must do is to make to sure that the wheels of capitalism keep turning. Some Marxists downplay this point because they centre-stage the related point that the wheels of capitalism are going to stop turning no matter what governments do, even if they give investors all the tax breaks, exceptions to environmental laws, subsidies, cheap labour, and so on that they ask for. To the extent that capitalism dominates, everybody's welfare depends on some people turning money into more money. Bowles and Gintis emphasize 'the exit power of capital', that is, the power to leave when it would be more profitable to be somewhere else. I focus on the key problem of achieving an open society by making capitalism governable, but many other things can be done to make societies more open.

So how can we liberate ourselves? Here I will take Amartya Sen as my guide. His ideas on how to tame capitalism can be taken both as advice on how to pave the way for human development and as advice on how to pave the way for the necessary transition to a green and open society. So my short answer to the simple question 'How will we get there?' becomes: 'We will get there by building an open society.' We will build an open society by liberating ourselves from domination by capitalism. We will liberate ourselves from domination by capitalism by following Sen's advice. Sen writes: 'Capitalism can generate mean streets and strained lives unless it is restrained and supplemented by other – often nonmarket – institutions.' Sen here offers a two-part formula for liberation. The first part is restraining capitalism, more commonly known as regulating it. The second is supplementing capitalism, often by nonmarket institutions. Let us consider the two parts one at a time. First, regulation:

- When we regulate or restrain we impose conditions.
- We decree, for example, that firms must either pay at least the legal minimum wage or cease to do business.
- Or we require that a factory must either cease to dump toxic waste into a nearby river or close.
- Or we pass a law that all shops must install ramps to accommodate people challenged with issues of accessibility. If they do not install the ramps, they lose their licences and must shut their shops.

You get the picture. Restraint and regulation give business a choice. Obey or quit.

Both logic and the historic failures of social democracy teach us that businesses often choose option 2. They quit. They stop doing business. Or they move somewhere else. Their workers lose their jobs. Whatever they were going to produce is either not produced at all, or it is produced somewhere else where there is less regulation.

My simple conclusion is that imposing restraints on capitalism will not by itself liberate us from domination by it.

That leaves the second part of Amartya Sen's formula: supplementing. Indeed, the more we restrain and regulate, the more we need to enlarge and supplement. This is true because the more businesses choose option 2 and close, the more we need to create supplementary livelihoods for the unemployed, and the more we need supplementary ways to supply the goods and services that the closed businesses are no longer supplying. We have to supplement. Regulation alone will not bring us freedom. Sen calls for supplementing capitalism, often with nonmarket institutions. Sen also implies that sometimes we supplement capitalism with market institutions that are not capitalist.

What could those nonmarket institutions be? What would be some examples of market institutions that employ people and produce goods and services but are not capitalist? One example would be the work of Matilda, the seamstress who lives in a house near mine and ekes out a living mending her neighbours' garments. Other examples would be the hawkers in South Africa around 1910 described by Mahatma Gandhi in his autobiography. Gandhi writes about them because they were prohibited from hawking their wares on the streets of Johannesburg because of their race. Such people are not capitalists and they are not employees of capitalists. They are not in business for profit. They are just using their labour power to generate enough cash to survive. Most of them make less money than they would make if they were working for wages in a modern factory run by a multinational corporation. In most Latin American and African countries they outnumber the people who find steady employment in the capitalist sector.

Their sector is usually called the informal economy although some of us prefer to call it the labour economy (because labour rather than capital is the main factor) or the people's economy. It sometimes happens, as happened towards the end of apartheid in South Africa, that 'Rising unemployment and the pressure of informal operators have forced policy-makers to move from suppressing to encouraging informal activities, often drawing ideas and proposals for action from academic work' (Richards, 2012). More often government response to the informal economy is a mixed bag: sometimes it is treated as tax-evading illegal activity to be suppressed by the police; sometimes it is encouraged and supported; sometimes governments dream that it will end when the country becomes 'developed' and everybody has a steady job at good wages in the formal sector. The Peruvian economist Hernando De Soto famously advocated formalizing what is now the informal economy, the linchpin of development policy. From the economic historian Karl Polanyi and others we learn that for most of the time human beings have lived on this planet their economies have not been market economies. There are non-capitalist traditional livelihoods that have existed for thousands of years and still exist.

Polanyi and other historians and anthropologists identify two main categories of pre-capitalist non-market economics. The first great traditional category is 'reciprocity' or 'reciprocal obligation'. Reciprocity is typically embedded in a whole worldview in which one might say, for example, 'The commons we share was left to us by our ancestors. We are its custodians and we must pass it on to our descendants.' Such talk comes out of a whole different worldview and sense of self. There is no simple way to translate it into the common sense of modern western normality. My proposed metanarrative insists on the legitimacy of such talk, but it does not by itself get past square one in understanding it.

Reciprocity is the principle that organizes families, clans, and tribes. Sir Henry Sumner Maine in his account of the transition from ancient to modern society called the principle of reciprocity in families 'status'. Everybody is born with a role and place in society, with a status, just because of being born a member of a certain family, clan, or tribe. Maine called the transition from ancient to modern called a transition from 'status to contract' (Maine, 1931). It is a generic category including what is known in the Bantu languages as *ubuntu*, or 'I am because you are'. Reciprocity was typical of the societies that Emile Durkheim called 'archaic' and to which he attributed high levels of social integration and *solidarité*. The second big generic category identified by Polanyi is redistribution. It was typical of the empires of Africa before European conquest. The classic example is Egypt, where the agents of the pharaohs gathered up the harvests, stored them, and from their granaries distributed grain in the seasons between harvests.

From Polanyi and other scholars we learn that we do not need to begin from scratch to find nonmarket supplements. We can rely on tried and true cultural resources that have functioned in practice for thousands of years to tame capitalism and to make it governable. The principle of *ubuntu* is not new. The principle of meeting basic needs from collective resources already existed three thousand years ago. It existed in Africa and you can read about it in the Bible.

Of course, cultural creativity did not end in the year zero, even though by then it had made a good beginning. In more recent times we have invented cooperatives, non-profit foundations, public–private joint ventures, worker-owned enterprises, permaculture, community currencies, neighbourhood food banks, asset-based community development, monasteries, to name a few. In another place Sen writes that markets are 'among the instruments that can be used to promote human capabilities'. Once again we see the importance of unbounded thinking. Within the conventional bounds of liberal economics the market is simply given as the normal framework of human activity. To move with Sen to the point where the market regarded as one instrument among many to be employed to reach the ethical goal of promoting human capabilities we need an unbounded curriculum. To supplement capitalism in practice we need unbounded organization.

Supplementing empowers regulating. Governability, which almost everyone regards as desirable, can be achieved when a mix of dynamics in a mixed economy loosens the grip of what Ellen Wood calls 'systemic imperatives' and Bowles and Gintis call 'the exit power of capital'. We will know that liberation from domination by capitalism has arrived when we can say: whatever may be the livelihoods that capitalism cannot generate with social and ecological responsibility, or cannot generate at all, we will generate some other way. We will be free when we can treat capitalism as one way among others to get the work of the world done. We can then use proper procedures to decide rationally and ethically what roles capitalism should play in a mixed economy. At long last we will be empowered to make the rules for capitalism instead of capitalism making the rules for us.

Living in a governable society will benefit everyone, even us capitalists. I take the liberty of calling myself a capitalist because I have a few investments. The conclusion that governability will benefit everyone, even those who are capitalists on a much larger scale than I am, follows from the claim that a truly open (and therefore governable) society is required to make the necessary transition to a green society. It can also be supported by the claim that an open society is more able to solve social problems that it is in everyone's interest to solve. Empirical studies show the welfare of all is improved when societies are more equal and less unequal.

An open society does not make universal and eternal rules. It makes provisional rules. It revises them periodically as it continues to learn from experience. It is important to note that there must be a certain degree of stability. Long-term investments (for example for the generation and transmission of electric power) cannot be made if the rules of the game change constantly. An unpredictable future makes it more likely that natural resources will be mined for immediate benefits and less likely that they will be enhanced for long-term benefits. Since an open society is by definition democratic, in the final analysis the people who will have the power to decide how to balance innovation and stability will be the same people who will benefit from getting it right and suffer from getting it wrong. Here I use the word 'people' not to refer to what Jean-Paul Sartre calls a 'series' of isolated individuals, but to refer to a cohesive nation whose identity includes its younger members who are not yet old enough to vote and its members who are not yet born. As a grandfather, I find it natural to believe that people will make sacrifices today for the benefit of their grandchildren tomorrow. I am not inclined to believe pessimists who believe that in a democracy, or in any form of government, whoever holds power will quickly discount the long-run future to a value of zero.

If my beliefs are right, then among the incentives citizens of a democracy will have to achieve a rational balance of innovation and stability will be the incentive of saving the earth and the benefits of their way of life for their descendants. Since decisions are provisional, there will be a tendency over time to make more right decisions and fewer mistaken decisions as the polity learns from its own mistakes. Let us remember too that a Popperian concept of democracy is inseparable from a concept of the social responsibilities of science. It requires not just that citizens and political leaders do their jobs, but also that we academics do our jobs. An open society has *two* pillars, democracy and science.

Let me now ask, 'What are some next steps?' I mean next steps for universities. Of course, I have already been implying curriculum transformation. Quite apart from the practical necessity to get *homo sapiens sapiens* off the endangered species list, at this point in intellectual history simple honesty requires an unbounded curriculum. The ethnocentric assumptions that framed the founding of the disciplines that constitute the modern university in Germany in the nineteenth century are simply false.

Simply counting on growing awareness of the unsustainability of the present world order to transform the university is unlikely to work as a next step. And there are also problems with relying on an appeal to intellectual honesty to transform the university. I do not think an epistemological critique calling on the university to change in the light of the present state of knowledge, like Edgar Morin's or like Catherine Hopper's and mine, provides a practical answer to the question 'What are some next steps?' Next steps have to be within the university's 'zone of proximal development.' Next steps in the zone of proximal development have to start where the university is and lead to where it is ready to go.

One can safely assume that in this day and age universities are mainly driven by epistemology in any form, not in the scholastic Aristotelian form of the medieval Christian and Muslim universities, not in its nineteenth-century Kantian–Humboldtian form, not in an early twentieth-century positivist form, and not in a contemporary post-modern or critical realist form. Epistemology is not where the university is today.

Henry Johnson Jr. wrote, 'In theory the university is in need of ontological, epistemological, and axiological rescue, but in fact it is uninterested in being redeemed. Its ontology is that of the business world, its axiology that of the account book, and the only truths it seeks are saleable truths. Worst of all, most of its members are by and large relatively happy with the way things are.' Like Lyotard, Johnson exaggerates. Some still believe that service to humanity and pursuit of truth are essential to the very idea of a university. The Socratic and Popperian ideal of unbounded enquiry making the university a place where all questions can be asked and all premises can be questioned is perhaps moribund. Iit is perhaps deceased, but it is not forgotten.

Nevertheless, thoughts like those of Henry Johnson ring true enough to move me to caution. Caution tells me that to be in the zone of proximal development of today's university I have to propose next steps that make business sense. I have thought of a next step that makes business sense, that contributes to transforming capitalism, and that connects my ideas to many of the ideas of other authors expressed in the following chapters of this book.

I start from two business premises. To design and market their products, universities are interested in employment opportunities for their graduates. Second, employment opportunities are scarce and getting scarcer as worldwide millions of university graduates flood the labour markets.

My suggestion for a next step is to promote social entrepreneurship. With respect to entrepreneurship generally, Harvard has led the way by communicating the message to its undergraduates that instead of hoping that somebody will hire them upon graduation they should go entrepreneurial and start their own enterprises. Fortunately, for the cause of rebuilding society and saving life on the planet, it happens that there is a specific growing field within the general rubric of going entrepreneurial called social entrepreneurship. It is sometimes called social enterprise. In social entrepreneurship people learn and invent innovative ways to mobilize resources to meet needs. They both get jobs and create jobs. They create jobs in ways that supplement the standard logic of capitalism. If we need to follow Amartya Sen's advice to save ourselves from ungovernable capitalism by supplementing, then we need more and better social entrepreneurs.

Here there may be an opportunity to eat our cake and have it, too: more emphasis on teaching and researching social entrepreneurship as it applies to the most salient social and ecological problems might well be a profitable next step for a university managed as a business. At the same time, social entrepreneurship builds nonmarket institutions that supplement capitalism and make it possible to restrain it.

The concept of the ecoversity developed in the following chapter lends itself to social entrepreneurship. 'Ecoversity' could be the label of a framework that would attract students who realize that either many of tomorrow's careers will be in social change or there will be no tomorrow.

Social entrepreneurship alloyed with tapping indigenous knowledge systems would be an even better business proposition and an even deeper social transformation. A social entrepreneurship diploma or degree featuring grounding in indigenous knowledge systems would differentiate the product of whatever university gets there first. It could be marketed as a premium-quality product different from those offered by competitors. This example of a plausible next step within the zone of proximal development of today's universities connects explicitly with Chapters 3 and 7 of this book. It connects implicitly with several other chapters in this publication.

'Social entrepreneurship' is not my conclusion. It is an example illustrating my conclusion. My conclusion is that universities can take next steps starting from where we (we academics) are here and now that lead towards where we (we human beings) are going. We are going (if we are going anywhere) to a global mosaic of green and open societies.

References

Andersson, G. (forthcoming). *Unbounded Organization: Embracing the Societal Enterprise*. University of South Africa Press.
Arendt, H. (1951). *The Origins of Totalitarianism*. New York: Harcourt Brace.
Bahti, T. (1987). Histories of the University: Kant and Humboldt. *MLN* 102: 437–460.
Berry, T. (1998). *The Dream of the Earth*. San Francisco: Sierra Club.
Bowles, S., and Gintis, H. (1986). *Democracy and Capitalism*. New York: Basic Books.
Cohen, G. (1978). *Karl Marx's Theory of History: A Defense*. Princeton: Princeton University Press.
Coser, L. (1956). *The Functions of Social Conflict*. New York: Free Press.
Debord, G. (1967). *La societé du spectacle*. Paris: Buchet-Castel.
Derrida, J. (1974). *Of Grammatology*. Baltimore: Johns Hopkins University Press.
De Soto, H. (1989). *The Other Path: The Invisible Revolution in the Third World*. New York: Harper & Row.
Foster, J., and McChesney, R. (2012). *The Endless Crisis*. New York: Monthly Review.
Foucault, J. (1966). *Les mots et les choses*. Paris: Gallimard.
Godway, E., and Finn, G. (eds) (1986). *Who is this 'We'? Absence of Community*. Montreal: Black Rose Press.
Hartsock, N. (1986). *Money, Sex and Power*. Boston: Northeastern University Press.
Fukuyama, F. (1992). *The End of History and the Last Man*. New York: Free Press.
Harvey, D. (1987). *The Condition of Postmodernity*. Oxford: Blackwell.
Heidegger, M. (1986). 'Jedes Fragen ist ein Suchen' ('Every question is a seeking'). In *Sein und Zeit*. Tübingen: Max Niemeyer. 1st edn 1926.
Hoppers, C., and Richards, H. (2012). *Rethinking Thinking: Modernity's Other and the Transformation of the University*. Pretoria: University of South Africa.
Huntington, S. (1996). *The Clash of Civilizations*. New York: Simon and Schuster.

Johnson, H. (1994). Review of *Prescribing the Life of the Mind* by C. Anderson. *Review of Politics* 56: 765–768.

Kant, I. (1963). *Idea for a Universal History from a Cosmopolitan Standpoint*. Indianapolis: Bobbs-Merrill. Original German edn 1784.

Kant, I. (2001). *The Conflict of the Faculties*. Cambridge: Cambridge University Press. Original German edn 1798.

Klare, M. (2002). *Resource Wars: The New Landscape of Global Conflict*. New York: Owl Books.

Lonergan, A., and Richards, C. (eds) (1990). *Thomas Berry and the New Cosmology*. Mystic, CT: Twenty Third Publications.

Lorenz, C. (2006). Will the Universities Survive the European Integration? *Sociologia Internationalis* 44: 123–151.

Lyotard, J. (1984). *The Postmodern Condition*. Minneapolis: University of Minnesota Press.

Magdoff, F., and Foster, J. (2011). *What Every Environmentalist Should Know about Capitalism*. New York: Monthly Review Press.

Maine, H. (1931). *Ancient Law*. London: Oxford University Press. 1st edn 1861.

Morin, E., and Kern, A. B. (1999). *Homeland Earth: A Manifesto for the New Millennium*. Creskill, NJ: Hampton Press.

Newman, J. (1907). *The Idea of a University*. London: Longmans Green.

Novek, J., and Kampen, K. (1992). Sustainable or Unsustainable Development: An Analysis of an Environmental Controversy. *Canadian Journal of Sociology* 17: 249–273.

Panayotou, T. (1985). *Green Markets*. San Francisco: Institute for Contemporary Studies.

Pimentel, D., and Pimentel, M. (2008). *Food, Energy, and Society*. 3rd edn. Boca Raton, FL: CRC Press.

Polanyi, K., et al. (1957). *Trade and Market in the Early Empires*. Glencoe: Free Press.

Popper, K. (1945). *The Open Society and its Enemies*. London: Routledge and Kegan Paul.

Luxemburg, R. (2003). *The Accumulation of Capital*. London: Routledge. Trans. Agnes Schwarzschild. German original 1913.

Rawls, J. (1971). *A Theory of Justice*. Cambridge, MA: Belknap Press.

Redclift, M. (1987). Sustainable Development: Exploring the Contradictions. London: Methuen.

Richards, H. (2012). Modernity's Other and the Transformation of the University: Short Answers to Simple Questions. Keynote talk, Sixth Annual Retreat on Development Education University of South Africa, 25 November. http://humiliationstudies.org/documents/RichardsSouthAfricaTalk.pdf (last accessed 14 January 2014).

Richards, H., and Swanger, J. (2006). *The Dilemmas of Social Democracies*. Lanham, MD: Rowman and Littlefield.

Sartre, J. (1976). *Critique of Dialectical Reason*. London: New Left Books.

Sen, A. (1982). *Poverty and Famines*. Oxford: Clarendon Press.

Sen, A. (2003). Sraffa, Wittgenstein, and Gramsci. *Journal of Economic Literature* 41: 1240–1255.

Sen, A. (2004). What's the Point of Democracy? *Bulletin of the American Academy of Arts and Sciences* 57: 8–11.

Sen, A., and Dreze, J. (1999). *The Amartya Sen and Jean Dreze Omnibus*. Delhi: Oxford University Press.

Sindane, N. (1993). South Africa's Informal Economy. *Africa: Journal of the International African Institute* 63: 143–144.

Trainer, T. (1996). *Towards a Sustainable Economy: The Need for Fundamental Change*. Oxford: Oxford University Press.

Wilkinson, R., and Pickett, K. (2010). *The Spirit Level*. London: Penguin.
Wood, E. (1995). *Democracy against Capitalism*. Cambridge: Cambridge University Press.
Wood, E. (2003). *Empire of Capital*. London: Zed Books. www.opensocietyfoundations.org
    (last accessed 14 January 2014).

Notes

1   Foucault (1966), Foucault targets 'l'homme', i.e., Kant's anthropology, i.e., the ethical basis of the Kantian–Humboldtian modernizing university, i.e., human dignity, respect for persons conceived as bearers of rights, knowledge contributing to rational progress towards freedom under law.
2   'The relationship between economic expansion and environmental protection remains fundamentally contradictory' (Novek and Kampen, 1992). This argument is further elaborated by many authors including Michael Redclift (1987). Further, as I will discuss below, economic expansion is an imperative of the dominant capitalist system, and consequently until that system is reformed, economic expansion will often trump environmental protection. See Magdoff and Foster (2011).

3

Indigenous and Western knowledge: a false dichotomy?

Margaret Sutherland

There is tacit agreement regarding the multi-dimensional nature of complex development issues facing society in the twenty-first century (United Nations, 2000). What is less clear is how we effectively and collectively address these issues. Talking within established educational institutional frameworks and in relation to the social and physical sciences, Sumner and Tribe (2008, p. 751) argue that wide-ranging perspectives relating to 'views on the world, knowledge and research processes' can hinder arrival at a collective approach to development issues. Sillitoe (2007) argues that we need to listen to the views and knowledge of others in order to enrich and enhance scientific knowledge and make it more culturally relevant. In this context 'others' refers to local communities whose knowledge, it is argued, will contribute to effective development initiatives since a sense of agency (Bruner, 1996) will have been engendered among the participants. Storey (2000) has argued that simply focusing on the local will not address the issues, as indigenous local knowledge is no more monolithic and hegemonic than Western science. Participation, according to Jakimov (2008), should be about generating local knowledge and not viewed as something that 'others' possess that might be useful to Western scientific knowledge. Whatever the context for development discussions, there is an imperative to work together to establish and develop a 'collective knowledge base that can lead to communal sense-making' (Boreham et al., 2000, p. 4). However, processes for achieving this are far from straightforward.

Knowledge transfer from the West was hailed as the solution to the difficulties faced by those living in poverty. This approach had its roots in the post-World War II modernist agenda (Dodds, 2002). This uni-dimensional tactic dominated development discourses, although post-colonial theorists began to question if such an approach to multi-dimensional issues had in fact hindered rather than supported development (Escobar, 1995). There was a growing awareness that indigenous knowledge had a role in development, but it was acknowledged that mining indigenous knowledge from its social and cultural context was problematic, as was the suggestion that indigenous knowledge could be applied generically to development studies (Sillitoe, 2007).

Indigenous, local, or traditional knowledge is sometimes cited to describe practice that is rooted in collective local community engagement with an understanding of the adjacent environment. This engagement and this understanding shape the responses to realities that the community faces on a daily basis (Gorjestani, 2000). Indigenous knowledge informs decisions about all aspects of daily life. It appears to offer developing communities agency in areas that directly affect them (Chambers, 2001). However, the conceptualization of indigenous, local, or traditional knowledge is problematic, and within the research community there is disagreement as to the precise meanings of these terms (Ellen and Harris, 2000). Underlying the various terminologies relating to local knowledge is the idea that this knowledge is bound by place and generated from a system outside the prevailing scientific knowledge system (Dove, 2000).

Western knowledge is accepted as representing that which is scientific, replicable, methodical, dispassionate, and unbounded (Ellen and Harris, 2000) and is, therefore, considered global. However, science is not monolithic and is equally ensnared in cultural complexities (Diawara, 2000). Although post- and anti-development theorists have called into question the transferability of scientific ideas, they argue that this worldview continued and continues to dominate the development scene (Escobar, 1995; Pretty, 1994; Nustad, 2001). There has been critique of Western knowledge as the dominant force in development (Sillitoe, 1998; Ellen and Harris, 2000; Kalland, 2000) and a move in some areas towards more participatory approaches, but this, too, is problematic, and mere participation will not automatically result in significant accrued benefits (Mayoux and Chambers, 2005).

The presentation of Western and indigenous knowledge as discrete and often mutually exclusive is perhaps then a false dichotomy, since issues of place and ownership transcend these domains. McFarlane (2006, p. 1416) argues that knowledge remains something that is exported to the Global South and calls, if we are to change, for a conception of learning that must be critically reflexive of the power relations between different groups, and that must be able to imagine the possibilities of learning between different contexts in ways that do not conform to historical patterns of colonization or to contemporary tendencies of aid-based conditionality.

Taking up McFarlane's call (2006) for a change in conceptualization of learning in and between different contexts will be challenging for universities with embedded institutional practices. Universities will have to explore this change internally and externally if there is to be a shift in thinking in the field of development. Cross-disciplinarity within institutions is proving challenging, and Sumner and Tribe (2008) suggest two main reasons for this: first poor communication between disciplines due to internal and established research structures which inhibit the flow of communication, and second the differing worldviews to which disciplines adhere. Cross-disciplinarity between institutions and the local community is equally demanding, with poor communication and differing worldviews as problematic in this context as they are within institutions. These issues are not solely based in Western institutions. Within communities there may be variation in the construction of knowledge between community members (Cleaver, 1999; Green, 2000), and thus there may be differences between community members that parallel the differences between university disciplines. A complex web of relational issues and worldviews emerges on all levels and across universities and communities alike. This chapter is not concerned with the continuum of cross-disciplinarity as described by Sumner and Tribe (2008), but considers instead the relational and human aspects that impact upon any collaborative work that is undertaken by institutions and/or local communities when creating collective knowledge. In particular, it will refer to learning theory and the work of Wenger (1998) and Engeström, Miettinen, and Punamäki (1999) in creating dynamic, reflexive responses to development (Jakimov, 2008).

Working together

Notwithstanding the aforementioned difficulties, in recent years there has been a clarion call for universities to work together, as evidenced through the setting up of institutes or the awarding of research grants which promote interdisciplinarity (Barrett, 2012). Simultaneously, the idea that communities should be involved in development issues is an assumption. A consequence of such situations is that people from both universities and communities find themselves working together in ways that are not understood and that in practice require relational skills outside the researchers' or community participants' frame of reference. Both parties bring situated knowledge to the table, but the ways in which knowledge can be shared, valued, and developed has resulted in one kind of knowledge (usually the scientific knowledge) outweighing the other (Jacobson and Stephens, 2009). However, Mercer (1995, p. 1) contends that while knowledge exists in the thought or 'the chest' of individuals (Sillitoe, 2010) it can also be shared and made available to others. As human beings we have the capacity to pool our mental resources in order to create knowledge through joint mental effort. Given that 'discovery, learning, and creative problem-solving are rarely, if ever, truly individual affairs' (Mercer 1995, p. 1), correspondingly universities and communities need to pay a good deal of attention to this communal construction of knowledge.

The bringing together of hitherto discrete disciplines, each with its own cadre of experts and knowledge to address common issues, would seem infinitely sensible when global concerns such as those outlined in the Millennium Development Goals (United Nations, 2000) are likely to remain after 2015 (Waage et al., 2010). This seemingly simplistic idea of 'coming together' belies the complexities that surround the practicalities of effective knowledge exchange endeavours. Experts, academics, local indigenous populations, and government and non-governmental organizations, to name but a few of the players in the field of development, bring to the development agenda wide-ranging views, experiences, and forms of knowledge. Perhaps this is the nub of the issue: how do disparate groups working together in a meaningful way when such institutional, geographical, cultural, and epistemological diversity exists?

The international context

Globalization diminishes variation between countries and is evidenced in the rise of multinational corporations, which are engaged in commercial activity across continents. Technological advances have resulted in the seamless flow of information, finance, and marketable goods on a global scale. This unprecedented inundation of fundamental fiscal activities gives rise to tensions between the local and the global, with the local frequently having to reconfigure and respond to global activity and pressure (Ozga and Jones, 2006). Education has not been immune from these global developments. A 2002 World Bank report *Constructing Knowledge Societies: New Challenges for Tertiary Education* asserts that tertiary education has a key role to play in addressing transnational issues such as poverty reduction. It regards knowledge as the emerging and major force of growth.

References to knowledge, knowledge exchange, knowledge transfer, and knowledge-driven economy, among others, have become common parlance in the literature relating to higher education and development. The *Oxford Dictionary* (online) suggests that knowledge is 'facts, information, and skills acquired through experience or education; the theoretical or practical understanding of a subject'. On the surface this explanation would seem to allow for divergent understandings of knowledge. Facts, information, and skills gained from experience or sensory based knowledge may differ from those gained through education (Classen, 2000 and 2005). While they do not have to be mutually exclusive, they may bring inconsistent insight to the same issues. Thus, there has developed a plurality of terms with diverse discourses associated with each. If cognizance is to be given to the different forms of knowledge, and if one is to learn from the other and practice is to change, it is imperative that reflective learning across epistemological, cultural, and institutional boundaries takes place, and this requires some form of collaboration between the often disparate groups.

Creating collective knowledge through collaboration

One response to this apparent disconnect between knowledges and across disciplines is the need for collaboration which emerges from a social constructivist theory of learning. Collaboration relates to the work of Bruner (1996), who postulates that learning is about understanding the minds of others. It relates to the work of Vygotsky (1978), who put social interactions at the heart of the learning process. It is the social element of the learning process which is crucial when groups work together to develop social transformation. We are all human beings. How we deal with people is a particularly important aspect of our professional and personal lives. In terms of professional collaboration, we need to 'separate the people from the problem' (Fisher and Ury, 1997, p. 11). We all have different perceptions, emotional responses, and communication abilities. In recognizing this and separating it from the issue we are trying to address, we have a better chance of a mutually agreeable arrangement being put in place.

The *Oxford Dictionary* (online) has two very different views of the collaborative process:

- the action of working with someone to produce something, and
- traitorous cooperation with an enemy.

While it is to be hoped that the first is the more likely candidate, the second does allude to some of the hazards which can be attached to the process. Difficulties in adopting a collaborative approach are associated with:

- suspicion of others' motives,
- vested interests in a particular outcome, and
- working with difficult people.

At a basic level, Head (2003, p. 50) suggests that there are 'individual activities which make up the procedural aspects of the collaborative process:

- coordinating,
- consulting,
- communicating, and
- cooperating.'

Societies or communities operate within these strictures. However, these actions are not mutually exclusive. If the activities remain at the level of these procedures, the net result may be efficiency, but by no means will all of the potential benefits of the collaborative process be achieved (Head, 2003).

Projects arise out of perceived identified needs, which Head (2003) calls the antecedent. This antecedent to collaborative work necessitates people working together effectively (the activity). The outcome of collaboration should be another activity or set of activities (the result). This process for collaborative working can be applied to both development and interdisciplinary Western scientific projects. For example, grappling with universal issues such as climate change or crop growing might require both the community and the scientific researcher to work together. It might also call for different disciplines within science to cooperate. If we accept collaboration in and between groups as crucial to addressing trans-national issues, then collaboration develops into a much more beguiling concept (Head, 2003) when considering:

- the antecedent–activity–result nature of the process,
- the diverse range of people who participate in the process, and
- the multiple activities involved.

In considering these aspects of the process, possibilities for achieving more than the efficiency signposted by its individual procedures become apparent. In other words, the activities mentioned above (coordinating, consulting, communicating, and cooperating) represent the serviceable aspects of collaboration, but there is also possibility for the conclusion of the process to be more than the sum of its parts. In this way, collaboration presents opportunities which transcend the procedural (Head, 2003). If we are to combine the view of collaboration as a means of more effective learning (Bruner, 1996; Vygotsky, 1978) with the notion that it has the potential to go beyond the procedural (Daniels, Norwich, and Creese, 2000; Scritic, 1991), then the primary outcome of any collaborative process must be about more than simply taking part in the process.

39

The social element of the learning process is crucial. Vygotsky (1978) suggests that when we learn there is a zone of proximal development (ZPD) which relates to how much we can learn from a given situation. The ZPD represents the distance between what a learner can achieve on her and his own and what can be learned in collaboration with more able or more experienced adults or peers. In a development context there is the potential for difficulties to arise when Western knowledge holders perceive themselves as, or are perceived as, the more able or experienced peers. Equally within a community context a male elder might consider himself to be more experienced or able than, for example, women from the community. The problem here is not the ZPD per se, but the stance that contributors take within it. Issues associated with power relations permeate both Western and indigenous knowledge constructs, and the interface between Western and indigenous knowledge are equally complex in nature (Briggs, 2005).

A cognitive interpretation of the ZPD (Daniels, Norwich, and Creese, 2000) would postulate that the learning that takes place within the ZPD, when we work alone, is much less than when we engage with others. Participatory models of development (Kapoor, 2004), with their emphasis on community, would seem to support this view arguing that it is together that progress will be achieved (Chambers, 2001). In addition, teams of researchers working on a scientific project may make greater gains than those working alone (Bok, 2003). Moreover, this coincides with what Bruner (1996, p. 3) has to say about the creation of meaning: 'however much the individual may seem to operate on his or her own in carrying out the quest for meanings, nobody can do it unaided by the culture's symbolic systems. It is culture that provides the tools for organizing and understanding our worlds in communicable ways.'

Alternative interpretations of ZPD exist. One such interpretation is the cultural model in which the ZPD is represented as the difference between what might be termed active knowledge (being owned by individuals and the result of their everyday experiences) and understood knowledge (being scientific in nature and gained through instruction) (Daniels, Norwich, and Creese, 2000). In development terms active knowledge would equate to indigenous knowledge, and understood knowledge is akin to Western knowledge. The issue for development studies is how these might intertwine so that everyday experiences may be influenced and shaped by instruction and vice versa. A second alternative interpretation views the ZPD as the distance between the everyday actions of individuals and collectively generated activity, the collectivist or societal interpretation (Lave and Wenger, 1991). Indigenous knowledge may be harvested collectively within a rural context, for example, but equally science may collectively garner knowledge. Again the issue here is how these bodies of knowledge connect and influence individuals' everyday actions in both settings, thus influencing the social structures in which they takes place. This brings us back to the perennial issue around dominant cultures and power constructs.

Working together to change practice

It could be argued that changing practice is at the heart of development. Western science, disciplines within Western science, and indigenous community knowledge bring centuries of different traditions and experiences to bear on an issue. Each of the players will have developed beliefs and values around her or his practice and from personal experiences, thus creating a framework of reference within which to operate. Encapsulating individual 'structures of feelings' (Williams, 1977) seems eminently sensible but is problematic in practice and does not lend itself to traditional social science research methodology dominated by a hegemony which takes little account of the 'ephemeral, indefinite, and irregular' (Law, 2004, p. 4). Gibson (1984, p. 62) contends that 'structures of feelings result in adults making judgments, explicit or implicit, on what is worthwhile and what is not' (p. 62). If we place value on particular ways of being, then in Western science particular structures of feelings might lead to the dismissing of indigenous knowledge and practice, deeming it to be outdated. Within the community there is potential for structures of feeling to lead to the dismissing of science as unconnected to 'real life'. If we accept that beliefs and frames of reference are drivers of practice, then we need to take account of these within and across any groups that work collaboratively.

This understanding of the beliefs of the individuals to address changes in practice does not necessarily dovetail with the universal hegemonic power associated with Western science. Within the field of education, authors such as Osberg and Biesta (2008) and Lenz Taguchi (2007 and 2008) have challenged the idea of universality in relation to educational goals and the standardization of curriculum. They argue that teaching and learning are a more nuanced activity and are linked to the local context. They argue that educators' values and goals will have to be renegotiated and that this renegotiation will result in 'rhizomatic logic' (Lenz Tagucchi, 2010, p. 19) and may result in an amelioration of the dominant values. Rhizomatic logic has its roots in post-structuralism and builds on the philosophical and cultural theories of Delueze and Guattari (1987). Rhizomatic logic suggests that beliefs and views should not be regarded as fixed, and in the context discussed here they would be part of what community and academics may become when they acknowledge the possibility of shifting multiple truths. However, careful consideration has to be given to the way in which disparate groups are brought together and how beliefs, values, and traditions are accepted, valued, challenged, negotiated, and changed in the light of the interaction. Further re-entrenchment of long-held beliefs across the groups may become the fall-back position when accepted norms are confronted.

Within educational contexts 'communities of practice' is a broadly used concept and is defined by Wenger, McDermott, and Snyder (2002, p. 4) as 'groups of people who share a concern, a set of problems, or a passion about a topic, and who deepen their knowledge and expertise in this area by interacting on an ongoing basis'. One of the defining aspects of this approach is its conceptualization of learning. Wenger (1998) argues that learning is not individualistic but social and located within social networks. Situating learning in a social context offers opportunities to explore this symbiotic relationship between learning and community participation. Situated learning as proposed by Lave and Wenger (1991) suggests learning takes place in the context in which it is applied. They argue that conflict within this process results in social transformation and that it is the negotiation and renegotiation within the process that drives change forward. Lave and Wenger (1991) suggest that when participants first join a community they learn at the margin of the community before moving towards the centre in what Wenger (1998, p. 11) calls 'legitimate peripheral participation'. In this way learning is not merely about acquisition of knowledge, but instead there is recognition that less experienced and more experienced participants work together through the socio-cultural practices of the community. In a development context this apprenticeship model ought to apply to holders of both Western and indigenous knowledge with the focus on the ways in which learning is 'an evolving, continuously renewed set of relations' (Lave and Wenger, 1991, p. 50).

Within communities of practice some of the dialogue and discussion about development will take place in a formal setting, for example, village meetings or presentations within universities. Other times it will be more informal in nature and may involve a chat in the local community with farmers, teachers, or health workers. These discussion points offer opportunities for all to share information. However, within a community of practice it is not simply about sharing information. These information exchanges should build and develop deeper understandings between groups so that all groups can assimilate and adapt their frame of reference. It is through this process that differences in understanding and of perception can emerge. This in turn offers opportunities for confronting the incongruity that might exist between the different factions allowing for what Engeström, Miettinen, and Punamäki (1999) might describe as a more inventive outcome. Communities of practice assume that the voices of all have a platform from which to be heard. Of interest to post-colonial theorists was the 'ontological and epistemological status of the voices of subaltern peoples in Western knowledge systems' (Briggs and Sharp, 2004, p. 664). For Hooks (1990) the apprenticeship model described above may be simultaneously problematic and opportunistic. It might be viewed as problematic because the marginalization of subordinate voice results in exclusion from the discourse. At best, minimal interpretation allows for input at the margins where unforeseen possibilities lie. However, Hooks's argument (1990) assumes that the centre is the place where power and prejudice reside. In a community of practice the centre is inextricably linked to the margin, with reciprocity of voices from the margin and the centre both informing and transforming the margins and the centre. This interactive flow of dialogue and renegotiation of differing worldviews presents challenges. For example, the dialogic process for Western science, disciplines within universities, and/or communities may result in an adaptation of hitherto accepted ways of being, doing, and understanding.

Conclusion

Communities of practice are not a panacea for interdisciplinary collaborative working. Nonetheless, they do start to challenge the hegemonic ideas that lurk behind the quixotic arguments for both indigenous knowledge and Western scientific knowledge and give voice and credibility to different conceptualizations of issues and possible solutions in a local context. The local focus of this approach is at variance with globalization and the universal quest for solutions to apparently universal issues. This is its strength.

Lave and Wenger (1998, p. 12) claim that social learning theory is of significance to 'a number of disciplines, including anthropology, sociology, cognitive and social psychology, philosophy, and organizational and educational theory and practice'. Perhaps it has even broader appeal and relevance. Talking about communities of practice opens up discussion about how human beings manage the complex interactions between them. The perennial issues surrounding dominant cultures, power constructs, voice, and collaborative working become relevant for all who work with human beings. Much of this chapter has talked about the intricate and oftentimes problematic relationship between Western science and indigenous knowledge. Interdisciplinary tensions within the university system are also suggested. The issues transcend knowledge boundaries – traditional Western notions of knowledge, disciplinary knowledge, and indigenous knowledge. While situated knowledge becomes the context for discussions, at the core are far deeper issues relating to human interaction. Just as we cannot assume universal hegemony in Western knowledge or indigenous knowledge, neither can we assume universal frames of reference and structures of feeling (Sillitoe, 2010). The communities of practice concept arises from a Western-based system and theory and could be accused of bias against the local. But if all players start from the view that 'learning is the vehicle for the evolution of practices and the inclusion of newcomers the vehicle for development and transformation of identities' (Wenger, 1998, p. 13), then it offers an optimistic outlook as dialogue starts from the familiar – the individual's frame of reference – and moves towards collective, communal meaning-making.

For some, such an approach will require a paradigmatic shift in thinking and practice. This seems a tall order given the established roots of the systems and structures in question. However, we are fast approaching 2015 and with it the realization that the laudable international development goals set in 2000 (United Nations, 2000) will not be met by Western science, indigenous knowledge, or indeed a hybridized version of the two (Waage et al., 2010). The 'collegial imperative' (Head, 2003, p. 60) to work together seems clear, and an examination of communities of practice and their collaborative nature to impact at a local level is worth exploring. In communities of practice, Western and indigenous knowledge will cease to be uneasy bedfellows in an interdependent world and instead will transform into an integrated developmental continuum.

References

Barrett, B. D. (2012). Is Interdisciplinarity Old News? A Disciplined Consideration of Inter-disciplinarity. *British Journal of Sociology of Education* 33 (1): 97–114.

Bok, D. (2003). Universities in the Marketplace: The Commercialization of Higher Education. Princeton, NJ: Princeton University Press.

Boreham, N. C., et al. (2000). Clinical Risk and Collective Competence in the Hospital Emergency Department in the UK. *Social Science and Medicine* 51: 83–91.

Briggs, J. (2005). The Use of Indigenous Knowledge in Development: Problems and Challenges. *Progress in Development Studies* 5 (2): 99–114.

Briggs, J., and Sharp, J. (2004). Indigenous Knowledges and Development: A Postcolonial Caution. *Third World Quarterly* 25 (4): 661–676.

Bruner, J. (1996). *The Culture of Education.* Boston: Harvard University Press.

Chambers, R. (2001). The World Development Report: Concepts, Content and Chapter 12. *Journal of International Development* 13: 299–306.

Classen, C. (2000). Other Ways to Wisdom: Learning through the Senses across Cultures. In L. King (ed.), *Learning, Knowledge and Cultural Context.* Dordrecht, Netherlands: UIL and Kluwer Academic.

Classen, C. (2005). *The Book of Touch.* London: Berg.

Cleaver, F. (1999). Paradoxes of Participation: Questioning Participatory Approaches to Development. *Journal of International Development* 11 (4): 597–612.

Daniels, H., Norwich, B., and Creese, A. (2000). Supporting Collaborative Problem-Solving Schools. In H. Daniels (ed.), *Special Education Reformed.* London: Falmer Press.

Deleuze, G., and Guattari, F. (1987). *A Thousand Plateaus: Capitalism and Schizophrenia.* London: Athlone Press.

Diawara, M. (2000). Globalisation, Development Politics and Local Knowledges. *International Sociology* 15 (2): 361–371.

Dodds, K. (2002). The Third World, Developing Countries, the South, Poor Countries in Desai. In R. B. Potter (ed.), *The Companion to Development Studies.* London: Arnold.

Dove, M. R. (2000). The Life-Cycle of Indigenous Knowledge and the Case of Natural Rubber Production. In R. Ellen, P. Parkes, and A. Bicker (eds), *Indigenous Environmental Knowledge and its Transformations: Critical Anthropological Perspectives.* Amsterdam: Harwood Academic Publishers.

Ellen, R., and Harris, H. (2000). Introduction. In R. Ellen, P. Parkes, and A. Bicker (eds), *Indigenous Environmental Knowledge and its Transformations: Critical Anthropological Perspectives.* Amsterdam: Harwood Academic Publishers.

Engeström, Y., Miettinen, R., and Punamäki, R. (1999). *Perspectives on Activity Theory.* New York and Cambridge: Cambridge University Press.

Escobar, A. (1995). *Encountering Development: The Making and Unmaking of the Third World.* Princeton, NJ: Princeton University Press.

Fisher, R., and Ury, W. (1997). *Getting to Yes: Negotiating an Agreement without Giving In.* London: Arrow Books.

Gibson, R. (1984). *Structuralism and Education.* London: Hodder & Stoughton.

Gorjestani, N. (2000). Indigenous Knowledge for Development: Opportunities and Challenges. Presentation, UNCTAD Conference on Traditional Knowledge, Geneva. www.worldbank.org/afr/ik/ikpaper_0102.pdf (last accessed January 2013).

Green, M. (2000). Participatory Development and the Appropriation of Agency in Southern Tanzania. *Critique of Anthropology* 20 (1): 67–89.

Head, G. (2003). Effective Collaboration: Deep Collaboration as an Essential Element of the Learning Process. *Journal of Educational Enquiry* 4 (2): 47–62.

Hooks, B. (1990). Marginality as a Site of Resistance. In R. Ferguson et al. (eds), *Out There: Marginalization and Contemporary Cultures*. Cambridge, MA: MIT Press.

Jacobson, C., and Stephens, A. (2009). Cross-Cultural Approaches to Environmental Research and Management: Response to the Dualisms Inherent in Western Science? *Journal of the Royal Society of New Zealand* 39: 159–162.

Jakimov, T. (2008). Answering Critics: The Potential and Limitations of the Knowledge Agenda as a Practical Response to Post-Development Critiques. *Progress in Development Studies* 8 (4): 311–323.

Kalland, A. (2000). Indigenous Knowledge: Prospects and Limitations. In R. Ellen, P. Parkes, and A. Bicker (eds), *Indigenous Environmental Knowledge and its Transformations: Critical Anthropological Perspectives*. Amsterdam: Harwood Academic Publishers.

Kapoor, I. (2004). Donor Participatory Governance Evaluation: Initial Trends, Implications, Opportunities, Constraints. *Journal of International Development* 16: 157–170.

Lave, J., and Wenger, E. (1991). *Situated Learning: Legitimate Peripheral Participation*. Cambridge: Cambridge University Press.

Lave, J., and Wenger, E. (1998). *Communities of Practice: Learning, Meaning and Identity*. Cambridge: Cambridge University Press.

Law, J. (2004), *After Method: Mess in Social Science Research*. London: Routledge.

Lenz Tagucchi, H. (2007), Deconstructing and Transgressing the Theory–Practice Dichotomy in Swedish Early Childhood Education. *Educational Philosophy and Theory* 39 (3): 275–290.

Lenz Tagucchi, H. (2008). An 'Ethics of Resistance' Challenges Taken-for-Granted Ideas in Early Childhood Education. *International Journal of Educational* Research 47 (5): 270–282.

Lenz Tagucchi, H. (2010). Rethinking Pedagogical Practices in Early Childhood Education: A Multidimensional Approach to Learning and Inclusion. In N. Yelland (ed.), *Contemporary Perspectives on Early Childhood Education*. London: Open University Press.

Mayoux, L., and Chambers, R. (2005). Reversing the Paradigm: Quantification, Participatory Methods and Pro-Poor Impact Assessment. *Journal of International Development* 17 (2): 271–298.

McFarlane, C. (2006). Crossing Borders: Development, Learning and the North–South Divide. *Third World Quarterly* 27 (8): 1413–1437.

Mercer, N. (1995). *The Guided Construction of Knowledge: Talk amongst Teachers and Learners*. Avon: Multilingual Matters.

Nustad, K. (2001). Development: The Devil We Know? *Third World Quarterly* 17 (2): 239–250.

Osberg, D. C., and Biesta, G. J. J. (2008). The Emergent Curriculum: Navigating a Complex Course between Unguided Learning and Planned Enculturation. *Journal of Curriculum Studies* 40 (3): 313–328.

Oxford Dictionaries. http://www.oxforddictionaries.com/definition/english/knowledge (last accessed March 2013).

Ozga, J., and Jones, R. (2006). Travelling and Embedded Policy: The Case of Knowledge Transfer. *Journal of Education Policy* 21(1): 1–17.

Pretty, J. (1994). Alternative Systems of Enquiry for a Sustainable Agriculture. *IDS Bulletin* 25: 37–48.

Scritic, T. M. (1991). Behind Special Education: A Critical Analysis of Professional Culture and School Organisation. Denver, CO: Love.

Sillitoe, P. (1998). Knowing the Land: Soil and Land Resource Evaluation and Indigenous Knowledge, *Soil Use and Management* 14: 188–193.

Sillitoe, P. (2007). Local Science vs Global Science: Approaches to Indigenous Knowledge in International Development. Environmental Anthropology and Ethnobiology. Oxford: Berghahn.

Sillitoe, P. (2010). Trust in Development: Some Implications of Knowing in Indigenous Knowledge. *Journal of the Royal Anthropological Institute* 16: 12–30.

Storey, A. (2000). Post-Development Theory: Romanticism and Pontius Pilate Politics. *Development* 43 (4): 40–46.

Sumner, A., and Tribe, M. (2008). Development Studies and Cross-Disciplinarity: Research at the Social Science–Physical Science Interface. *Journal of International Development* 20: 751–767.

United Nations (2000). Millennium Development Goals. www.un.org/millennium/declaration/ares552e.pdf (last accessed 8 February 2014).

Vygotsky, L. (1978). *Mind in Society: The Development of Higher Psychological Processes.* Boston: Harvard University Press.

Waage, J., Banerji, R., Campbell, O., Chirwa, E., Collender, G., Dieltiens,V., Dorward, A., Godfrey-Faussett, P., Hanvoravongchai, P., Kingdon, G., Little, A., Mills, A., Mulholland, K., Mwinga, A., North, A., Patcharanarumol, W., Poulton, C., Tangcharoensathien, V., and Unterhalter, E. (2010). *The Millennium Development Goals: A Cross-Sectoral Analysis and Principles for Goal Setting after 2015.* London: London International Development Centre.

Wenger, E. (1998). *Communities of Practice: Learning, Meaning and Identity.* New York: Cambridge University Press.

Wenger, E., McDermott, R., and Snyder, W. M. (2002). *Cultivating Communities of Practice: A Guide to Managing Knowledge.* Boston: Harvard Business School.

Williams, R. (1977). *Marxism and Literature.* Oxford: Oxford University Press.

World Bank (2002). Constructing Knowledge Societies: New Challenges for Tertiary Education. Washington, DC: World Bank.

4

Guerrilla geography: describing and defending place for a living (or the renaissance of 100–mile geographers)

Briony Penn

In 1969, the bicentenary of the geographer and naturalist Alexander von Humboldt slipped by largely unnoticed in North America. Given his contributions to the study of the earth, it was a surprising descent into relative obscurity. A medical researcher writing in to the *Journal of the American Medical Association* had expressed his dismay that Humboldt was 'no longer accorded the recognition he enjoyed during his lifetime' (Frankel, 1964). Frankel was remembering Humboldt's style of collaborative enquiry during famous expeditions to the crater of Vesuvius in the autumn of 1805 accompanied by his friends and colleagues, the chemist Joseph Louis Gay-Lussac, the geologist Christian Leopold von Buch, and the Latin American politician Simón Bolívar, who was encouraged by Humboldt to win independence from the repressive Spanish Empire – the namesake for the current Bolívar revolution in Latin America. They were looking at the live eruptions of Vesuvius but the conversation, undoubtedly, covered the geological, atmospherical, geographical, biological, and humanitarian equivalent of eruptions. As Humboldt wrote in *Cosmos*, 'Nature ... is a unity in diversity of phenomena; a harmony blending together all created things, however dissimilar in form and attributes; one great whole cosmos animated by the breath of life' (Humboldt, 1858). Frankel's hope for a fitting bicentenary never materialized; the political climate of the cold war in North America had left little appetite for 'a champion of the liberation of Latin America from the yoke of colonialist oppression' (Rupke, 2005, p. 136).

As a young girl in 1969, my thoughts were not yet straying to Humboldt and his cohort cohort, nor to my own small role in North American colonial oppression. I was sitting on another extinct volcano, Christmas Hill, on the far western edge of the continent on Vancouver Island innocently looking out over the capital of British Columbia named after the empress herself, Victoria. I was in a remnant patch of native oak meadow deemed by the first colonial leader, Sir James Douglas, 'a perfect Eden', and pondering a basic biogeographical question: what was the story of this place? It was a task towards which the 1805 cohort would have been well placed to bend their collective minds. But it was the mid-twentieth century, and the descriptive study of place was temporarily out of fashion. Academic trends towards quantification and spatial economic theory found footholds in institutions bowing to the financial pressures of globalization. I was in the middle of the generation or two in which regional knowledge, description, and engagement were considered quaint, feminine, or dangerous, and/or were relegated to obscurity like Humboldt and Bolívar.

Almost until the close of the twentieth century, this drought-adapted ecosystem, now the focus of research on ecosystem resilience in the face of climate change, had lost its name, its cultural identity beyond a Christian Eden or Little England, had little recognition from academia, and had no protection – despite being one of the most endangered ecosystems in Canada. Helping a community to articulate the uniqueness and relevance of their place became a task for a new cohort of elders, poets, conservation biologists, naturalists, palaeobotanists, activists, and guerilla geographers who asked the thornier questions. This chapter presents a case study in the Garry oak ecosystem where a return to localism and demand for regional enquiry helped build a more resilient community. The mapping of place, the naming of place and the telling of stories that made sense of our relationship to the land were important tools in achieving this. It is written as a personal narrative because community activism has little theoretical context – it just happens. Latterly, academia folds itself around the movement and makes sense of it. Humboldt, in this regard, was in fact the original trailblazer. The intention of this chapter is to encourage university students wishing to chart a course of meaningful work in a dynamic time to find a way to support themselves as they pick up the lost stories of their place and weave them with the new. It identifies the increasing role for the young guerrilla geographers in their respective places around the globe. It also suggests ways for the academic community to support, educate, and legitimize the next generation of guerrilla geographers.

The origins of a guerilla geographer

During that spring of 1969, I would sit for hours gazing at these meadows of stunning spring wildflowers full of butterflies from one of the gnarled Garry oak trees. The essence of Garry oak meadows is that they occur on sunny, warm, south-aspect slopes, distinct from the rest of the coast, which is typically shrouded in cloud. These meadows are reliant on geology. The tectonic plates of that Pacific edge have piled up mountains like suitcases on a conveyor belt, forming a unique rainshadow from the deluges of the open ocean. I dwelt in an island ecosystem within an island. In 1969, the Garry oak ecosystem was four years away from being named and described by Western botanists botanists (Hans Roemer was to complete his Ph.D. on 'Forest Vegetation and Environments on the Saanich Peninsula, Vancouver Island' in 1973 from the University of Victoria. Roemer was trained in Germany as a landscape ecologist). Meanwhile the indigenous language describing the species and the well-established culture that had inhabited it for millennia was flickering at the edge after a century of colonial prohibition of the language. I was looking out over a sea that lay in the same peculiar limbo, unnamed and unstoried by the latest colonists while the indigenous stories and names were lingering in memories and ethnographies (see Figure 4.1).

Figure 4.1 Sitting on a Garry oak branch

Source: Illustration by Briony Penn

Of those features that had been named, few made sense to me. The glacier-capped mountains that captured the clouds were called the Olympics, evoking images of ancient Greek gods and sporting spectacles, far from the tectonic drama that was happening in front of my eyes. The volcanoes to the east, one of which was to erupt a decade later, were visibly steaming from their vents and 'Baker' or 'Saint Helen' seemed mild appellations for these forces of nature under which we perched. The city that lay below was named Victoria after a long-dead monarch who had never gazed on this island, and nor had the monarch, George, after whom one of the straits of water was named. The tree I sat in was named after a benefactor from the Hudson's Bay Company in a fort three thousand kilometres away from the tree's most easterly distribution. The hill itself, Christmas Hill, was named at the time when my colonial forebears were locating a new fort site for the company. The Indian chief's baby at the time had been 'stolen' by an eagle, but 'found' on top of this hill by company men on Christmas Day – for which we were to give thanks for the Christianizing influence on the natives. I remember doubting the veracity of that Christmas story and its motives even then. There was no shortage of incomprehensible stories for that day.

My love and defense of this place were absolute. I constructed forts of my own to create strongholds against brothers and neighbourhood bullies who came armed with rocks, sticks, and matches. I defended the alligator lizards that lived in the rocky outcrops, the nighthawks that nested on the mossy knolls, and the meadows of camas, shooting star and Easter lilies – native wildflowers for which only a grandmother and her elderly garden companion, Mr Raven, could produce names and affection. The camas bulbs would blossom and die for several more decades, before I learned that they had once carpeted the region and that children, like myself, had been playing in these places enjoying the views and warmth, while their mothers harvested the bulbs for millennia.

The key to the entire landscape, I later learned, were the women who owned and harvested these meadows, feeding their communities and trading the rest up the coast. They were cultural landscapes of enormous appeal for their aspect, their beauty, and their importance for survival.

The biggest threat to the Christmas Hill camas meadows came in 1971 with a proposal for Victoria's new hospital. I wrote my first letter to the editor stating that they should not put hospitals where people were healthy and happy already. It was a political awakening and proved accurate when the links between aboriginal health and food sovereignty became clear, decades later. The hospital went elsewhere, but what followed was a steady onslaught of proposals for malls and urbanization, about which I had little ability to articulate my distress, other than that these sprawling monotonous landscapes felt dull, ugly, and heavy on my heart. Cars, I had an intui-tive sense, were causing untold damage in the atmosphere, yet there was no credible vocabulary to integrate a discussion of nature, climate, and aesthetics with the compartmentalized technological male domain of energy and transportation. My intuitions lay in the realm of anecdote, and to even mention the words 'feels wrong' and 'ugly' had no place in societal discourse until I arrived as an undergraduate at the the University of British Columbia (UBC) geography department in 1977.

Despite the quantification revolution, a handful of geography professors were bravely assigning Yi-fu Tuan and Allen Van Newkirk to their undergraduates. Tuan was reintroducing ideas of a humanist persuasion like the concepts of place and placelessness out of Columbia University, while the biogeographer Allen Van Newkirk, living in a rural community outside Halifax at the time, had rebranded an old concept in 'bioregionalism'. Van Newkirk was pointing out the tendency for human cultural communities to thrive when they organized themselves around ecological communities that shared physical and ecological associations. Bioregions were mapped by overlaying descriptions of watersheds, land forms, traditional territorial boundaries, patterns of flora and fauna, climate, and economic linkages. In 1971, Van Newkirk collaborated with the cultural activist Peter Berg, from San Francisco, to expand the concept of the 'bioregion' to a political organizing unit. 'A bioregion refers both to geographical terrain and a terrain of consciousness – to a place and the ideas that have developed about how to live in that place' (Berg, 1977, p. 2). Berg, the ecologist Raymond Dasmann, and the Pulitzer prize-winning poet Gary Snyder began to share their common interest in inspiring a process of social change on the North American continent around the integrated concept of bioregions. But although the theorists for local community engagement were there, the skills, tools, and political will to implement them at the university level were not. As an aspiring geographer eager to do service in a region and for its community of inhabitants, I was out of a job. Was there a profession for a geographer wanting to tell the story of place? Unlike Humboldt, I had no personal fortune to pursue the task.

It was not until I was working on a Ph.D. in geography at Edinburgh University in Scotland, looking at legal and perceptual constraints of public access to the land, that I stumbled upon the concept of community mapping as a tool for public engagement and the means to employ it. The inspiration had nothing to do with the formal cartographic courses with theodolites, cadastral maps, and geographic information systems designed for resource mapping and allocation. Nor was there much chance of grants assisting graduates in community mapping, as much of the funding at Edinburgh in cartography during the 1980s was funded by Ministry of Defence. One of my colleagues was working on the early digital modelling of landscapes for cruise missiles. Inspiration came from my informal education gleaned at the breakfast table every Sunday morning. I would open up the *Sunday Times* magazine to find a beautifully illustrated map of a local area or parish somewhere in Britain. Local residents and artists had collaborated to map and record everything they cherished about their place, from badger sets to heritage apple orchards and from historic pubs to familiar landmarks. The process was called the Parish Maps Project. Following initiation in 1987 by an organization called Common Ground, the founders, Sue Clifford and Angela King, provided a template to describe and ultimately defend what was important to communities at the very personable scale of the parish. Parishes, in some regards, were the ancient jurisdictional forerunner of the bioregion.

The fundamental premise of mapping as pioneered by Common Ground was that whoever draws the maps controls the fate of the land; maps typically drawn by professionals delineate property lines, the ownership of scarce resources, or zones defining certain activities. Community maps, on the other hand, provide a geographical and historical record of what makes a place unique and liveable. They record the special information that is not included on commercial maps or does not have commercial values. What the parish maps project demonstrated was that if someone has taken the time and effort to record community information, then the maps took on a life of their own and had power. People become aware of and sensitized to these values of attachment, and they become advocates. The application to my home islands off the west coast of Canada seemed obvious.

I arrived back from Scotland eager to introduce this idea and very quickly came up against some challenges. The first was nailed to the Christmas Hill oaks, declaring a developer's application for rezoning from Agricultural Land Reserve to urban zoning – the death knell to this plant community. I was eight months pregnant and crawled along a ditch by the side of the meadows in the dead of night to erect my own sign, which said 'Zone for Garry oaks'. At the University of Victoria, where I had started teaching part-time as a sessional instructor, an equally unique remnant of the Garry oak meadow on campus was designated for a new Centre for Innovative Teaching. To the sign declaring this new development, I added an 'Un-' before 'innovative' and signed it. If I had briefly considered a career as an academic, my engagement in activism eliminated that option. It was neither the first nor the last time that a university, with schools of environment, biology, and political science, failed to put the pedagogy into practice. Academic David Orr has taken up that critique (Orr, 1997).

Community mapping in 1991 had little place else to go in Vancouver Island than the non-profit sector, so we started projects under various banners. We set up the Garry Oak Meadow Preservation Society to raise awareness about the ecosystem and trees, which were the focal point of the movement. Community volunteers mapped the ancient trees using street maps, documenting the lack of young ones coming up. The word 'meadow' was added to 'Garry oak' to create a friendly 'meme' for the ecosystem, playing to an agrarian nostalgia. A publisher of a local independent magazine (*Monday Magazine*) took a real interest in the issue and provided a space for me to write a weekly column on the natural history and geography of the region, which continued for sixteen years. As a group that included ecologists, we had substantial support inside and out for the provincial government to do a Sensitive Ecosystem Inventory, which local governments could integrate into their Official Community Plans with new planning tools, like development permit areas and natural area tax incentives, to guide development away from these sensitive areas. From the inventories, we identified high-risk areas that were under threat of development and lobbied for legislation to establish land trusts that could help conserve these lands lying in private ownership. We set up a provincial land trust, the Land Conservancy of British Columbia, with an active membership, to acquire these critical areas using the new stewardship tools like conservation covenants. Covenants were voluntary legal agreements between landowners and conservation organizations to protect areas with legal baselines and with penalties for non-compliance attached to the land title itself with some tax incentives for lowered property value.

In 1993, Doug Aberley, who had been at Heriot-Watt University in Edinburgh at the same time as me (although we had never met there), brought his brand of community mapping to the School of Community and Regional Planning at UBC, which was headed by Professor Bill Rees of 'ecological footprint' fame.In his *Boundaries of Home: Mapping for Local Empowerment* Aberley outlined his 'kitchen table' approach of encouraging public input through outreach and digital tools, stirring up the rarefied air of regional planning offices. Aberley developed a particular expertise in assisting first nations to map their own resources, place names, and traditional uses of their territories. Meanwhile, I worked with the community organizer Sheila Harrington and the geographer Kathy Dunster on the first artists' show on the Gulf Islands in 1995, called 'Mapping Cherished Places', an exhibition of twenty maps by local artists of their treasured home places. Islanders loved the maps, and mapping caught on in the region.

As Sue Clifford and Angela King successfully demonstrated in the 1980s, purely scientific arguments for conservation of the unique and the rare were less successful for public engagement than artistic celebrations of what we hold dear. The Renaissance tradition of marrying the microscope with the mandolin drew people in with an accessible celebration of place. Common Ground artists picked up the tradition that had been continued by artist-geographers like Heywood Sumner, a major figure in the Arts and Crafts Movement in the 1880s and 1890s, when he chronicled the disappearing landscape of the New Forest in southern England. The result of the Parish Project was a stunning collection of maps that were as effective in their parishes as they were as a collection. The maps each accurately locate on land those places that local people valued, while providing some space on the paper for the artist to express what those values were. With increasing land use conflicts, the parish map idea had fuelled a renaissance of mapping, as it could also express the pain of placelessness.

With the demand for a handbook coming out of the original exhibition of 'Mapping Cherished Places', *Giving the Land a Voice,:Mapping our Home Places* was produced with a growing collaboration of community mappers. The contacts and expertise evolved out of the shows and workshops, and the handbook sold worldwide, building on the growing movement of bioregional mapping with a special emphasis on 'barefoot mapping' – making maps from scratch with a simple compass and tape measure. What followed was a rich decade of workshops, developing methodology, curriculum for schools, and training sessions. Schoolyard mapping was popular with teachers as a way to integrate arts and sciences in the curriculum, assist with greening schoolyards and getting children outside through the curriculum.

In Vancouver, the following year, the Institute for the Humanities at Simon Fraser University initiated a mapping project called 'In Our Own Backyard: Mapping the Grandview-Woodland Community', which drew wide participation. This was a popular project and generated many maps and community mappers. In the absence of an academic engagement at the University of Victoria, a North American version of Common Ground, a grassroots community mapping network, was started in Victoria under Maeve Lydon, assisting community associations to produce their own maps of what they identified as important. Well over a dozen regional maps of what neighbourhoods valued were produced over the next decade, and these integrated both the simple mapping of special places with the more scientific ecosystem mapping laid over official community plans. This helped to raise awareness in ways in which typical planning and zoning maps fail to do. Finally in 2006, the network was brought to the University of Victoria by Lydon when she took on a role in the new Office for Community-Based Research. The project also developed a hold, albeit tenuous, in the geography department under the digital and artistic guidance of the cartographer Ken Josephson and graduate students.

Not surprisingly, the shift of community mapping towards digital media helped to expand the movement. Some innovative government scientists, like Brad Mason with the federal government, began to see the power and fiscal advantage of harnessing citizen-collected data for sensitive ecosystems, from eel grass beds to the Garry oak meadows, and set up digital community mapping networks online. In the independent filmmaking world, Heather McAndrew and David Springbettt produced a documentary series and book on community activism including a segment called 'Maps with Teeth', featuring the work of the community mapper Doug Aberley and myself. The writer and editor Alan Morantz wrote his book *Where is Here? Canada's Maps and the Stories They Tell* in 2002, documenting the flourishing of the artistic and community mapping in Canada and placing our west coast efforts in the broader Canadian context. 'Communities too', he writes, 'are taking charge of their own maps, with equally intriguing results. These maps have the ineffable quality to synchronize with the emotional currents of individuals and communities, and to give visual expression to hard-to-get-at impulses' (Morantz, 2002, pp. 216–217).

With growing grassroots support, the scientific community acquired a small measure of political support and opportunities opened up federally with a Minister of Environment, David Anderson, who had himself been raised in a Garry oak meadow and pushed through a 'federal species at risk' act. The listing of over 100 species at risk associated with this endangered ecosystem led to a prioritization of federal funding for its conservation. The Garry Oak Ecosystem Recovery Team was formed and took on the more systematic scientific inventory to meet federal requirements, making use of federal grants to compile its inventory.

Throughout this time, the community mapping projects flourished with the diversity of its tellers, especially first nations. For thousands of years, the wildflower meadows of camas and fritillarias had fed coastal communities. River otters and nesting birds like oystercatchers also loved these areas. The crops grew luxuriously with crab and fish fertiliser and equal doses of spring sun and showers. The large bulbs were harvested after the seeds dropped in the summer and smaller bulbs were replanted back in the earth. Every autumn just before the rains, the islets were burned to enrich the next year's harvest and suppress any conifers.

When colonists converted camas patches and deer hunting grounds to agricultural plots of potatoes and pigs, camas culture with its associated flowers, butterflies, birds, and human traditions shrank to a mere 1 percent of the former range. The only places where camas culture survived were the tiny Indian reserves, the smallest islets, parks set aside as pleasure grounds in the early part of the twentieth century, and the inaccessible rocky patches of hillsides where I grew up. These areas became islands of biodiversity in a sea of urban development – perfect laboratories for theories of island biogeography.

It was this shared landscape that brought Cheryl Bryce, from Songhees First Nation, and me together. The two of us, a cultural mix of potato and camas cultures, were in our own cultural solitudes, rooting out the white fleshy camas bulbs in these isolated remnant patches while we looked over encroaching shopping malls and subdivisions. Her tradition of digging camas had all but gone, remaining as just memories of being taken as a small child to the parks with her grandmother to dig the bulbs early in the morning to avoid arrest. The traditional diet of camas, cooked slowly in pits to break down inulin, with high proportions of seafood from the Salish Sea, had disappeared with the loss of access to camas and salmon. With restricted access came 'loss of cultural knowledge relating to the production, harvesting, processing, and use of the food – the knowledge that has sustained generations of people in their home territories for thousands of years' (Bryce, 2013). Cheryl produced a documentary called *Diabetes: Then and Now*, highlighting the impacts of lack of access to traditional foods on indigenous health – 60 percent of Lekwungen people having contracted type 2 diabetes.

Cheryl used ethnographic accounts and worked on restoring the tradition of camas culture on her reserve, reinstating the harvesting in the summer, the feasts and the burning of the meadows in the fall. In restoration projects, with the support of the Restoration of Natural Systems at the University of Victoria, she worked with graduate students on traditional harvesting patterns and the relationship to ecosystem health. Control sites of burned area and non-burned areas identified how certain activities benefitted certain species. Increasingly, however, the responsibility and 'liability' for species at risk – applicable only to lands under federal jurisdictions like Indian reserves – was falling on first nations' hands, with no responsibility being borne by lands under private control.

In 1999, one of the largest, most intact Garry oak meadows left in British Columbia (well over 600 hectares) that had been mapped and identified for conservation was acquired by a corporation that intended to develop it. There was no protection afforded to the species or ecosystems at risk under the federal act, so the only option for conservation was to stop the development and buy it. Salt Spring Islanders rallied around and for two years raised awareness and over a million dollars. CBC and the National Film Board filmed a documentary on the issue called *Ah the Money, the Money, the Money*. The money raised leveraged another $15 million from federal, provincial, and regional governments to buy 1,800 hectares of Garry oak meadows and Douglas fir forest. Nine people went to jail and thousands participated in demonstrations, walks, and fundraising activities. As a guerilla geographer, my task was to create maps that would integrate the scientific rationale with the community's emotional response to the land. My role also shifted into media stunts as the realization dawned that science had little to engage media. Two more projects were born out of this time.

In 1999, Sheila Harrington, Judi Stevenson, and I launched a mapping project for the millennium. It was a five-year project and brought together community members, elders, historians, geologists, biologists, artists, fishers, farmers, ethnobotanists, and a cross-section of the community to map the rich natural and cultural history of the islands at the turn of the millennium. Funding came from a variety of sources, which were documented with the methodology in the final atlas to provide a template for other communities. Three thousand people from seventeen islands had brought their paintbrushes, computers, compasses, pastels, binoculars, fabric, clay, plaster, plant books, hiking boots, water samples, heritage registrars, traditional knowledge, and stories to the task, producing a set of maps that became a travelling exhibition and a book, *Islands in the Salish Sea: A Community Atlas*, which was nominated for two British Columbia book awards. The reviewer Coll Thrush wrote of the atlas:

> *Islands in the Salish Sea* is a model for thinking critically about our part of the world, for doing good research, and for actively building community and engaging in advocacy of place. Just imagine: what if every place in British Columbia, from Oak Bay to the Downtown Eastside, from Surrey to Fort Nelson, from Haida Gwaii to Whistler, was home to something like this? What if community groups, schools, and universities throughout the province (and beyond) engaged in this kind of work? Then where (pun intended) would we be? (Thrush, 2006, p. 1)

The other project was to solidify the name and concept of the bioregion, around which islanders not only from Canada but from the American islands could rally. Central to that objective was to support the work of Bert Webber, a Canadian-American biologist originally from Vancouver, who conceived the idea of naming the unnamed inland sea after the Coast Salish, the common linguistic name for the people sharing the sea in the early 1970s. 'I was working on a paper to describe the ecology of the region for the U.S. Fish and Wildlife Branch and didn't have a name for what I was describing, so I proposed the Salish Sea.' Webber had spent the last ten years looking at potential impacts from oil spills, which do not recognize international boundaries or confine themselves to one strait or pass. He found his colleagues in the USA were starting to use the name Puget Sound to refer to all the northern Canadian waters, which confused the Canadians. The *Bellingham Herald* got hold of Webber's story in 1988 and published the first article on the proposal to name the unnamed sea (Penn, 2001).

The idea did not die. After the initial newspaper article, Webber was asked to submit an application to both the Canadian and the US agencies for a geographical place name in 1990. These applications were circulated quite widely for review and received a variety of comments. Many people and groups who recognized the ecological rationale for the name supported it, for example, first nations, naturalists, scientists, ecotour companies marketing particular regions, and so on. 'People who wanted to create a shared sense of place liked the idea.' Others felt there was no need for a new name, while others, who had misinterpreted the proposal and thought old names would be changed, were opposed. The proposal was shelved for a while on the grounds that there was not enough common usage – yet – and the name persisted.

Tom Sampson, elder of the Tsawout First Nations and instigator of the Coast Salish Sea Aboriginal Council, brought the name officially to government. The council continues to bring native leaders from both countries together on a biannual basis through the Salish Sea Conference. Sampson said that he first brought up the general notion of regional identity with the Premier of British Columbia, Mike Harcourt, in 1979, as a way of recognizing this distinct region of over eighty tribes that share resources, ceremonies, language, kinship, and traditional technologies. Although the Salish-speaking nations had no name other than 'saltwater' for the sea, Sampson championed the new name back in 1990, as did George Harris, of the Chemanius First Nations.

When I first met Webber in the early 1990s, his proposal hit a chord. I introduced the name into my weekly column in *Monday Magazine*. Over the next twenty years, it slowly worked into all sorts of places, from songs to tourist literature. Folk singer Holly Arntzen and I introduced the idea to Parks Canada, which adopted it in its school outreach programmes for the new national park and proposed national marine conservation areas. That project culminated in the writing of new songs, a CD called *The Salish Sea*, and a big festival of 400 school kids, who all sang songs about the Salish Sea. When we pitched the project to map the islands, the project naturally became 'The Islands of the Salish Sea'. The rationale for the Salish Sea name was to honour the common language of the Coast Salish people who had inhabited these shores for millennia and had a different ethic of stewardship for waters, lands, and animals. The sea as a partly enclosed body of water is more vulnerable to pollution and degradation than the open ocean. Protected waters like seas are also places of rich biodiversity because they afford shelter from the biggest oceanic storms; animals come in for sanctuary to overwinter, breed, and raise young. In 2010, the name Salish Sea was declared the official name of the sea by both countries and the Salish First Nations.

With the successes, there was also the increasing realization that community mapping and guerilla geography were surprisingly slow to get legitimacy in the academic world. Bill Reese, from UBC, writes, 'the modern university is at a tipping point. It can either continue its contemporary flirtation with the corporate world and submit to its assigned role as enforcer of the status quo or it can reassert its claim to leadership on society's intellectual frontier' (M'Gonigle and Starke, 2006, p. i). From the trenches, I have watched maps of love posing a threat to those who have traditionally controlled the content of maps. Cartographers have been trained to turn land and nature into polygons of commodities. Academic funders have rarely been citizens of a place anxious to recognize all the values. The majority of funders of academic institutions have been companies or agencies intent on extracting resources or delineating property in British Columbia. The profession has not been devoid of, to use writer Wendell Berry's coined expression, 'professional vandals' who are rarely in the position to question the oversimplification of a landscape of which their funds have little knowledge or love. The systemic problem is, of course, that in corporate-funded universities nobody funds the local, as there is no perceived benefit or economy of scale in the local.

The answer is to recognize again the role of the citizen and the public funding of research. There is growing cohort of researchers who are delving into the rebranded Humboldt tradition of community and participatory research with a passion. They are providing tools, methodologies, evaluations, links to grants and researchers, space, workshops, and encouragement. The specialists of place are cross-fertilizing with specialists of subjects, and interdisciplinary vigour is strengthening. As the writer Eudora Welty famously wrote, 'One place comprehended can make us understand other places better' (Welty, 1978).

Conclusion

As a case study, the Garry oak ecosystem within the Salish Sea is useful in many regards. From an island biogeography perspective, it echoes any urbanized landscape where only islands of the natural world remain. The significance of mapping, naming, and fully telling the stories of these 'islands' becomes more important as the impacts of climate change are felt. Trees and the rest of the plant community are the only means by which carbon is sequestered. Natural ecosystems also provide the only genetic resilience to changing climates, and the bigger and more connected these remnants are, the better chance we have of adapting. Garry oak ecosystems are the forefront of resilience to climate changes like drought, as they are already adapted to drought. E. O. Wilson and and R.H. MacArthur articulated for all of us the particular tensions of life on an island. On the one hand, you are vulnerable and isolated on your refugia in the sea, but on the other hand you are blissfully separate and insulated from the continental forces, which can range from glaciers to trans-Canada highways. Occasionally, ferries, winds, and tides bring in new blood to the island, but just as easily they can take it away. From an evolutionary point of view, you are either going to be among the next to disappear off the face of the earth or the only ones to survive. We need as many early experiments as we can get.

From a sociological perspective, the Garry oak meadow was a grand place to fall in love with. When you fall in love you do what lovers do when threatened. Guerilla geography provided a way for me to help map and chronicle the stories of these meadows by the Salish Sea; to forge the links between beauty, health, flowers, geology, atmospheric carbon, lizards, queens, sanctuary, and volcanic eruptions. The writer and grassland ecologist Don Gayton wrote, 'Artists let themselves be frightened by mechanism, just as scientists shrink from myth, and from imagination. But the worlds of myth and mechanism do finally come together on the common group of our natural landscape' (Gayton, 1992, p. 15).

It has been meaningful work in a dynamic time; and there have always been ways to earn a living bypicking up the lost stories and weaving in the new. There are places that need young guerrilla geographers to tell and retell the stories. And this next generation of guerrilla geographers need the academic community to support, educate, and legitimize them. The question back to the academic community of how to best nurture these young geographers is being answered through the growing discourse on community and participatory research. From the perspective of those of us out here in our place, the most important contribution is kind encouragement in a manner that is as heartfelt as Humboldt's invitations to his friends to walk upon the volcano, and as tangible as the bark of the oak. To the institutions I offer a plea to support this kind of welcoming academics: your survival may depend on it.

References

Apostol, D., and Sinclair, M. (2006). *Restoring the Pacific Northwest: The Art and Science of Ecological Restoration in Cascadia*. Washington, DC: Island Press.

Arntzen, H., McNaughton, D., Penn, B., and Snively, G. (2001). *Salish Sea: A Handbook for Educators*. Victoria: Parks Canada.

Berg, P. (1977). Strategies for Reinhabiting Northern Californai Bioregion. *Seratim: Journal of Ecotopia* 1 (3): 2–8.

British Columbia, Ministry of Environment (2014). *Sensitive Ecosystem Inventory*. www. env.gov.bc.ca/sei/ (last accessed 27 January 2014).

Bryce, C. (2013). *Lekwungen Food Systems*. http://lekwungenfoodsystems.org/portfolio/ kwetlal-camas-harvesting/ (last accessed 27 January 2014).

Common Ground (2013). www.commonground.org.uk/ (last accessed 8 April 2013).

Crouch, D., and Matless, D. (1996). Refiguring Geography: Parish Maps of Common Ground. *Transactions of the Institute of British Geographers*. new series 21 (1): 236–255.

Deur, D., and Turner, N. J. (2006). Keeping it Living: Traditions of Plant Use and Cultivation on Northwest Coast of North America. Seattle: University of Washington Press.

Elliot, D. (1990). *Saltwater People*. Victoria: School District 64.

Frankel, W. D. (1964). Humboldt Bicentennial. Letter, 22 June. *Journal of the Americal Medical Association* 188 (12): 1091.

Gayton, D. (1992). *The Wheatgrass Mechanism: Science and Imagination in the Western Canadian Landscape*. Saskatoon: Fifth House Publishers.

Gordon, K. (2010). Lost in Translation. *Focus Magazine*, December. http://focusonline. ca/?q=node/146 (last accessed 27 January 2014).

Harrington, S., Aberley, D., Dunn, M., and Penn, B. (1995, 1999). *Giving the Land a Voice*. Salt Spring Island: Land Trust Alliance of British Columbia.

Harrington, S., and Stevenson, J. (2005). *Islands of the Salish Sea: A Community Atlas*. Victoria: Touchwood Editions.

Higgs, E. (2003). *People, Natural Processes and Ecological Restoration*. Cambridge, MA: MIT Press.

Humboldt, A. von (1858). *Cosmos: A Sketch of the Physical Description of the Universe*. Trans. E. C. Otte. Vol. 1. New York: Harper & Brothers.

Land Conservancy of British Columbia. http://blog.conservancy.bc.ca/ (last accessed 27 January 2014).

MacArthur, R. H., and Wilson, E. O. (1967). *The Theory of Island Biogeography*. Princeton, NJ: Princeton University Press.

McEwen, C. (2009). *Community Action on Saltspring Island*. Community Research Connections. http://crcresearch.org/forum_archive/saltspring.htm (last accessed 25 January 2014).

M'Gonigle, M., and Starke, J. (2006). *Planet U: Sustaining the World: Reinventing the University*. Gabriola Island: New Society Publishers.

Morantz, A. (2002). Where is Here? Canada's Maps and the Stories they Tell. Toronto: Penguin.

Newkirk, A. (1975). Bioregions: Towards Bioregional Strategy for Human Culture. *Short Communications in Environmental Conservation* 2 (2): 108.

Orr, D. (1997). Architecture as Pedagogy. *Conservation Biology* 11 (3): 597–600.

Penn, B. (1991). *Maps to Murrelets*. Canadian Rainforests Resource Guide Grades 8–12. Victoria: Sierra Club of British Columbia.

Penn, B. (1991–2007). 'Wild Side' columns. *Monday Magazine*. Victoria.

Penn, B. (1998). Mapping the Last Blank Space. *Orion Afield*, December, pp. 20–24.

Penn, B. (1999). *A Year on the Wild Side*. Victoria: Horsdal and Schubart.

Penn, B. (2001). The Salish Sea. *Beautiful British Columbia Magazine*. Spring, p. 47.

Ransen, M. (2001). *Ah the Money, the Money, the Money: The Battle for Saltspring*. Documentary film. National Film Board of Canada.

Rippy, J. F., and Brann, E. R. (1947). Alexander von Humboldt and Simón Bolívar. *American Historical Review* 52 (4): 697–703.

Rupke, Nicolaas. A. (2005). *Alexander von Humboldt: A Metabiography*. Chicago: University of Chicago Press.

Simon Fraser University, Institute for the Humanities (2014). *Our Own Backyard: Mapping the Grandview-Woodland Community*. www.sfu.ca/humanities-institute-old/archive/backyard.htm (last accessed 27 January 2014).

Thrush, C. (2006). Review of Islands in the Salish Sea: A Community Atlas. *BC Studies* 149 (1): 94–96.

Tuan, Y. (1974). *Topophilia: A Study of Environmental Perception*. Columbia: Columbia University Press.

University of Victoria Community Mapping Collaboratory. http://mapping.uvic.ca/ (last accessed 27 January 2014).

Welty, Eudora (1978). *The Eye of the Story*. New York: Random House.

5

Universities in transition: overcoming barriers and creating pathways for sustainability

Jesús Granados Sánchez

Introduction

One of higher education's greatest challenges in the upcoming years is to materialize the contribution made by co-creation of new knowledge to build a sustainable future for society. Sustainability involves the development of a new culture, encompassing an analysis of knowledge itself, reviewing the assumptions that sustain our understanding of the world and the human dynamics in it.

The mission of the Global University Network for Innovation (GUNi) is to strengthen the role of higher education in society by contributing to the renewal of the visions, missions, and policies of higher education across the world within a framework of public service, relevance, and social responsibility. One of the main areas in which GUNi works is to find an adequate response to the challenge of (un)sustainability in higher education institutions (HEIs) by strengthening community university engagement.

GUNi's commitment to sustainability in higher education is manifested in different ways. In 2010, GUNi organized the International Barcelona Conference on Higher Education, a forum for debating the state of the art of sustainability in higher education institutions. In 2011 GUNi published the report *Higher Education's Commitment to Sustainability: From Understanding to Action*, which brought together eighty-five authors from thirty-eight countries. Additionally, research projects have been undertaken on the same issue: two investigated the promotion of sustainability in universities of Sub-Saharan Africa and the latest explores the transition of universities towards sustainability.

This chapter presents the findings of two GUNi studies on barriers, solutions, and actions identified in higher education institutions when they try to implement changes in their performance for achieving sustainability. The first study, made with the participation of sustainability scholars and experts from various parts of the world, identifies the main barriers and possible solutions to embedding sustainability into higher education. The second study is centred on the experience of Spanish universities and suggests actions to build their transition towards sustainability.

Universities in transition towards sustainability

Sustainability is a frame of mind (Bonnet, 2002). Sustainable development can be metaphorically compared to action by viewing things through a three-lens telescope in which the lenses represent the environment, the society, and the economy (Granados, 2011). Tilbury (2007) argues that to successfully transition society to sustainability requires that one envisions sustainability itself. As an inherently vague concept, the need to give 'sustainability' meaning in a specific context involving multiple stakeholders makes the concept attractive to educators. An educational perspective requires joint meaning-making, co-creation of new knowledge, collaborative learning, and critical enquiry (Granados et al., 2012).

In terms of sustainability, higher education can play a leading role in the domains of education, understanding, and action. But if the higher education sector is to be transformative, it needs to transform itself first. The present and future of higher education institutions can be seen from three different perspectives: continuity, transition, and radical change. Continuity refers to a state in which things remain the same while ignoring unsustainability. This is not a desirable option. Radical change is a scenario that implies a total reformulation of universities – a challenging and risky proposition. Transition seems to be the most plausible option as it consists of a gradual reform of the current system. The concept of universities in transition towards sustainability takes into account contributions such as the transition movement (Raskin, 2012; Hopkins, 2008; Chamberlin, 2009) and stages of sustainability (O'Riordan, 1996). Transition is about a process in which sustainability is progressively included in higher education, but the overarching question is whether we can change fast enough (Raskin, 2012). For that reason, the main features of transition are time, level of commitment, and the degree of transformation.

Since the 1970s, universities worldwide have increasingly embraced sustainability through the launching of environmental engineering programs, and in the 1990s by greening campuses through efforts such as minimizing waste and energy consumption, developing low carbon buildings, and modelling sustainability to influence the behaviour of students and staff. Many academic institutions worldwide have signed international declarations towards implementing sustainability through environmental literacy initiatives, curriculum development, research, partnering with governments, non-governmental organizations, and industry in developing sustainability initiatives (Wright, 2004). A third wave (Wals and Blewitt, 2010) at the turn of this century was the convergence of the environmental, social, and economic spheres, the blurring of the disciplines, and the reconceptualization of teaching and learning. In the last decade, we have seen a rise in more complicated research methods, where the investigator becomes both expert and partner through research on and with people. Research is inter- and multi-disciplinary while discipline-focused, with academic and social impacts that both inform and transform. These initiatives represent tangible transitions towards sustainability especially in changing views on how we work, moving from isolation in our approach to collaboration. Some catalysts towards the sustainability objective are the United Nations Decade of Education for Sustainable Develop-ment (2005–14) and the establishment of Regional Centers of Expertise (2011).

However, much remains to be done for sustainability to become genuinely and fully implemented at universities and for universities to become sustain-ability leaders (Waas, Verbruggen, and Wright, 2010). For Tilbury (2012) there is evidence to suggest that higher education does not fully understand the true nature of the challenges of sustainability. For her, achievements have been random and mostly disconnected from the core business of higher education, usually engaging minority groups and failing to reach the core staff, students, and stakeholders or to influence the culture of institutions. Initiatives influencing core university personnel are rare and seldom impact on students' formal learning opportunities.

This final reflection suggests that universities are taking a slow pace in their sustainability transition. It appears that there are a number of barriers in higher education institutions that affect their ability to respond to the challenges associated with sustainability. The main contributions to the study of institutional barriers that have influenced our research studies include Bolman and Deal (2008) and Miller (2012). Their analytic framework for organizational change consists of four components: the structural, human resource, political, and symbolic. In our case, we started delimiting four institutional areas: management, research, teaching and learning, and community engagement, but in the end, we found that barriers and solutions could transcend more than one area and even affect or be part of all of them. For this reason it is better to analyse sustainability from a more holistic angle and not by separating areas that are interrelated.

Methodology

This chapter presents two interconnected research studies. The first study engaged a group of higher education representatives from a number of countries in defining the barriers and solutions to sustainability. The second research study was conceived as a continuation of the first one, but instead of having a global focus it centred on the case of Spain.

The first one had four working phases: a discussion among experts to develop an initial set of barriers, workshops to establish a final list of barriers and solutions, a poll, and a final expert working group at the GUNi Knowledge Community. Phase 1 of the study began with an experts' group discussion on the main barriers encountered in the implementation of sustainability in higher education institu-tions. As a result, an initial set of barriers was defined and used as a starting point for the discussions in the parallel workshop sessions during the Fifth International Barcelona Conference on Higher Education, 'Higher Education's Commitment to Sustainability: From Understanding to Action'. The aim of the workshops was to offer a forum for collective discussion and proposals for overcoming the main barriers in the transformation of higher education systems towards sustaina-bility. These workshop discussions were based on an interactive and participative methodology driven by recognized academics in the field. The 115 participants from across the world were divided into seven groups and asked to identify the barriers and solutions they considered most important and appropriate. New barriers were added to the initial proposal, and final lists of twenty-one barriers and twenty-eight solutions were defined (see Tables 5.1 and 5.2 below). The list of solutions was based on general criteria and not intended to match the barriers on a 'one-to-one' basis. Thus, some solutions are related to one or more barriers, and one barrier may imply more than one solution.

The GUNi poll 'Breaking Barriers for Transformation' was based on the final list of barriers and solutions. The poll was distributed to experts in sustainability in higher education worldwide and was completed by 201 in all. Its purpose was to evaluate the degree of relevance that each of the respondents gave to each of the barriers and solutions. It also aimed to shed some light on the general trends that led to the inclusion of sustainable development in higher education institutions.

Poll respondents were asked to rate each barrier and solution according to its level of importance (from 1 to 5, where 1 is 'not important' and 5 is 'very important') and then to choose the five most relevant barriers and solutions they considered as a priority in their own particular context. In terms of professional posts, professors were the biggest group of respondents (with 73 responses). They were followed by the group of researchers, directors, and vice-chancellors (each of the three groups had about 30 respondents). There was a lower rate of participation by administrative staff (18), practitioners (11), and students (6). In terms of regional representation, the largest number of respondents was from Europe (80). Asia Pacific (37) and Latin America and the Caribbean (33) were the regions with the next largest numbers of respondents, while in the case of North America (19), Africa (18), and the Arab states (14) the participation was lower. The intention of the poll was not to have a proportional representation of all regions, but rather to gather worldwide experts' views on sustainability in higher education institutions.

The analysis of the data and the concluding findings were done collaboratively in a working group within the GUNi Knowledge Community, which was composed of the same experts who participated as facilitators in the conference workshops.

The second research study consisted of two workshops carried out at two separate events with the participation of 105 Spanish scholars working on sustainability (from different disciplines and faculties): at the conference 'Universities in Transition: Transformations for Sustainability', organized by GUNi in Barcelona in November 2011, and at the Seventh Environmental Education Seminar, 'Miradas' at the Spanish National Centre of Environmental Education (CENEAM) in Segovia in May 2012. The workshops were intended to discuss the following questions: What are the most important barriers to address first and why? What are the most relevant solutions and why? What actions could be carried out as a priority?

The process was the same for both workshops. Participants were divided into small groups of five to six people, and they first had time to present the initiatives on sustainability in which they were involved at their universities. Secondly, a brick wall was built to illustrate metaphorically an obstacle that is preventing the advance towards sustainability with each brick representing a barrier. Each group's main task was to deconstruct the wall by choosing the main barriers and to remove them from the wall. At the same time, participants were asked to find the main solutions to such barriers, and to define what actions they found appropriate and feasible to begin overcoming the barriers in their own institutions. The bricks were used to build a new path based on actions. Once all the groups were finished, all the pathways were described and common reflections and concluding remarks were shared.

Main findings

In the first study, 'Breaking Barriers for Transformation', there appeared to be a general consensus among respondents and participants that sustainability in higher education is of great relevance. As a result of the research study, a list of twenty-one barriers (Table 5.1) and a list of twenty-eight solutions (Table 5.2) have been identified.

Table 5.1 The main barriers to embedding sustainability into higher education

Barrier	Description
1	Lack of a common understanding of education for sustainability in higher education.
2	Supremacy of technological and instrumental knowledge versus human and social knowledge.
3	Absence of culture-specific knowledge, indigenous knowledge, and knowledge of traditional ecological systems.
4	Sustainable development is perceived as an 'add-on' to education, not a built-in aspect in higher education.
5	Pedagogical processes focused on the transmission perspective (knowledge transfer) rather than on the 'transformation' perspective.
6	Lack of vision and prioritization of sustainable development at the leadership level of higher education.
7	Lack of consensus in higher education institutions about the way to introduce education for sustainable development.
8	Higher education institutions are too compartmentalized. Lack of departmental autonomy and coordination, and too many offices and units.
9	Difficulties in acquiring integrative thinking, transdisciplinary learning, and interdisciplinary cooperation in universities.
10	The dynamics of academia hinder change, giving rise to disconnects between mission, vision, and reality.
11	Difficulty of sustainable processes in non-sustainable civilizations, institutions, and organizations.
12	The educational system tends to make teachers prioritize research and publications over education and pedagogical practices.

Barrier	Description
13	High pressure to focus higher education activities on short-term market needs and on profitable activities, thus making higher education institutions factories for degrees and publications.
14	Unconscious introduction of unsustainable practices in curricula.
15	The pedagogical model strengthens the separation of knowledge from experience.
16	Research places more emphasis on science-for-impact factors than on science for social impact.
17	Higher education has been confined to devoting financial support to science and technology, thus making it difficult to finance education for sustainability.
18	Lack of coordination and vision to change sustainability policies and education at the governmental level.
19	Isolation of universities and of universities from their communities.
20	Absence of higher education stakeholders who influence governments on development and innovation.
21	Absence of professional resources and pedagogical training.

Source: Granados et al. (2012), p. 200.

Table 5.2 Possible solutions for facilitating the embedding of sustainability into higher education

Solution	Description
1	Developing an institutional understanding, vision, and mission on sustainable development in higher education institutions, taking into account faculty, students, and external parties by engaging in open dialogue with all of them.
2	Designing a management mechanism for organizations as a whole to create a comprehensive vision of sustainable development, on the basis of which experts (teachers) will be able to work on projects to develop competences in interdisciplinary, integrated social relationships.
3	Encouraging analysis, synthesis, process, and critical thinking as well as action-oriented competences by using sustainable development tools for learning and communication on issues from a problem-solving perspective.
4	Involving internal stakeholders in such a way that leads to ownership, empowerment, participation, and willingness to contribute to and be responsible for change. Communicating and sharing more information (e.g. through team-building, coffee breaks, awareness-raising about issues of education for sustainability, etc.).

Solution	Description
5	Opening up the learning process to base sustainability on different cultures and perspectives. Knowledge of native, indigenous, and marginalized cultures. Integrating alternative courses (drama, arts, yoga); introducing service-learning activities; and running accredited extra-curricular activities for students.
6	Having educated and selected leaders at all management levels to facilitate and support collaborative and democratic dialogue processes on the social responsibility of higher education.
7	Carrying out volume-based research into sustainable development education, focusing both on processes and outcomes.
8	Changing the incentive system and quality indicators to encourage and promote multidisciplinary work, interdisciplinary teaching, theses, projects, etc.
9	Developing institutional policies to appraise the approach to sustainability in higher education institutions by means of compulsory indicators.
10	Reviewing the mission and vision statements of universities.
11	Creating leadership units to help reduce bureaucracy and its processes; creating common physical and intellectual spaces where interaction becomes possible; acting as an expert and consultancy unit; helping to integrate sustainable development in universities; monitoring the design and implementation of sustainable development content in curricula; and offering awareness-raising and/or training programs on sustainable development for all university teaching, research, and administrative staff.
12	Overhauling selection criteria and the recruitment of senior managers and leaders in universities; recognizing transformative leadership in a global context using the global interconnectivity of technology in such a way that injects new blood into institutions.
13	Having an assessment mechanism or indicator of an active institution and good education for sustainability practices to evaluate universities. Promoting good-practice institutes.
14	Having scheduled sustainable development meetings at universities (e.g. starting working days with project presentations, holding an annual meeting of university faculties to discuss the development of sustainable development at the university).
15	Running new programs on sustainability that include extra-curricular activities.
16	Linking research to sustainability.
17	Applying for government funding.

Solution	Description
18	Making research grants available for cross-disciplinary research.
19	Securing financial resources from the business sector that can be earmarked for higher education activities related to sustainability.
20	Offering services that are beneficial to society and at the same time generating financial resources to invest in sustainability projects at the institutional level.
21	Ensuring the proper management and use of financial resources at the institutional level.
22	Building a culture of sustainability by involving and engaging the local community, universities, families, schools, and other stakeholders in sustainability issues and projects. Including active learning courses and action research with local community projects that take students out of the classroom.
23	Creating academic programs that help the interrelationship of society and higher education institutions.
24	Submitting policies on sustainable development to governments and organizations through university research and partnerships with local communities.
25	Developing joint initiatives and having direct communications at the national, international, and local level (non-governmental organizationss, higher education institutions, civil society, Regional Centres of Expertise in Education for Sustainability, other universities, etc.).
26	Drawing up guidelines for governments and organizations for developing policies and programs that promote the role of universities as change agents for sustainability.
27	Having international agencies and committees to implement and monitor national levels of ESD accreditation that also have an influence on national governments.
28	Sharing knowledge with other HEIs and with the governments on which they depend.

Source: Granados et al. (2012), p. 200.

The main thematic areas appearing in the barriers and solutions are:

- the common understanding of sustainability and funding and support for education for sustainable development (ESD),
- integration of diverse knowledge,
- interdisciplinarity,
- overcoming inertia,
- new pedagogical approaches,
- unsustainable structures and new institutional set-ups,
- unconscious unsustainability,

- short-term market needs,
- the relationship between theory and practice,
- government sustainability policies and how to influence them, and
- moving from isolation to networking and collaboration.

There is a relationship between the barriers that were voted the highest number of times as priorities and the main responses they received on the level of importance in overcoming the barrier. Thus, there was general agreement among the participants about the barriers that most urgently need to be broken down, which are:

- Difficulties in acquiring integrative thinking, transdisciplinary learning and interdisciplinary cooperation in universities (barrier 9);
- Sustainable development is perceived as an add-on to education, not a built-in aspect of higher education (barrier 4);
- Lack of vision and prioritization of sustainable development at the leadership level of higher education (barrier 6);
- Lack of a common understanding of ESD in higher education (barrier 1);
- The lack of coordination and vision to change sustainability policies and education at the governmental level (barrier 18).

The five solutions that were considered priorities as starting points at the respondents' institutions were:

- Developing an institutional understanding, vision, and mission on sustainable development in higher education institutions, taking into account staff, students, and external parties, and engaging in open dialogue with all of them (solution 1);
- Changing the incentive system and quality indicators for encouraging and promoting multidisciplinary work and interdisciplinary teaching, theses, and projects (solution 8);
- Building a culture of sustainability by involving and engaging the local community, universities, families, schools, and other stakeholders in sustainability issues and projects. Including active learning courses and action research with local community projects that take students out of the classroom (solution 22);
- Involving internal stakeholders in a way that leads to ownership, empowerment, participation, and willingness to contribute to and be responsible for change. Communicating and sharing more information through team-building, awareness-raising of ESD issues, etc. (solution 4); and
- Monitoring the design and implementation of sustainable development contents in curricula, offering awareness-raising and/or training programs on ESD for all university academic and administrative staff (solution 11).

If we compare the relationship between the priority barriers and the priority solutions, it can be seen that they more or less focus on the same two big issues. One is introducing and monitoring sustainability as a priority by reaching a common understanding and facilitating interdisciplinarity for knowledge creation and learning. In this matter leadership is key. The second one is policy change at the government level that would encourage and promote the transformation of the way higher education works.

The main difference between the priority barriers and the priority solutions is that the barriers are mainly about institutional internal matters, while the main solutions integrate community–university engagement as a key element for achieving sustainability.

In the case of the second study, the main urgent barriers agreed for the Spanish context present some differences when compared with the results of the global previous survey. Barrier 1 (understanding of sustainability and ESD) and barrier 8 (compartmentalization of the university) were chosen as the most important and urgent ones. Three solutions were related to them: the recognition of world leaders in the transformation of higher education institutions towards sustainability, the necessity of well-trained leaders in sustainability at institutional level, and the creation of special units to lead the implementation process at universities. The proposed feasible actions to undertake were:

- Identifying reference projects, their dissemination among teachers and their adaptation to context;
- Requiring experience in sustainability for candidates to strategic positions at the university;
- Developing regular sustainability meetings that allow social interaction and that open the institution to society; and the creation of interdisciplinary units that are cross-departmental.

The difficulty of teaching students integrative and cross-disciplinary thinking (barrier 9) and the emphasis on the academic impact above the social relevance (barrier 16) were identified as the following main obstacles, and for the participants in the workshops, these two barriers share solutions and actions in the same direction. The main solutions were related to changing the incentive system and quality indicators for encouraging and promoting interdisciplinary teaching, introducing cultural perspectives, and developing initiatives with community stakeholders. The specific actions defined were:

- CRUE (the conference of vice-chancellors from Spanish universities) must act as a lobby to promote the government's recognition of interdisciplinary projects and also those projects that entail participation with the community.
- Social responsibility should be included as a requisite in all research projects.
- The overhead expenses for cross-disciplinary projects should be reduced.
- Networking within and outside the universities should be promoted among scholars from different departments to enable them to collaborate in cross-disciplinary projects.

The last barrier that was identified as relevant for the Spanish context was the isolation between universities and their communities. To overcome this difficulty it was proposed to build a culture of sustainability with the local community where the university is based. The specific action to be addressed was the creation of 'communities in transition' that bring together people from different sectors of society and the university (or group of universities when possible). The group can be coordinated by a social responsibility office which also can help with the mobilization of the knowledge and initiatives that have been created.

Sustainability in higher education in Spain is increasingly perceived to be linked to initiatives that involve engagement with the community. But most of the sustainability scholars that participated in the study did not know much about the community–university engagement movement, and approaches for the integration of teaching, research and engagement are still in an early stage.

Conclusions

One of the greatest challenges of our times is the combination of community–university engagement with the introduction of sustainability in higher education. Over the years, the function of engagement within the higher education sector has come to be expressed as the 'third mission', a concept which derives from the common description of the role of universities as being teaching, research, and service to community or society (Inman and Schuetze, 2011). We believe that the nature of the global unsustainability crisis facing humanity is of such seriousness and complexity that higher education must transform itself once again to move beyond the limited understandings of a third mission towards an 'engaged sustainable university'. In so doing, the earlier separate functions of teaching, research, and engagement are transformed into a shared space capable of radical innovation, co-creation of knowledge, visibility for alternative ways of sustainable living, a deeper holistic comprehension of reality and its dynamics, and an inclusive form of active citizenship at both the local and global level.

As we have seen through the barriers and solutions analysed in this chapter, the alternative way of doing things must integrate changes in higher education institutions' internal organization and management, in pedagogical approaches, in the way of doing research, and in community engagement. These changes require an integration of new perspectives on the role of knowledge in the service of the common good, and imply an evaluation of what role the university wants in relation to knowledge, what to teach and with what purpose, what to research and with whom, and how we do all this. Higher education institutions have made substantial progress in embedding sustainability and many barriers have been overcome. The present and future journey towards sustainability may be compared to a bicycle. As bicycles have two wheels that move together simultaneously, there exist two key elements for creating a sustainable society: knowledge and partnership.

There are at least six changes to incorporate into the way we handle, use, build, and understand knowledge:

1. Move from a mono-culture of scientific knowledge to an ecology of knowledge;
2. Move from rational knowledge to integral human knowledge;

3. Shift from descriptive knowledge to knowledge for intervention;
4. Change from partial knowledge to a holistic and complex knowledge;
5. Abandon the isolated creation of knowledge to building a social co-creation of knowledge; and
6. Replace the conception of a static use of knowledge with one of a dynamic and creative knowledge.

The partnership is the main consideration in shaping a truly engaged university. The main elements for a successful partnership are: the creation process; a vision of engagement and sustainability (which implies defining the mission, the type of community, and the level of integration); the partners and their roles (which involve mutual understanding and trust, definition of leadership, and participation in decision-making); the outcomes (which assume reciprocity and mutual benefit); and the sustainability or continuance of the partnership (which requires evaluating difficulties and weaknesses, revising agreements, and contemplating people's replacement).

Universities are already making some of these shifts. A practice of knowledge democracy linked to a sustainable society would be supported by myriad creative examples of community–university engagement that are arising now in universities in literally every part of the world. It would build on a vision for a new architecture of knowledge and an activist sense of social responsibility in higher education.

References

Bolman, L. G., and Deal, T. E. (2008). *Reframing Organizations: Artistry, Choice, and Leadership*. San Francisco, CA: Jossey-Bass.

Bonnet, M. (2002). Education for Sustainability as a Frame of Mind. *Environmental Education Research* 8 (1): 9–20.

Chamberlin, S. (2009). *The Transition Timeline for a Local, Resilient Future*. Dartington, Devon: Green Books.

Global University Network for Innovation (GUNi) (2011). *Higher Education's Commitment to Sustainability: From Understanding to Action*. London: Palgrave Macmillan.

Granados, J. (2011). Teaching Geography for a Sustainable World: A Case Study of a Secondary School in Spain. *Review of International Geographical Education On-Line (RIGEO)* (1/2): 158–182.

Granados, J., et al. (2012). Moving from Understanding to Action: Breaking Barriers for Transformation. In GUNi (2011): pp. 191–207.

Hopkins, R. (2008). The Transition Handbook: From Oil Dependency to Local Resilience. Dartington, Devon: Green Books.

Inman, P., and Schuetze, H. G. (eds) (2011). *The Community Engagement and Service Mission of Universities*. Leicester: National Institute of Adult Continuing Education.

Miller, J. M. (2012). Framing Sustainability. *Journal of Sustainability Education* 3.

O'Riordan, T. (1996). Democracy and the Sustainability Transition. In W. Lafferty and J. Meadowcroft (eds), *Democracy and the Environment: Problems and Prospects*. Cheltenham: Edward Elgar.

Raskin, P. (2012). Higher Education in an Unsettled Century: Handmaiden or Pathmaker? In GUNi (2011): pp. 12–15.

Raskin, P., et al. (2002). Great Transition: The Promise and the Lure of the Times Ahead. Boston, MA: Tellus Institute.

Tilbury, D. (2007). Learning Based Change for Sustainability: Perspectives and Pathways. In A. E. G. Wals (ed.), *Social Learning towards a Sustainable World: Principles, Perspectives and Praxis*. Wageningen, The Netherlands: Wageningen Academic Publishers.

Tilbury, D. (2012). Higher Education for Sustainability: A Global Overview of Commitment and Progress. In GUNi (2011).

UNESCO (2009). Bonn Declaration. UNESCO World Conference on Education for Sustainable Development, 31 March–2 April 2009, Bonn, Germany. www.esd-world-conference-2009.org/fileadmin/download/ESD2009_BonnDeclaration080409.pdf (last accessed 4 February 2014).

Waas, T., Verbruggen, A., and Wright, T. (2010). University Research for Sustainable Development: Definition and Characteristics Explored. *Journal of Cleaner Production* 18: 629–636.

Wals, A. E. J., and Blewitt, J. (2010). Third Wave Sustainability in Higher Education: Some (Inter)national Trends and Developments. In P. Jones, D. Selby, and S. Sterling (eds), *Sustainability Education: Perspectives and Practice across Higher Education*. London: Earthscan.

Wright, T. (2004). The Evolution of Environmental Sustainability Declarations in Higher Education. In P. B. Corcoran and A. E. J. Wals (eds), *Higher Education and the Challenge of Sustainability: Problematics, Promise and Practice*. Dordrecht, Netherlands: Kluwer Academic Publishers.

PART II

Studies of environmental sustainability

6

Sustainable local food systems and environmental sustainability

Sandra Streed

We begin with a simple truth. How we eat determines how the earth is used.
(Wendell Berry, 1990)

Berry's statement provokes questions about the connections and relationships among food, our earth, and our environment. Where does food come from? Where and how is it grown? How is it harvested, packaged, delivered to us? What is its value and what is its cost? Is it a sustainable system? What food systems are in place? What is a sustainable food system? What is sustainability? What is environmental sustainability?

The role of food systems in environmental sustainability will be discussed in the context of the engaged curriculum of Northland College in Ashland, Wisconsin. This will include a discussion of the components of its thriving local food system.

Sustainability is 'the ability to endure, relating to, or being a method of harvesting or using a resource so that the resource is not depleted or permanently damaged'. The definition of sustainability in the 1987 Brundtland report brings it to a more personal level: 'Meeting the needs of the present generation without compromising the ability of future generations to meet their needs' (WCED, 1987). This sentiment is reminiscent of the Native American Seventh Generation philosophy that leaders must consider the effects of their actions through to the seventh generation of their people.

The principle of the three pillars of sustainability says that for complete sustainability to be achieved, all three pillars must be sustainable. The three pillars are social sustainability, environmental sustainability, and economic sustainability. Of the three pillars, the most important is environmental sustainability. If this is not addressed, the other two pillars will not survive. Environmental sustainability is made up of the rates of renewable resource harvest, pollution creation, and non-renewable resource depletion that can be continued indefinitely. In other words: 'The fate of the living planet is the most important issue facing mankind' (Gaylord Nelson).

Part of the solution can come from sustainable agriculture which forms the core of a sustainable local food system. Grace Communications Foundation defines sustainable agriculture as

the production of food, fiber, or other plant or animal products using farming techniques that protect the environment, public health, human communities, and animal welfare. This form of agriculture enables us to produce healthful food without compromising future generations' ability to do the same.

Sustainable agriculture does not utilize chemical pesticides, synthetic fertilizers, or genetically modified seeds or participate in practices that might contaminate the air, water, or soil. Sustainable farmers grow a variety of crops, use crop rotation, and manage waste which benefits not only the ecosystem but also the farm workers, consumers, and general public.

Food systems are composed of all of the components involved in the farm-to-table voyage – from choosing and planting the seeds, through the growth cycle to harvest, to processing, packaging, distribution, purchasing, and consumption. One view of food systems categorizes them as local, regional or global. A local or regional food system infers a geographical area and is usually considered sustainable and environmentally friendly since all operations are located relatively close to consumers. This enables products to be picked or prepared close to maturity for ultimate freshness and nutritional value and to travel short distances to consumers, thus conserving energy, reducing pollution, and minimizing potential product damage. Having food system operations located close to each other also provides employment opportunities and encourages community interaction and development.

One important point involves the definition and use of 'local'. As stated, 'local' is a geographical reference; it does not necessarily mean sustainable. Nor does it mean that the food is fresher, more nutritious, or grown sustainably. One must be cautious and careful, ask for additional information, and remember *caveat emptor* – 'let the buyer beware'.

It is the view of the Grace Foundation's Sustainable Table that the global food system relies upon industrial agriculture by necessity since the quantities of food needed for production are so large. Rapid advances in transportation such as the refrigerated rail cars, intensive mechanization, increased production of food on mammoth farms supported by inexpensive energy, and the use of fertilizers, antibiotics, and chemicals for larger yields and extended shelf life have created a corporate-dominated food system that offers food sold at low prices that do not reflect the true costs of producing them. These costs are significant: monetary cost for the seed and fertilizer that must be purchased each year; the 'necessary' chemicals and fuel; social costs such as worker injuries from machinery; health issues related to unavoidable chemical ingestion; and the environmental costs of loss of biodiversity, soil degradation and erosion, air pollution, and water contamination. Increased consolidation has resulted in difficulty of traceability; increased risks of improper handling or processing, food safety issues, contamination, and the danger of possible intentional tampering to large quantities of food. Although industrialized agriculture provides food for billions of people, the total cost is of increasing concern.

J. I. Rodale wrote in 1954: 'Organics is not a fad. It has been a long-established practice – much more firmly grounded than the current chemical flair. Present agricultural practices are leading us downhill.' If this is true, all three pillars may be in danger.

Equally important and destructive is the loss of knowledge and appreciation of the process of farming, of nature, and of the land itself. Social indifference to the farmers and farm workers who grow food reflects our disinterest in and disconnectedness to nature and season. The lack of concern about ever-increasing urban sprawl; erosion of topsoil; contamination of air, water, and soil; climate change; and loss of small farms further demonstrates our increasing disregard with nature. In the words of the renowned farmer Abraham Lincoln:

> The ambition for broad acres leads to poor farming, even with men of energy. I scarcely ever knew a mammoth farm to sustain itself; much less to return a profit upon the outlay. I have more than once known a man to spend a respectable fortune upon one; fall and leave it; and then some man of modest aims get a small fraction of the ground and make a good living upon it. Mammoth farms are like tools or weapons which are too heavy to be handled. Ere long they are thrown aside, at a great loss.

Over 100 years later, in 2002, the agricultural development leader Jules Perry concurred but was more ominous: 'If a system of production has negative side-effects, and cares not about the resources on which it relies, then we have taken a path leading ultimately to disaster.' One must add: and to the collapse of the pillars.

Both agriculturists are describing unsustainable agricultural systems. What could serve as an alternative? There is significant agreement that a food network of local-based and regional-based systems of diversified farms using sustainable practices to produce fresh, nutritious food is a solution. Shorter travel time from farm to table would maximize taste and nutritional value, reduce carbon footprints and layers of handling, stimulate local economies, and support interactive community relationships.

Increased public awareness of the problems caused by the current industrialized food system has resulted in extensive and growing support for sustainable agriculture. In addition to having access to healthy food, many consumers want to know where their food comes from, how it was grown, and who grew it. They want to know about the entire food chain. This awareness and demand for information is creating a vibrant, resilient, creative market for sustainable foods and prompting demands for changes in agricultural policies and regulations.

Leading civic and business organizations have commissioned studies and committed resources, leading to the inclusion of local food systems in local and regional planning efforts. In 2007, the American Planning Association released its first food systems paper. This was followed by a meeting in June 2010 of the Academy of Nutrition and Dietetics (formerly the American Dietetic Association), American Nurses Association, American Planning Association, and American Public Health Association to develop a set of shared food system principles. This declaration is the result: 'We support socially, economically, and ecologically sustainable food systems that promote health – the current and future health of individuals, communities, and the natural environment (American Planning Association, 2103).

To support the 2040 regional plan of the Chicago Metropolitan Agency for Planning (CMAP), the Chicago Community Trust in 2009 commissioned a food systems study that was conducted by the Chicago Food Policy Advisory Council, the City of Chicago Department of Zoning and Planning, and a group of advisors. An in-depth section on building a local food system is now being included in CMAP's *Go to 2040* plan (2010). Other Illinois counties including DuPage, Lake, and Kane and cities such as Cleveland, Detroit, Madison, Kansas City, and Seattle are including local food systems in their planning. As more and more people begin to understand the economic, social, cultural, and environmental elements of a local food system, progress is being made towards including a sustainable local food system as a core element and important planning tool of a sustainable development plan.

The leaders and supporters of sustainable local food systems and environmental sustainability come from small and large communities, government, non-profits, regulatory agencies, business and industry, and academia. All play important roles but institutions of higher learning are particularly well equipped to play a unique role in the development, growth, and maintenance of sustainable local food systems. Their mission is to teach, to educate, to prepare students to address current issues and to meet the challenges of the future. They provide technical assistance, develop innovative technologies and equipment, and then engage the community to share the knowledge and deliver the resources.

Northland College

With the acceptance of the value of sustainable local food systems, many educational institutions have conducted research on sustainable local food systems and the connections to environmental sustainability. Northland College in Ashland, Wisconsin represents a unique endeavour that has been leading the way to environmental sustainability for over 100 years, and sustainable local food systems are a critical component of the future of the college and the region.

Northland College was founded in 1892 by community members who wanted to provide a unique educational opportunity for residents of the region. The founders created a learning environment that emphasized moral and spiritual values, placed high value on free enquiry, and recognized each individual's intrinsic worth. This value system spurred Northland's commitment to sustainability and good stewardship, demonstrated by its adherence to the core principle of sustainability – conservation of resources for future generations.

The deep connection with nature and appreciation of the environment that permeate Northland may be due in part to its location close to Lake Superior and its proximity to nearly a million acres of the Chequamegon National Forest. But it is also a result of the way the administration, faculty, and students view the human–nature relationship. They value exploring human nature in order to tap into the resources of this relationship, then utilize those findings to solve existing problems creatively and develop innovative strategies for our increasingly interdependent world.

Since its beginning, Northland has been a pioneer, charting a different course for itself. Long before people were discussing green issues and climate change,

Northland was building its national reputation as a leader in environmental and sustainability issues. Sustainability at Northland is practised through education, research, awareness, and implementation. Students test theories on campus and throughout the community, working on real world projects that have real risks, real rewards, and real impacts. Embedded in all of the college's activities is stewardship of resources. Practising stewardship on a daily basis can equip students to help move larger systems toward long-term environmental sustainability.

In 1970 the Northland Board of Trustees initiated the development of the Environmental Studies Program. All of the programs at Northland College place a strong emphasis on the environment and sustainability. Many classes focus on specific environmental issues. The natural settings around and near the college are utilized as classrooms and laboratories where students become agents of positive change.

Northland exhibited its environmental leadership once more in 1971, when it hosted its first environmental conference slightly more than a year after the first Earth Day. The two key speakers were Wisconsin Senator Gaylord Nelson, the 'Conservation Governor', and Sigurd Olson, professor, author, environmentalist, and one of the foremost US conservationists. In addition to environmental presentations and exhibits, regional problem-solving workshops were held on issues and impacts affecting the Apostle Islands.

It was Senator Gaylord Nelson whose 1969 national teach-in increased environmental awareness and focused political attention on environmental issues. This led to the establishment of the first Earth Day on 22 April 1970. Sigurd Olson was born in Chicago but grew up in northern Wisconsin, where he developed his lifelong interest in the outdoors and his love of the wilderness. He studied agriculture, botany, geology, and ecology at Northland College, the University of Wisconsin–Madison, and the University of Illinois, and spent most of his life in the Ely area connected to Northland, teaching and writing about area history, ecology, and outdoor life.

Following the conference, Malcolm McLean, Northland's recently appointed president, who strongly believed that the institution should address society's challenges, distanced the college from traditional academia by taking the visionary step of embedding its environmental focus in its mission statement and curricula. He recognized the need to train future generations in environmental stewardship and enlisted support from Nelson, Olson, and many others including Robert Matteson. Matteson had held many positions in academia and various departments of the US federal government but was at heart an avid environmentalist. Citing the conference as the instrument of origin, he became the driving force for the creation of the Sigurd Olson Environmental Institute (SOEI), which was founded in 1972 and serves as the outreach and extension arm of the college. The SOEI advisory board was created and the environmental outreach charter designed at that same time. Also in 1972, the college enrolled the first class of environmental studies students.

Northland is a member the Association for the Advancement of Sustainability in Higher Education (AASHE), which advances sustainability by engaging diverse representatives of the higher education community, providing a frame-

work for understanding sustainability in higher education, facilitating information sharing, and providing valuable resources and materials. AASHE created the
Sustainability Tracking, Assessment & Rating System™ (STARS), a transparent,
self-reporting framework for colleges and universities to measure their sustainability performance. Northland College began its partnership with STARS in 2008
and has a silver rating.

Today, Northland is taking its leadership a step further. The current president,
Michael Miller, who was appointed in 2010, has continued to build upon the Northland traditions of community engagement, strong curricula, and environmental
sustainability. While many entities focus on sustainability at the scale of the institution or the single municipality, Northland is actively engaged in regional-scale
sustainability initiatives with a broad range of community partners.

Currently, these collaborations are focused on two critical and interconnected
regional sustainability issues: fostering a dramatically expanded local food system,
and expanding carbon neutral energy production and energy efficiency. Northland's enhanced focus in these two areas is intended to help build the region's
self-sufficiency and resiliency in the face of climate change, political instability,
and economic turmoil; provide new educational opportunities; and strengthen
the connection between the college and the regional community. A broadened
focus on energy and food also will be leveraged as a distinctive economic development driver for the region by focusing social entrepreneurship on the quadruple
bottom line of people, planet, profits, and place.

Northland has utilized a systems approach in order to integrate sustainability
into different areas of operations and academics. There are eight sustainability
initiatives: Local Food; Composting; Energy; Reduce, Reuse, Recycle; Bikes and
Transportation; Native Landscaping; Green Buildings; and Community, which
demonstrate the breadth of their sustainability spectrum and the potential for the
future. It is all about choice: 'What we choose to buy, where we choose to shop,
even whether we choose to be part of campaigns ... all this is not an homage to
some weighty obligation; it's a celebration of the world we want ... My choices as
a consumer used to feel so small, but now I'm convinced they have real power.
Together we are a sleeping giant and, awakened, we can really stir things up.' Each
of these initiatives is described below.

Local Food

Supporting the development of a significantly expanded local food system is
Northland's highest sustainability initiative. Northland has actively engaged
regional community partners in increasing the sale and consumption of local
food products at the college and within the community. The college is partnering
with the University of Wisconsin Extension, the Chequamegon Food Co-op,
the Bayfield Regional Food Producers Cooperative (BRFPC), the Chartwells,
and several area farms. Northland sees this as a significant step in building the
region's self-sufficiency and resilience. Northland has a long-term goal of sourcing
80 percent of food consumed on campus.

This project is the result of a 2012 proposal from the BRFPC to the Chequam-egon Food Co-op requesting that the cooperative serve as intermediary between the farmers and area schools. Farmers deliver their products to the Chequa-megon Food Co-op, which serves as an aggregation, storage, and distribution site, or 'food hub'. Then Chartwells picks up the food from the cooperative and delivers it to Northland College and to the Ashland School District. This not only provides local schools with access to more fresh produce, but also supports the local food economy, its farmers, and its families. This collaboration streamlines the entire process for both the farmers and the schools, relieving them of much time-consuming logistics and paperwork, reducing or eliminating fuel costs and waste, and creating jobs in the community.

This project involves thousands of pounds of local food going to local consumers and thousands of dollars going to local famers, and is the result of over five years of steady growth in the local food market. It is anticipated that the program will expand to provide other area institutions such as hospitals, other school districts, and public service organizations. The initiative is building stronger connections between the college and the regional community and is on track to develop into a scalable and replicable model.

Northland is also a signatory of the Lake Superior Good Food Charter and the Superior Compact Purchasing Commitment, which are parts of the Lake Superior Good Food Network Region. The Western Lake Superior Food System covers 18.4 million acres spread over fifteen counties and is based on the research by Stacey Stark, David Syring, and David Abazs, through funding provided by the Healthy Foods, Healthy Lives Institute at the University of Minnesota. Their research demonstrates that the region has the potential to grow sufficient amounts of healthy food and has the economic potential to add thousands of jobs to the local economy. The non-farm portion of the food dollar and the health care savings of embracing a 100 percent local food system are over $1 billion per year for the Western Lake Superior Region.

Participants in the charter advocate economic resilience, community health and food justice, food knowledge, and culture and ecological health. They recog-nize that:

- Lake Superior and its bioregion play an influential role in agriculture and diet,
- The local food system plays a critical role in the overall health, security, and prosperity of area communities and environment,
- The development of a vibrant, dynamic local food system is an integral foundation to ensure the health and prosperity of our region.

The Superior Compact Purchasing Commitment asserts that the Western Lake Superior Region has the agricultural potential to produce adequate supplies of healthy food necessary for a balanced diet and supports a goal of locally sourcing 20 percent of food purchased by 2020. The compact is predicated on the beliefs that a local food system can:

- Create jobs and increase regional economic resilience;
- Provide fresher and healthier foods that can address critical health issues;
- Reduce food transportation costs, soil erosion and ground water contamination;
- Increase relationships between farmers and consumers;
- Revive small towns; and
- Support the development and diversification of the rural infrastructure throughout our region.

Composting

Recognizing that 10 percent of municipal waste consists of food scraps, a Northland student volunteer launched a composting program on campus in 1993 and has kept tens of thousands of pounds of food waste out of the landfill. Compost is collected from the cafeteria and from bins located in all dorm kitchens and other campus buildings. The finished composted material is used in the campus garden to grow food consumed in the campus cafeteria, for native landscaping, and for other uses on and off campus.

Northland College recently constructed a new compost building on campus that will be a focal point of the college's commitment to sustainable operations by reducing campus waste. Northland hired for the project several contractors from the local community, who all worked together to attain the highest levels of sustainability throughout the building process. The new building will operate more efficiently than the old compost shed, which will remain in use to compost the food waste from the campus cafeteria. Northland students financed the facility through the Renewable Energy Fund, which is funded by an annual $80 contribution per student as part of tuition and fees.

Energy

Energy efficiency has always been a leading focus but has now taken on more importance as the college works to expand carbon-neutral energy production and energy efficiency as part of its strategic regional development plan. Since most of Northland's greenhouse gas emissions come from buildings, the college has committed itself to making the buildings as energy-efficient as possible. The recently renovated Dexter Library, featuring a photovoltaic array and geothermal heating and cooling, was one of the first buildings in Wisconsin to achieve Leadership in Energy and Environmental Design Gold certification. Recent additions to the campus are the student-built Strawbale Demonstration Energy Lab, which operates off the grid, and the McLean Environmental Living and Learning Center (MELLC). The campus also features two wind towers, four hot-water arrays, five photovoltaic arrays (including one installed by students at the president's house), and geothermal heating and cooling in the Ponzio Campus Center.

Nationally, Northland is a signatory of the American College and University Presidents' Climate Commitment (ACUPCC) and a participant in the Billion

Dollar Green Challenge. The ACUPCC is a national initiative undertaken by a network of universities that have made institutional commitments to eliminate net greenhouse gas emissions from certain campus operations and to promote research and education to re-stabilize the earth's climate. Participants recognize the responsibility that institutions of higher learning have to serve as role models for their communities.

The Billion Dollar Green Challenge ('The Challenge') encourages colleges, universities, and other non-profit institutions to invest a combined total of one billion dollars in self-managed revolving funds that finance energy-efficiency improvements. Participating institutions will achieve reductions in operating expenses and greenhouse gas emissions while creating regenerating funds for future projects. The Sustainable Endowments Institute, in collaboration with sixteen partner organizations, has launched The Challenge to help non-profit institutions achieve sizeable energy savings through the use of green 'revolving funds', which invest in energy-efficiency projects to reduce energy consumption on campus and reinvest the money saved in future projects. They are called 'revolving funds' because the funds loan money to specific projects, which then repay the loan through an internal account transfer from savings achieved in the institution's utilities budget.

Reduce, Reuse, Recycle

The 'Reduce, Reuse, Recycle' initiative is one of Northland's most basic sustainable practices. Work-study students monitor campus waste and recycling, create educational campaigns, and operate an on-campus 'ReUse Room'. Plastic, aluminium cans, glass, mixed paper, cardboard, batteries, and ink cartridges are collected for recycling, and an electronics recycling event is held annually for the community. Food waste is collected and composted on site.

A new and expanded ReUse Room recently opened in the basement of the Townhouses. Students and community members can peruse the displays in search of treasures. All items are free and donations may be placed in a drop-box outside the Ponzio Campus Center.

Bikes and Transportation

Since the mid-1990s, Northland's Sunshine Community Bike Shoppe has served as a hub for bike enthusiasts. The shop has tools, parts, and plenty of advice to offer people who need to repair or want to build a bike. A template for other campus communities, the shop is a reminder of the potential of bicycles to bring us closer to sustainability.

The Northland College Student Association (NCSA) partners with Bay Area Rural Transit to provide expanded services and free bus passes for students, faculty, and staff. Northland is measuring greenhouse gas emissions from field trips, sporting events, and college-related air travel to develop the best methods to offset this impact. NCSA provided a new hybrid car for the admissions office out of its renewable energy fund.

Native Landscaping

Northland's campus has many chemical-free lawns for lounging and games. However, in keeping with the mission of environmental sustainability, large areas of campus have been restored to native plant communities. The college is working to instil the distinct character of northern Wisconsin habitats into its grounds in order to connect the campus further with its surroundings. White pine, graceful grasses, wildflowers, and the songs of indigenous birds combine to form a landscape pleasing to all the senses. Signage describing the various habitat areas and plantings is sprinkled throughout the campus.

Green Buildings

Strawbale Building

Northland's commitment to green buildings began in the 1990s. During the winter semester of 1998, a straw bale design workshop was conducted. During the May term, several students built a structure constructed entirely of locally produced materials. Straw bales provide excellent insulation, and the ceiling is insulated with cellulose from recycled newspapers. All south-facing windows capture passive solar heating, and a one kilowatt wind generator and three 75 watt solar photovoltaic panels supply electricity to the building's batteries. In-floor heat is provided by four hot-water solar panels. The building is now the home of the Sunshine Community Bike Shoppe.

McLean Environmental Living and Learning Center

Opened in 1998, the McLean Environmental Living and Learning Center is a unique residential space for students and was an early model for green design. Students were active participants in the building's design process and helped to select environmentally-friendly materials including recycled carpet, furniture made from recycled milk jugs and recycled steel, bio-composite counter-tops, windows with low-emissivity coated glass, and natural-based linoleum floors. Walls, ceilings, and windows received increased amounts of insulation. Three photovoltaic solar arrays provide efficient active solar energy collection. Motion sensor lighting and high-efficiency light fixtures, motors, and appliances reduce electricity use. Two waterless composting toilets and low-flow water-saving fixtures throughout the building help conserve water. Fourteen solar panels placed on the roof of the south wing heat water for residential use. Heat recovery comes from exhaust air, and high-efficiency boilers are used for space and water heating.

Dexter Library

The library was renovated in 2008 and was one of the first LEED Gold-certified buildings in Wisconsin. To receive a Gold-level certification, the renovators had to control not just what they built, but what they threw away. Of the total construction and demolition waste, 75 percent was diverted from landfill. These materials were either recycled or reused, reducing the burden on landfill and the demand for virgin resources. Recycled content carpet was used, and 30 percent of the furniture and furnishings were reused and/or refurbished. Of the new wood-based products and materials, 50 percent were FSC-certified, and 20 percent of the building materials were manufactured within 500 miles. There is a 14–kilowatt photovoltaic solar array on the roof, and geothermal heating and cooling are used. Energy-efficient lighting with occupancy sensors, increased roof insulation, and low-flow plumbing fixtures were installed. There was extensive use of materials low in volatile organic compounds (VOCs).

Community

Community and sustainability are inseparable and omnipresent at Northland: 'community – the place where we live and work. We are committed to sustainability and good stewardship, in order to conserve this place for the generations that will follow us'. It is appropriate to conclude with a few comments that demonstrate the college's ongoing commitment.

Community engagement has been a leading priority and driving force at Northland since its founding. Northland strives to interact with the community to achieve local and regional growth in a sustainable manner. Examples have been provided of Northland's commitment to sourcing local food, hiring area contractors and service providers, and working with multiple groups and institutions to form and implement strategies for regional well-being. Northland supports and promotes social entrepreneurship and the quadruple bottom line of people, planet, profits, and place in order to achieve regional resiliency and self-sufficiency.

In 2012, Northland joined public, private, non-profit, and tribal leaders to create a comprehensive plan for regional development based on the belief that economic development is more successful and more powerful when partnered with community development. Northland brings to the table its long history of community engagement, established partnerships, economic development initiatives, and its commitment to and expertise in utilizing environmental sustainability. Michael Miller, President of Northland and board member of the Ashland Area Development Corporation, served as chair of the steering committee. Four community work sessions were held to define the community vision, identify goals for the future, and develop an action plan that would address the focus areas the community thought were most important. On 5 November 2012, the committee hosted a community celebration, and the guest of honour was the one-page, four-point Strategic Plan.

Northland has a long and close relationship with nearby Native American communities and offers college access and readiness programs for Native Americans and indigenous youth; courses focusing on Native American history, language and culture; and a degree in Native American studies. In 2011, the Native American Indigenous Culture Center (NAICC), an extension of and successor to the long-standing Native American Studies Program, was established at Northland. It promotes awareness of and creates programs to appreciate and understand further Native American and indigenous cultures, traditions, and languages.

The NAICC serves as a resource centre and a gathering place for community meetings, cultural exchanges, presentations, and social events. It endeavours to form partnerships and connections in order to increase the capacity of the college and the community to develop solutions to issues and problems.

Northland College is a sponsoring partner of the Chequamegon Bay Area Partnership, a coalition of fourteen regional municipalities and tribal governments, state and federal agencies, and non-profit organizations working toward the restoration of Lake Superior. Since September 2010, the partnership has won more than $1 million in competitive grants from the Great Lakes Restoration Initiative to fund habitat restoration, outreach, and education and environmental survey initiatives. This amount includes two grants totalling nearly $500,000 awarded in August 2011. The college is also part of the Eco League, a five-college consortium that enables students to spend semesters at Alaska Pacific University, Green Mountain College, Prescott College, and College of the Atlantic.

Northland College continues to examine itself and apply its traditions, environmental mission, and sustainable practice to shape a world where human and all biological communities can thrive together indefinitely. They are guided by the words of Chief Seattle:

> Whatever befalls the earth, befalls the people of the earth. Man did not weave the web of life; he is merely a strand in it.

References

Abazs, D., Stark, S., and Syring, D. (2010). Defining the Agricultural Landscape of the Western Lake Superior Region: Realities and Potentials for a Healthy Local Food System for Healthy People. Healthy Foods, Healthy Lives Institute, Department of Food Science and Nutrition, University of Minnesota. www.round-river.com/LAFS/HFHL_FINAL-REPORT.pdf (last accessed 2 February 2014).

American Planning Association (2013). *Principles of a Healthy Sustainable Food System.* www.planning.org/nationalcenters/health/foodprinciples.htm (last accessed May 2013).

Berry, W. (1990) *The Pleasures of Eating.* New York: North Point Press.

Chicago Metropolitan Agency for Planning (CMAP) (2010). *Go to 2040: Comprehensive Regional Plan for Metropolitan Chicago.* Chicago. www.cmap.illinois.gov/2040/main (last accessed 7 February 2014).

Daly, H. E. (1990a). Boundless Bull. *Gannett Center Journal* 4 (3): 113–118.

Daly, H. E. (1990b). Toward Some Operational Principles of Sustainable Development. Ecological Economics 2: 1–6.

Grace Foundation Communications (2013). *Sustainable Table.* www.sustainabletable.org/ (last accessed May 2013).

Lake Superior Good Food Network (2103). http://goodfoodnetwork.org/ (last accessed May 2013).

Lappé, A., and Lappé, F. M. (2002). *Hope's Edge: The Next Diet for a Small Planet.* New York: Jeremy P. Tarcher/Putnam.

Lincoln, A. (1859). Speech at Wisconsin State Fair, 30 September. www.abrahamlincolnonline.org/lincoln/speeches/fair.htm (last accessed May 2013).

Nelson, G. (2002). *Beyond Earth Day: Fulfilling the Promise.* Madison: Wisconsin Press.

Northland College (2013). www.northland.edu/about-northland-mission-vision.htm (last accessed May 2013).

Northland College Magazine (2012), Fall, p 18.

Pretty, J. (2002). Agri-Culture: Reconnecting People, Land, and Nature. London: Earthscan. www.earthdinner.org/pdf/EarthDinner_booklet.pdf, p. 46 (last accessed 7 February 2014).

Rodale Institute (2013). www.rodale.org (last accessed April 2013).

Seattle, Chief, Suquamish Tribe (1854). Speech to Territorial Governor of the State of Washington. Attributed. http://epubl.ltu.se/1402–1773/2007/074/LTU-CUPP-07074–SE.pdf, p. 23 (last accessed 8 February 2014).

United Nations, World Commission on the Environment and Development (WCED) (1987). *Our Common Future.* www.un-documents.net/our-common-future.pdf (last accessed 14 January 2014).

7

Higher education intervention in the management of soil erosion and agricultural practice in Nigeria

Idowu Biao and Roseline Tawo

Introduction

Soil erosion is a major ecological problem in Nigeria in general, but particularly in south-eastern Nigeria. In addition to being a major issue, the incidence of soil erosion in Nigeria is a long-standing problem and has been the subject of numerous high-level discussions since the beginning of the twentieth century. For example, Ofomota (2009) indicated that the Udi Forest Reserve and an anti-erosion plantation, also at Udi, were created in 1922 and 1928 respectively, with a view to combating soil erosion in the country.

Poor agricultural practice is one of the suspected causes of soil erosion in the country. Yet concerted efforts to tackle this menace effectively seem to be lacking. One weakness in the process of tackling soil erosion in Nigeria is linked to the supply of fertilizers for purposes of agricultural practice.

This chapter examines the interrelationship existing among soil erosion, agricultural practice, and access to fertilizers in Nigeria. It also describes an ongoing engagement by a university in the south-eastern part of Nigeria with local communities which aims at reducing the nefarious effect of soil erosion. Finally, it calls attention to the role that Nigerian and African higher education may play in improving the quality of the environment in Africa and in proffering solutions to other social challenges.

Nigeria

Created in 1914 by the British colonial conquerors and ruled and managed for a significant length of time by Lord Lugard (Crowder, 1980), Nigeria is a west African country that holds the largest population of black people on earth. Nigeria's population represents one-sixth of Africa's total population. It is expected to grow at the rate of about 2.5 per cent to about 185 million inhabitants in 2015 and to about 390 million in 2050 (United Nations, 2010). Almost equally divided between men and women, Nigeria's population is made up of a large active segment comprising 41 per cent of persons aged up to fourteen years and about 56 per cent of persons aged between fifteen and sixty-five years (United Nations, 2010).

Much of this population occupies a large portion of the 910,770 square kilometres in land area of the country, which includes a variety of features such as:

- the Niger Delta,
- the Coastal Lowlands,
- the Undulating Plains of the Interior Lowland,
- the Scarplands of South-central Nigeria,
- the Niger-Benue trough,
- the Sokoto Plains,
- the Chad Basin,
- the Western Uplands,
- the North Central Plateau, and
- the Eastern and Northeastern Highlands (OnlineNigeria, 2012).

About 85 per cent of Nigeria's land is said to be agricultural land, that is, arable and cultivable on either a temporary or a permanent basis (Tradingeconomics, 2012). However, erosion makes agricultural practice difficult as all parts of Nigeria are prone to erosion, albeit to different degrees (Ofomata, 2009; Igbokwe et al., 2008).

Soil erosion and agricultural practice in Nigeria

Soil erosion and agricultural practice are two interrelated phenomena in Nigeria. Poor agricultural practice engenders erosion and, ultimately, erosion ends up hampering agricultural practice. Erosion is both a process and a result of topsoil loss. It is a 'process under which soil is bodily displaced and transported away faster than it can be formed' (Igbokwe et al., 2008). A number of natural and man-made agents account for this phenomenon. Among natural agents are running water, glaciers, waves, wind, and rainfall droplets. Man-activated agents include poor methods of farming, bush burning, and wood harvesting (Imoke et al., 2010; Ofomata, 2009; Igbokwe et al., 2008).

A number of methods have been employed or recommended for combating erosion; however, it has been observed that some of these methods complicate and aggravate the original situation. Hence, Ofomata (2009) suggests that a distinction should be made between 'actual erosion' and 'potential erosion' as a way of driving home the view that without sufficient knowledge, techniques to fight erosion may lead to worsening states of erosion.

In Nigeria, the erection of soak-away pits and tree trunk dams is a common way of controlling and preventing soil erosion.

> Soak-away pits are constructed outside the farm but are meant to limit runoff into and within the farm. Labour spent desilting these pits is part of the cost of sediment and erosion control (SEC). None of the farmers used concrete structures. Most of the SEC measures were integral parts of the agronomic (tillage) practices in the area. Only soak-away pits and tree trunk dams were found to be applied not as part, but as independent, of general tillage practices. What farmers achieve with the measures described above are both SEC and soil erosion prevention (SEP). That is, if we define SEP measures as those that are established more or less before erosion occurs while SEC measures are put in place largely when erosion is already occurring. More often than not, farmers do not institute measures for SEC but for SEP. We did not see any much evidence of post tillage soil amendment meant specifically for SEC. We also

found that if at all farmers put SEC measures in place, they were directed at points on the farm where crops were clearly under threat. (Okoye, 2009, p. 3).

Soak-away pits are relatively shallow holes dug in the ground around farms with a view to collecting waters that may run into farms from all directions. This reduces the number of water currents traversing the farm and consequently topsoil wash-off is reduced, minimizing erosive activities of water and other particles.

At the University of Calabar, the desire to become involved in agricultural practice is driven by two main needs, namely, to promote relevant community engagement activities and to protect the university's unoccupied land against erosion.

The University of Calabar and its needs

The University of Calabar is one of Nigeria's second-generation universities. In addition to the provision of the Act mandating the university to engage in teaching, research, and community service, the university developed a strategic plan (revised in 2011) that encouraged all faculties and departments to engage with communities around the university and in Cross River State for the purpose of exchanging ideas and improving skills in all aspects of living (Ita, 2011).

Within the framework of the university's strategic plan, a series of collaborative community engagement activities involving the Departments of Soil Science and Adult and Continuing Education and farmers in Calabar has been going on for about five years. A report of a community engagement effort that focused on an agricultural training for livelihood for women farmers around the university has been made elsewhere (Biao et al., 2011). However, the project described here specifically showcases efforts aimed at protecting the yet to be exploited land of the University of Calabar against soil erosion.

The University of Calabar's project against soil erosion

Of the large expanse of land belonging to the University of Calabar, only seven hectares have been developed. The remaining nearly fourteen hectares of land lie fallow as a result of lack of financial resources to develop it. Since any abandoned and unattended land in south-eastern Nigeria is prone to erosion and degradation, the university has evolved a system for looking after its undeveloped land by leasing portions of it to farmers. They may exploit it for livelihood as long as the university does not have a need for the land. The lease is carried out without written agreement, and the financial benefit that the university derives from the lease is token and insignificant as the lease is primarily designed to remind farmers that the land belongs not to the farmers, but to the university.

However, while all the farmers are grateful to the university for allowing them to derive livelihood from farming on the land, only a few of them are aware of methods that may be employed to protect the land against erosion. Hence, the university's Departments of Soil Science and Adult and Continuing Education developed an integrated education programme for farmers which aims to help them to derive healthy yields and to protect the land against erosion.

Two major strategies were adopted in educating farmers on how to protect the soil against erosion. The first consists of providing the farmers with information regarding steps to be taken to protect the land against erosion. The second consists of taking the farmers through demonstrations relating to the specific ways in which these steps are to be taken to maximize their effectiveness.

A basic lesson in the educational programme is that the land should always be covered with some kind of vegetation, in particular, fine grass or crops. Bush burning should always be avoided, and the slopes between the ridges should be dammed with sizeable pieces of wood to prevent fast-running waters from eroding the soil. The practical aspect of the community education includes demonstrations of how farmers should erect dams and keep grass low on the portions of the land they are not planning to use.

However, while grass may grow naturally on much of the land in south-eastern Nigeria, crops need more than rain to grow healthy and be economically profitable. Therefore, for the farmers and the university to succeed in their collaboration, it became necessary for them to examine jointly the issue of successful cropping. Inorganic fertilizer and its availability are major factors in agricultural practice and success in Nigeria. Unfortunately, inorganic fertilizer has proved a difficult commodity to access since Nigerian independence.

Agriculture has always been the mainstay of the Nigerian economy. Even between the 1970s (the period during which petroleum revenue began to be a part of the country's budget) and the present time, agriculture has remained the backbone of the nation's economy. For example, in 1999, 2000, 2008, and 2010, agriculture contributed 41 per cent, 43 per cent, 42 per cent, and 32.5 per cent of Nigeria's GDP respectively, against 18 per cent and 20 per cent from petroleum (Banful, Nkonya, and Oboh, 2009; Index Mundi, 2013). Additionally, 70 per cent of Nigerians are still engaged in subsistence farming (Ragasa et al., 2010).

Yet Nigeria remains unable to produce enough food to feed its increasing population, largely as a result of a low supply of inorganic fertilizer. Although a national campaign to use inorganic fertilizer did increase the demand among farmers from the 1970s, studies have shown that only 30 per cent of subsidized fertilizer ever reached farmers in Nigeria (Liverpool-Tasie, Banful, and Olaniyan, 2010; Banful, Nkonya, and Oboh, 2009).

A number of strategies have been devised by authorities to increase access to fertilizer and the level of its use among farmers. These strategies include the establishment of Village Extension Agents (VEAs), the adoption of a fertilizer voucher programme, the introduction of fertilizer distribution monitoring services, and the yearly review of fertilizer distribution mechanisms (Liverpool-Tasie, Banful, and Olaniyan, 2010; Banful, Nkonya, and Oboh, 2009). In spite of these efforts, fertilizer use in Nigeria remains extremely low, principally because farmers are not able to access it (Nmadu and Amos, 2009; Liverpool-Tasie, Banful & Olaniyan, 2010 and Banful, Nkonya, and Oboh, 2009).

Yet farmers need a certain amount of fertilizer in order to engage productively and meaningfully in agricultural production. Where farmers are not able to circumvent the scarcity of fertilizer, they are not able to protect the university's land against erosion. It has been necessary to evolve another partnership that would bring the university and the farmers together to work on a project that would enable them to access fertilizer all year round.

While the supply of inorganic fertilizer is controlled by government and para-government institutions, organic fertilizer is a product which farmers can produce with little support and guidance. Consequently, through a number of learning sessions, the university's Departments of Soil Science and Adult and Continuing Education have taught the farmers the techniques of mixing in appropriate quantities of both organic waste and human and/or animal urine to obtain the right quality of fertilizer. In order to ensure an uninterrupted supply of organic waste, an organic waste bank was established within each of the farm sites to which the farmers contributed domestic waste on a daily basis. This process made fertilizer available all year round, and this availability motivated farmers to work for themselves and thus benefit the university by preventing soil erosion on its land.

The use of compost is not without its consequences. Composting has implications for the quality of air and water within the immediate environment. It equally has effects on the soil and crops which are better avoided (Baldwin and Greenfield, 2009; Strantton, Baker and Rechcigl, 1995). However, the singular aim of the project discussed here was to provide the farmers with an alternative source of fertilizer, and no effort was made to assess the possible consequences of this new process. The need to study the consequences of the new process of sourcing fertilizer will ultimately arise as the project matures.

Contribution of the project to international programmes

The United Nations' Millennium Development Goals remain the most influential development programme rolled out by the international community in recent times. Each of the eight goals of this programme has associated targets that are expected to be met within the first fifteen years of the twenty-first century. Two of these goals and a number of their targets have been addressed by the current project. Specifically, goal 1 seeks to eradicate extreme poverty and hunger by the end of the millennium, with targets of halving the proportion of people who suffer from hunger and live on less than $1.25 a day, and to achieve decent employment for all, including women and young people, by 2015 (United Nations, 2013).

Goal 7 advocates environmental sustainability and targets the enactment of policies and practices that reverse the loss of environmental resources as one way to do this. It also seeks to reverse the loss of biodiversity by substantially increasing the land area covered by vegetation or forest (United Nations, 2013).

CONFINTEA (the Conference Internationale sur l'Education des Adultes, or International Conference on Adult Education) is another international programme that is relevant to this project. CONFINTEA is a convening of adult educators organized by UNESCO to review achievements within the field of adult education and learning, and to determine future directions of adult education theory and practice. On the basis of the premise that not all of the education needed for a happy, functional, and successful life in the twenty-first century can be obtained within a specified time-space period, CONFINTEA VI recommended that lifelong learning should be adopted by all societies to promote development in all of its ramifications (Ahmed, 2010; Bissio, 2010; Eldred, 2010; Varavarn, 2010; Walters, 2010).

By providing opportunities for the production of food, this project is contributing to the reduction of hunger and unemployment, albeit minimally. The partnership between the university and the farmers also is contributing significantly to saving a prime environmental resource (land) from degradation while income made from the farm activities is helping to reduce extreme poverty.

Evaluation of the programme

While a full-fledged evaluation of this project has not yet been conducted, two formative evaluation exercises carried out have revealed three facts:

1. While many more farmers than those currently engaged by the university would have loved to partake in the present project, the university management position favours keeping the number of farmers to engage to a manageable level. By limiting participation to a modest number of farmers of honourable disposition who are capable of keeping to the terms of unwritten agreements, the university is able to ensure that the programme does not become too unwieldy and too large to control.

2. For their part, farmers wished that the token fees being collected from them by the university could be reduced further. Indeed some of the farmers would like the token fees to be eliminated altogether. As one farmer stated:

   The university recognises that the majority of us are poor and unemployed by government. Yet, we have mouths to feed and children to train. By letting go of the fees we currently pay, the university would have been helping to ameliorate our conditions. After all, our labour is currently contributing to the maintenance of the university land. Why would they then not show some compassion towards us?

3. Participating farmers have made two other suggestions. One is that the university uses the collections it makes from them to supplement the supply of the equipment (hoes, cutlasses, boots, etc.) that they need. Second is that the university helps bring local government authorities to assist the farmers working on university land in accessing farm implements cheaply or at no cost.

Higher education and community engagement in Africa

Higher education in Africa includes all post-secondary education institutions. Examples of these institutions are polytechnics, colleges of education, colleges of health sciences, colleges of agriculture, and universities. While the polytechnics and colleges produce middle-level manpower in their domain of expertise, the expectations from the universities are higher and numerous. The universities are expected not only to produce a sizeable number and categories of high-level personnel, but also to collaborate with industries and to add value to life in African communities through the process of community engagement. Consequently, as a result of high expectations from universities, they alone (to the exclusion of colleges) have come to connote higher education in the mind of most Africans.

Between 1827, the year of the establishment of the first university in Africa (Teferra and Knight, 2003), and the beginning of the twenty-first century, the number of universities on African soil has run to about 1,000 (Association of African Universities, 2013). Teaching, research, and community service (community engagement) remain the three core activities known to African universities. While teaching and some level of research work have been known to have been carried out by universities in Africa, their level of community engagement remains poor (Preece, 2011; Preece et al., 2012). Community engagement is a process of university–community partnership that seeks to generate a two-way basket of benefits for the two partners.

By the beginning of the twenty-first century, the neglect of university-community engagement had reached such a noticeable and disturbing scale that the Association of African Universities put out a call for a research into the extent to which African universities promote community engagement. That project, which was christened ITMUA (Implementing the Third Mission of Universities in Africa), was implemented by university colleagues drawn from four African countries (Botswana, Malawi, Lesotho, and Nigeria).

The result of the investigation, which lasted for about eighteen months, showed that, of the three missions of the African universities, teaching, research, and community engagement, university-community engagement was the most neglected. Indeed barely 3 per cent of African universities were found to be involved in any meaningful community engagement activities (Preece, 2011).

From the perspective of this less than encouraging performance, the effort of the University of Calabar may be viewed as laudable and worthy of encouragement. The following policy recommendations therefore are designed to urge the University of Calabar to greater community engagement work in the future, but also to carve some way forward for the community engagement efforts of African universities.

Policy recommendations

Flowing from the preceding discussion are the following recommendations:

- The farmers should be encouraged to organise themselves into an association with the view to engaging the university in discussion, instead of the current practice of the university dealing with the farmers mostly on an individual basis. The advantage of such an approach is that the university would become more visible and more likely to be seen by the community as contributing meaningfully to community welfare.
- The university should revisit its budget for community service ('community service' is still in use in the official documents of most Nigerian universi-

ties) with a view to increasing it so that the academic departments involved in such work may benefit from a certain amount of material and financial support from the university. At present, only departments that are able to access external funds are involved in community engagement efforts, and they are few in number. Usually, external funds are unable to cover all necessary costs of projects, which makes the need for the university to maintain a generous community service fund more pressing.

- The university should revise its community service policy to take into account the dimensions recently introduced by the concept of 'community engagement', namely, those of 'frank and mutually beneficial partnership' between communities and the university, and 'service learning' and 'integrated development', which have the potential to increase the relevance of African universities to the African milieu.
- African universities avoided their third-mission responsibilities as a result of World Bank policy discouraging such activity from 1960 to 1990 (Preece, 2011, p. 2). Since old habits die hard, the period since the 1990s continues to record low participation of Nigerian and African universities in the area of community engagement. Yet greater external support now exists for such activity than before. It is, therefore, recommended that Nigerian universities should become more involved in community engagement during the twenty-first century. Additionally, it is through such university-community engagement efforts that the environment in Africa can be improved and other social issues addressed, to the benefit of African populations.

Conclusion

This project has revealed four facts. First, it has proved that, even in its early state of community engagement, the University of Calabar was able to initiate some collaborative work with the communities surrounding it. Second, the university can lead initiatives for the creation of employment (no matter how initially low-paid) for communities around it. Third, the university is able to provide hands-on training in the field of agriculture with a view to ultimately increasing the supply of food within its immediate communities and the country. Fourth, and most important, this project has proved that the university, in collaboration with its surrounding communities, is capable of supplying local solutions to local problems.

In view of the foregoing, the current battle against soil erosion using relatively cheap methods will be sustained if a few additional techniques for combating soil erosion are taught to the farmers and if the farmers' produce is moved to markets where it may attract higher revenue than it does at the moment.

Although environmental challenges are not the only issues offering themselves for community engagement, it is within an environment that can sustain life and promote decent and healthy living that other community engagement issues can be dealt with. Consequently, while soil erosion remains an issue in south-eastern Nigeria, other issues such as girls' education, the education of boys who are out of school, adult illiteracy, and youth unemployment continue to constitute major challenges in other parts of the country.

Each of these challenges is begging for attention, and it is hoped that, with a bit of internal reorganization and support from within and outside the country, Nigerian higher education in general, and universities in particular, will in the future be able to take on more social and environmental issues through the implementation of their third mission. The need to make itself more relevant to the nation and earn greater social respectability should encourage the leadership of Nigerian higher education to address the aforementioned policy recommendations with a view to eventually selling them to national and international donor agencies.

References

Ahmed, M. (2010). Facing the Truth about Literacy. *Adult Education and Development* 75: 107–112.

Association of African Universities (2013). *Number of Universities in Africa*. www.aau.org (last accessed 19 September 2013).

Baldwin, K. R., and Greenfield, J. T. (2009). *Composting on Organic Farms*. www.cefs.ncsu. edu (last accessed 10 April 2013).

Banful A. B., Nkonya, E., and Oboh, E. (2009). Constraints to Fertiliser use in Nigeria: Perspectives and Insights from the Agricultural Extension Service. IFPRI Brief No. 6. www.ifpri.org/sites/default/files/publications/nsspbr06.pdf (last accessed 29 July 2012).

Biao, I., Akpama, S., Tawo, R., and Inyang, E. (2011). Female Farmers in a University-Led Agricultural Training Programme in Calabar, Nigeria. In J. Preece (ed.), *Community Service and Community Engagement in Four African Universities*. Gaborone: Lentswe La Lesedi (Pty) Ltd.

Bissio, R. (2010). Multiple Crisis, One Solution: Put People First. *Adult Education and Development* 75: 91–96.

Crowder, M. (1980). *The Story of Nigeria*. London: Faber and Faber.

Eldred, J. (2010). Adult Learning, Literacy and International Development: Hope or Hypocrisy? *Adult Education and Development* 75: 101–104.

Igbokwe, J. I., Akinyede, J. O., Dang, B., Alaga, T., Ono, M. N., Nnodu, V. C., and Anike, L. O. (2008). Mapping and Monitoring of the Impact of Gully Erosion in Southeastern Nigeria with Satellite Remote Sensing and Geographic Information System. *International Archives of the Photogrammetry, Remote Sensing and Spatial Information Sciences* 37 (B8).

Imoke, E. D., Ibu, U. J., Omonya, O. C., Nwabueze, O. J., and Njar, G. N. (2010). Effects of Land Degradation on Soil Productivity in Calabar South Local Government Area, Nigeria. *European Journal of Social Sciences* 18 (1): 166–171.

Index Mundi (2013). Country Facts. www.indexmundi.com (last accessed 23 June 2013).

Ita, B. (2011). Unical Vice-Chancellor Hinges Academic Progress on Strategic Plan. www. unicaledu.com (last accessed 2 February 2014).

Liverpool-Tasie, S. L. O., Banful, A. B., and Olaniyan, B. (2010). *Assessment of 2009 Fertiliser Voucher Programme in Kano and Taraba, Nigeria*. IFPRI Policy Note No. 30. www.ifpri. org/sites/default/files/publications/nssppn30.pdf (last accessed 20 July 2012).

Nmadu, J. N., and Amos, T. T. (2009). Effect of Fertiliser Consumption in Nigeria and Rate of Naira Exchange to the US Dollar on Sorghum Acreage between 1960 and 2006. *Journal of Human Ecology* 26 (1): 41–45.

Ofomota, G. E. K. (2009). Soil Erosion in Nigeria: The Views of a Geomorphologist, No. 7. Inaugural lecture, University of Nigeria, Nsukka, 2009.

Okoye, C. U. (2009). Soil Erosion Control and Damage Costs in Nigerian Small Farms: Implications for Farm Growth. http://ageconsearch.umn.edu/bitstream/53079/2/068. pdf (last accessed 29 July 2012).

OnlineNigeria (2012). Land-Nigeria. www.onlinenigeria.com/links/ (last accessed 7 May 2012).

Preece, J. (2011). Universities, Community Service and African Contexts. In J. Preece (ed.), *Community Service and Community Engagement in Four African Universities*. Gaborone: Lentswe La Lesedi (Pty) Ltd.

Preece, J. (ed.) (2011). Community Service and Community Engagement in Four African Universities. Gaborone: Lentswe La Lesedi (Pty) Ltd.

Preece, J., Biao, I., Nampota, D., and Raditloaneng, W. (2012). Community Engagement within African Contexts: A Comparative Analysis. In J. Preece, P. G. Ntseane, O. M. Modise, and M. Osborne, *Community Engagement in African Universities: Perspectives, Prospects and Challenges*. Leicester: National Institute of Adult Continuing Education.

Ragasa, S., Babu, A., Abdullahi, B., and Abubakar, B. Y. (2010). Fertiliser Market Situation in Nigeria. www.ifpri.org/sites/publications/pdf (last accessed 29 July 2012).

Strantton, M. L., Baker, A. V., and Rechcigl, J. E. (1995). Soil Amendments and Environmental Quality. www.cabdirect.org (last accessed 10 April 2013).

Teferra, W., and Knight, J. (2003). *Higher Education in Africa: The International Dimension*. Ghana: Association of African Universities.

Tradingeconomics (2012). *Land Area in Nigeria*. www.tradingeconomics.com/nigeria/land-area (last accessed 7 May 2012).

United Nations (2010a) *The Millennium Development Goals Report*. New York: United Nations.

United Nations (2010b). *World Populations Prospects*. New York: United Nations.

University of Calabar (2011). *Strategic Plan 2011–2015*. Calabar: Unical Printing Press.

Varavarn (2010). Towards Lifelong Learning. *Adult Education and Development* 75: 25–43.

Walters, S. (2010). The Bridge We Call Home: Putting People First. *Adult Education and Development* 75: 97–100.

8

The importance of women's leadership programmes in developing a sustainable economy

Morgan Chawawa and Wapula Raditloaneng

Ba Isago University College and community engagement

Universities the world over are coming to terms with their new mandate of making a contribution towards addressing critical community development issues through what is termed 'community service'. Over the past decade universities have been connecting with disadvantaged communities to eradicate poverty and sustain development in the African region through their involvement at the grassroots level. During the same time it has become increasingly apparent that university engagement requires a community-led approach to build trust and raise aspirations. The case study covered in this chapter is the result of the community engagement experience of Ba Isago University College, one of the thirteen private colleges registered by the Tertiary Education Council in 2006. Botswana is a country of 1,900,000 with a per capita income of about US $14,000. The country had one public university, with a capacity of 15,000, prior to the introduction of private colleges.

Ba Isago University College undertook a study of the minority San communities in Botswana with the aim of fulfilling one of its mandates as a tertiary education provider in Botswana, that is, community engagement. Universities in Botswana are expected to work with communities to address socio-economic problems in one way or another. This is an important role that they play in the fulfilment of the government of Botswana's strategic plan for the nation termed VISION 2016. VISION 2016 calls for an 'educated and informed Nation' as well as a 'compassionate and caring Nation'. After conducting an extensive needs assessment on the needs of minorities, the college decided to work with the San women in the D'kar Farm community, Ghanzi District (see Figure 8.1). Botswana is addressing poverty and lack of employment in that community.

The college approached the Kellogg Foundation of the USA for funding and then initiated its community engagement programme in the D'kar Farm San community, Ghanzi District. Botswana then transformed the lives of San women and their families. It is important to note that the San, traditionally called Bushmen, live by and large in abject poverty because of their nomadic lifestyle, in spite of massive financial investments in their community by international donors. On the D'kar Reformed Church Farm, a village of about 2,000 residents of San tribe

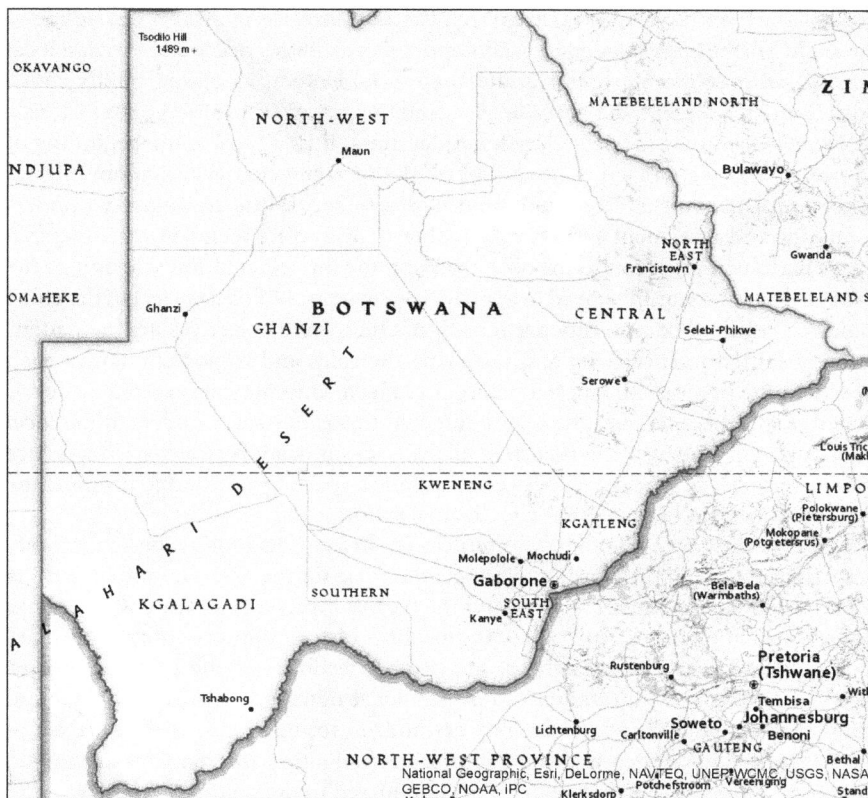

Figure 8.1 Map of Botswana

origin has grown, without any tangible means of employment. The farm has a shop where handcrafted Bushman articles can be bought. The money is then used to help the people of the Kalahari. It houses a school and a clinic. The D'kar community is governed by the D'kar Trust under the umbrella of the Kuru Development Trust. The trust provides sanctuary for the San, who are running away from exploitation by commercial farmers who use them as poorly paid labour for their operations. The farm has been serving as a community organizer as well as a food source and is administered by the San women. The San women in D'kar developed leadership and work skills through Ba Isago University's Community Capacity Building Programme. This programme achieved this while developing sustainable business opportunities for economic transformation. The women formed a cooperative that started producing tie-and-dye (Batik fabric) products while undergoing training in business and leadership skills.

The Kellogg Foundation was chosen as a partner in this community engagement initiative on basis of the way it operates, especially its application of the 'zooming' approach. This approach builds local capacity in youth, women, and families. The capacity to self–drive is developed by supporting rural communities to self-start, self-assess, and self-correct. Furthermore, the approach was designed to build business and leadership skills and the capabilities needed to provide local people with economic opportunities and employment. Zooming builds confidence and resources that people need to lead their own social and economic transformation. A multi-faceted approach to learning, it is argued, is the beginning of a participatory approach that would link the disconnected D'kar community to the rest of the world. The foundation works to secure the community's understanding and agreement with its values, objectives, and strategies. Local leadership pays particular attention to the objectives and the implementation schedule of the zooming process, as they need to approve the capacity-building aspect of the effort and the required community participation. Once these objectives are met, attention is shifted to specifying and clarifying the roles and responsibilities of each party in the process. The model is supported by a communication strategy developed by the steering committee and targeted to various stakeholders of the local development process. The objective of the communication strategy is to reduce the differences in perception between the various participants and to promote the cohesion needed for a successful collective action.

Approaches used for the communication strategy include using community meetings to spread the word, providing a rationale for the exercise, and informing stakeholders of the different steps and the parties involved. Community meetings offer the opportunity to learn about the locality's history, opportunities, challenges, and achievements. Community forums provide feedback on the zooming process and its outcomes. Community radios and local newspapers provide timely and ongoing information about the process and its results. Once the objectives of the exercise are defined and the appropriate facilitation mechanisms are agreed upon, a systematic needs assessment is conducted to define the support required for successful completion of the zooming process. Following this assessment, a planning grant is made to the community or to the facilitation agency to allow for the more detailed visioning and planning that follows. This generates a comprehensive multi-year programme to be supported by the Kellogg Foundation and other partners.

Fifteen San women in D'kar Farm community ran a cooperative making art, crafts, and tie-and-dye products. This cooperative had been operating for ten years but had failed to take off because of a lack of leadership and business management skills. It had a part-time business manager, and the members of the cooperative were not committed to the project. Members came to work on the project only when money was needed. A number of donors from the Netherlands had injected some funds into the tie-and-dye project, but because of lack of leadership and business management skills, the project could not grow. The intervention of Ba Isago University, with the financial support of the Kellogg Foundation, transformed the cooperative by giving it strong leadership and business management skills.

The women needed practical skills that they could use to make quality products to sell and make money for their families. The Kellogg Foundation and Ba Isago University College provided trainers, raw materials, and a training facility where women were given special training in making tie-and-dye goods, which many tourists like to buy and display in their homes. During a two-week training period, the women were busy making the goods. Tourists came and bought large quantities of their products, which was very encouraging for the women who were engaged in the project. The trainer and project coordinator gave lectures and demonstrated how to make specific patterns and pictures with objects used to block out the sunlight. Learners were involved in all aspects of the training and were encouraged to solve problems themselves by assessing the facts (e.g., hearing from an experienced craft distributor about the market value of their products) and then finding solutions as to how to improve. Participants were told to gather the objects they wanted to use and plan the design on a piece of paper. When this was done, outside space was cleared for each person to put her fabric in the sun. The participants then applied the dye and arranged their objects according to their planned design.

The leadership role of San women

In the D'kar Farm San community, most households are headed by women. Women look after families without material support from the men, most of whom do not have formal employment. Many do not live with the families in the village. There was an urgent need to equip women with skills to start their own businesses so that they could support their children. They have traditionally relied on men for leadership in the home and in community development projects. This is generally true for the San communities. But it was thought that the women needed to develop their own leadership skills in this project because they would be the drivers of the project. The skills of leading, directing, and supporting organizational goals were covered during the training sessions. At the end of the training sessions, a number of changes were observed among the participants. Leading is the management function of influencing people to act or not act in a certain way. It is the process of getting members of the project to work together in a fashion consistent with the goals of the project. Major aspects of leading include motivating employees and managing group dynamics, both of which are closely related to major areas of organizational behaviour. The San people are not good at 'leading' because everything among them must be done by consensus. When families decide on any activity or function, they must agree as a family; otherwise nothing happens. The training sessions gave the participants a new perspective on this aspect of their life. Initially, it was difficult to convince them of a need for someone to provide leadership in their business undertaking. The tie-and-dye business demands that the leader communicates with other businesses on behalf of the other members of the cooperative. The San tend to be suspicious of each other. They are wary of being cheated or short-changed in business dealings. So all decisions are referred to the group, which must agree or else the project is abandoned. After the training sessions, this thinking changed. They group chose a woman to be their leader and began to refer some decisions to the leader when they felt it was necessary to do so. The meetings were chaired by the leader and decisions from their meetings were carried out with the support of the leader. After the training sessions, the leader was able to encourage her colleagues to complete project goals. Although initially the leader was not comfortable giving instructions to the other members of the project, she gradually accepted the responsibility for achieving the project objectives. As a result of the training sessions, she began to play a major role in moving projects forward and in motivating other women by ensuring good communication between the members of the cooperative. We saw the leader giving direction when it came to matters of finance, when it involved sharing of profits at the end of the month, and when products had been sold and monies banked. Although the group decided how much each member should receive, the leader decided how to use the rest of the funds left in the project. We also witnessed the leader playing a major role in the implementation of the business plans including expansion of the business operations, purchasing additional equipment, and adopting new marketing techniques.

Leadership training infused energy into the project, motivating its members to get things moving and keep them moving. Leadership was important in passing information to colleagues, explaining the mission, allocating tasks and giving instructions, consulting with staff, and supervising their work – whatever was necessary to raise production, discipline staff, or handle conflicts. The practices though which information is gathered and used in the San community are interesting. Traditionally, the San people do not share much in terms of 'information'. They believe that power lies in how much you know and how much others depend on you. As a result, they operate by and large on a 'need to know basis', so the more you know, the less you want to share that information. In the training sessions, the facilitator spent some time on the importance of information for all members of the cooperative and why it had to be shared. The training sessions encouraged cooperative members to offer ideas on matters pertaining to their business operations. These included ideas on increasing production, motivating staff, knowledge of their business, and communication aimed at improving performance and increasing productivity.

Participants also were given an understanding of the fundamental differences between a manager and a leader. Good managers lead their projects to greater achievement, productivity, and ultimately, profitability. Managers have the authority to enforce order and direct the activities of others. This includes issuing orders and being responsible for their execution. A leader has the authority, but gets results without using force. The women discussed several different types of leadership styles, some more prevalent in their community than others. The workshops also addressed autocratic style. In the autocratic leadership style, all decision-making powers are centralized in the leader. The leader does not entertain any suggestions or initiatives from colleagues. Autocratic management has been successful as it allows for quick decision-making. One person decides on behalf of the whole group and keeps each decision to herself until she feels it needs to be shared. This is not true in the San community, where consensus is highly respected. During the workshops, the participants were highly critical of this model of leadership, and discussions focused on why it should not be used in their project. The women wanted this type of leadership model in their homes when disciplining children, but not in the cooperative. Young female members of the cooperative were very critical of the views expressed by the older women. They felt that it was abusive for men to make decisions and that the practice should be stopped in Botswana. They wanted to be involved in making decisions that affected their lives. The participative or democratic leadership style was also discussed at length during the workshops. In contrast to the unilateral decisions of the autocratic leader, the democratic leader consults with the group before making a decision, thereby winning cooperation of the group and providing effective and positive motivation. Members of the cooperative were very excited about this form of leadership because it is prevalent in the San community. What seemed to be lacking in their view of this leadership was 'accountability'. All wanted to be consulted when decisions were being made, but no one wanted to be account-able for the results of those decisions. They wanted the leader to be accountable. Because in the San community women do not normally hold leadership positions, the participants, who were all women, were not prepared to lead the group. In the end, some incentives had to be introduced to encourage one woman to accept the leadership position. The leader was given a small monthly allowance and less work on the production line since she had to work with all of the customers, suppliers, and shops associated with selling the cooperative's products.

A third leadership style covered during training was *laissez-faire*, or 'free rein'. This style of leadership raised many questions during the workshops. This was the dominant leadership style when Ba Isago University began its community engagement initiative. According to the trainer, a free-rein leader does not lead but leaves the group entirely to itself, allowing maximum freedom to colleagues in deciding their own policies and methods. Although it is prevalent in the San community, cooperative members felt that this type of leadership was not going to give them the best business relationship and that they would fail if they supported it. During the discussions no one wanted to admit that it was under this leader-ship style that the cooperative had run its business in the past, and that that is why they had failed to grow their business operations. Many donors had poured money into the cooperative, but because of *laissez-faire* leadership very little had come out of the investments.

The workshops also discussed what is called 'toxic leadership': leadership that abuses workers and leaves the organization in a worse condition. The participants appeared to be familiar with this type of leadership, giving examples of commu-nity leaders who were not good leaders because of the way they made decisions that affected the whole community. The leaders met with donors and the govern-ment of Botswana and decided on projects that had failed to take off because 'toxic leadership'. The examples given pointed to San men holding traditional positions who unilaterally made decisions on behalf of the community as they worked with project funders or government officials. The women of the cooperative raised their voices during this discussion and passionately expressed their disenchantment with this type of leadership, but they were not prepared to declare their views in the presence of the traditional leaders, who were not represented at these workshops.

The facilitator of the workshop allowed women to vent their anger on this topic because it was evident the participants did not want this type of leadership in their community and even less in their cooperative. They described in detail why they felt the traditional chief was a 'toxic leader', using examples of decisions he had made without consulting the people. The discussion was helpful in understanding how the leader was going to motivate members to work cooperatively with her. During the project, there was little need to worry about such destructive leadership because it had been fully discussed in the training sessions.

During the training sessions, the women learned how to work as a team. The workshop came up with strategies to ensure that individuals, board members, and management would engage in good governance that avoided bribes, kick-backs, and so on. Workshop participants were taught that good governance practice involves social responsibility based on an understanding of the community's expectations of an organization. This 'social contract' may include public reporting, openness to complaints about services, or tips regarding illegal actions of employees. The women learned that providing a vehicle for suggestions advances social responsibility. In the world of governance, better-educated citizens are constantly raising their levels of expectations for its leaders. Rules, principles, and social responsibility guidelines can help ensure that managers, board members, and/or political leaders raise expectations and rebuild faith in leadership. This is important for the sustainability of our communities and the sustainability of our trusts.

In the San community product prices are not determined by supply and demand or any commercial factors. Product price depends on whether you know someone or not. The price is higher when you do not know someone. The workshops covered pricing factors on the products. Participants were divided into two groups. After the workshop facilitator provided the women with the price of materials used, labour, transporting materials from the distributer or the product to the market, and administrative support, they had to set prices based on this information. Participants now understood how pricing works and had a sound strategy to determine prices for their products. After the training on pricing, members of the cooperative began to charge higher prices for their products because they had acquired more information on their actual costs. The cooperative began to make more money. At the end of the month, the profits were higher, allowing members to receive a bigger share for their families. This was great news.

The concept of marketing was unknown to the cooperative. The workshop facilitator invited a distributor for crafts based in Maun to visit the cooperative to assess the marketability of its products. In anticipation of this, she asked the participants to iron their fabrics and lay them out on display. After viewing their fabrics, the distributor told the cooperative members that the market was overstocked with tie-and-dye products from the rest of Africa and Indonesia. If they wanted to sell their fabrics, they should make them unique. For example, they should sew on beads, draw animals unique to Botswana, or make other articles from them. She did not recommend making clothes from the fabrics, but rather fashioning them into cushion covers, bedspreads, or table linen.

Final improvements

The participants made decisions informed by the lessons. For example, they agreed that sewing ostrich eggshell beads, a symbol of their culture, onto some of the tie-and-dye fabrics was an attractive idea. This did improve and add extra interest to the fabrics. Each participant finished six pieces of fabric over a three-week periods. They selected two to keep for themselves and sold the rest at the Kuru Art Centre.

The women of D'kar Farm were fortunate to have undergone special training in tie-and-dye and game farming self-help commercial projects because of the keen interest and passion they expressed in the community capacity building workshops sponsored by the Kellogg Foundation in partnership with Ba Isago University College. These women are now able to look after their families, send their children to school, and improve their diet. The Kuru Development Trust benefited immensely from this training, particularly in good governance and effective leadership. A spirit of natural resource conservation has taken firm root in this community to the extent that monthly conservation meetings are held to discuss relevant issues in the field of natural resource conservation on the farm. The women in D'kar are now good leaders of their families and better managers of their financial resources.

The future of the projects

After intensive discussions at the end of the community engagement programme, a forum was created for the women of the San cooperative to map their way forward. They decided to expand the scale of the cooperative and to seek external funding for that. They identified a number of priorities including hiring a trained manager for the tie-and-dye project, sourcing materials on a large scale to cut costs, and expanding their working space (they were located in the art studios and some artists were a bit upset about their intrusion). They identified a market, strategically located to attract tourists, and someone to sell the products. Other priorities included setting up a bank account and focusing on customer satisfaction. In general, they wanted to work towards a sustainable project and to diversify production to include curtains, table cloths, bags, dresses, quilts, cushion covers, and sofa covers, and planned to hire someone to sew articles from the fabrics. For marketing, they tasked the art project manager to market their fabrics to local hotels, government departments, craft shops, and places that attract tourists. Their marketing strategy included a website to advertise their work on the internet. Some participants felt they wanted to portray their culture in the fabrics, much as the Kuru artists do in their paintings.

For Ba Isago University College, the Kellogg Foundation, and the D'kar San tribe, the community engagement initiative was a major success. The San women were empowered to change their own lives and became leaders in their own community. They learned to express their own views and contribute to the welfare of their families and the community at large. However, Ba Isago University

College became more aware after this experience that community development and community engagement must be a multi-sectoral effort for long-term sustainability. The government of Botswana is cognizant of this fact and is involving all key community development departments, including civil society organizations and educational institutions like Ba Isago University. By the same token, the process calls for a multi-faceted approach to learning, the formal classroom being one of them. Because most of the key participants in the rural areas have had no exposure to tertiary education, and many may have dropped out of elementary school, other forms of engagement must be employed. This may include translation of community engagement learning materials or the use of pictures to express ideas. The challenges faced by Ba Isago University staff were many. Working with a community situated 700 kilometres from Gaborone, where Ba Isago is based, was a challenge in terms of effective communication with field staff, providing logistical support, transporting materials and consultants for the project, effecting timely payments to vendors, and making important decisions on the project operations. With funds being released annually by the Kellogg Foundation, sometimes the project experienced operational difficulties due to gaps in the disbursement of monies. However, the project owes its success in part to the funding from the Kellogg Foundation.

Ba Isago's community engagement gave the San women in D'kar the power of self-recognition that energizes communities to seek to transform their reality to a better quality of life, to plan for it, and to strategize for access to opportunities that allows them to achieve an improved quality of life. What was needed at the local level was an 'I can do' attitude. The women were able to develop their ability to collectively articulate a vision for their future and collaborate with other stakeholders to find feasible and compatible answers to common challenges. The women in D'kar needed innovative programmes and activities that promoted new ways of doing business and empowered the poor so that they could take charge of their own affairs.

References

Ba Isago University College (2008). Annual Report for the Tertiary Education Council, Botswana. Ba Isago: Ba Isago University College.

Bridges, William (1991). *Managing Transitions, Making the Most of Change*. Boston, MA: Addison-Wesley Publishing Group.

Burns, James MacGregor (1978). *Leadership*. Harper Torchbooks. New York: Harper & Row.

Burns, James MacGregor (2002). *Transforming Leadership: A New Pursuit of Happiness* New York: Atlantic Monthly Press.

Central Intelligence Agency (2009). Botswana.World Factbook Download. www.cia.gov/.../download/download-2009/index.html (last accessed 3 February 2010).

Covey, Stephen R. (1992). *Principle Centered Leadership*. New York: Simon and Schuster.

International Development Research Council (IDRC) (2002). *A Training Guide on Outcome Mapping*. Ottawa: International Development Research Council.

Ndiame, Fadel, and Magome, Kgobati (2008). Guidelines for Building the Self-Drive Mindset and Community Visioning as Imperatives for Sustainable Development of

Rural Communities: The W. K. Kellogg Approach. Battle Creek, MI: W. K. Kellogg Foundation.

Warner, Michael, and Sullivan, Rory (eds) (2004). *Putting Partnerships to Work: Strategic Alliances for Development between Government, the Private Sector and Civil Society.* Sheffield: Greenleaf Publishing.

West African Rural Foundation (2004). Report on Team Building Training Programme for Participatory Intergrated Watershed Management Project, Bakau, The Gambia, 23–28 April 2007. www.fidafrique.net/IMG/pdf/NORPREP_TB_Report.pdf (last accessed 4 February 2014).

W. K. Kellogg Foundation (2004).*W. K. Kellogg Foundation Update 2004. Logic Model Development Guide.* Battle Creek, MI: W. K. Kellogg Foundation.

W. K. Kellogg Foundation (2005*). W. K. Kellogg Foundation Report 2005. From Ideas to Action.* Battle Creek, MI: W. K. Kellogg Foundation.

9

Becoming part of the solution: engaged research on sustainability

Linda Silka

Higher education has splintered into disciplinary enclaves for which research has become little more than meeting disciplinary aims. On topics such as sustainability there is an urgent need for research that is interdisciplinary, engaged, and solutions-focused. How will this be achieved? Maine's Sustainability Solutions Initiative (SSI) offers an exemplar for how to address complex environmental problems through interdisciplinary research that is attuned to stakeholder needs. This chapter uses SSI to give an in-depth view from one university's experience of how campuses can change their practices. This example highlights both the opportunities and the challenges to higher education's becoming more relevant and useful.

Higher education and its shortfalls in creating useful, usable research

Universities have become discipline factories (Viederman, 2006). As Viederman (as well as many others) has noted: 'the world has problems; universities have disciplines ... Sustainability is about the whole, about the sum of the relationships among the parts of systems. Universities excel at parts, not the whole' (Viederman, 2006, p. 22). As threats to sustainability become more pronounced, universities need to generate integrated knowledge that will help to solve these increasingly complex problems.

Critics have called attention to many practices in academia that are obstacles to university research contributing to solutions. Consider six practices that have been the focus of much commentary. First, Bok (1982) and others have pointed out that research has become so specialized that piecemeal knowledge generation is the result. Second, researchers continue to choose problems that lend themselves to existing research methods rather than difficult problems that might require innovative new approaches (Kreuter et al., 2004; Rittel and Webber, 1973; Silka, 2010). Third, university faculty often assume that the state of current knowledge is insufficient to guide action and that more research is always needed (Cash, Bourk, and Patt, 2006; Kreuter et al., 2004). Fourth, university research is often framed in ways that are not attuned to application. As Campbell (2012) points out, 'the work of academics is generally regarded as too abstract (and theoretical) to have practical applicability' (pp. 349–50). Fifth, results are not aligned to solutions, because researchers rarely involve stakeholders in the selection of the research topic or the design for its investigation (Fischer, 2000; Trickett and Ryerson Espino, 2004). Sixth, critics have argued that universities have become too focused on disciplinary publication. As Campbell (2012) puts it in her role as a journal editor, to whom does what we publish matter? She notes that publication is no longer a public good but has become a private benefit, too often simply helping individual faculty achieve acclaim among their peers. As a result, university faculty rarely communicate their knowledge beyond their disciplinary walls (Shanley and Lopez, 2009; Watkins, Shepard, and Corbin-Mark, 2009).

Critics sum up these points by calling for changes that include academics taking on complex problems rather than merely those that are easy to study, avoiding the limitless generation of low-impact studies, finding ways to bring disciplines together, and ensuring that research is pursued in ways that will inform policy, involve stakeholders, and communicate outside our disciplines.

Are universities up to this? Some critics, such as Viederman (2006), hold out little hope that universities can become partners in arriving at solutions to complex sustainability problems. Others see universities as capable of change and look to endeavours such as Maine's SSI as promising experiments attempting to address all the above six problematic practices in an integrated way.

Sustainability is a key topic for considering whether universities can meet the challenge of helping to solve complex problems. As Senator George Mitchell, one of the architects of many US federal environmental laws, has noted: 'Regardless of the specifics, these issues are inherently challenging because they involve complex connections between human well-being and environmental protection, between local and global, between present and future, and especially between knowledge and action' (2012, p. 8). Sustainability is a challenge that requires universities to rethink key aspects of how they pursue their knowledge functions: who devises the research problem? How should disciplines work together? What roles should stakeholders play? How much focus should be put on solutions, and how much on the fundamental understanding? The Maine SSI is attempting an experiment that addresses all of these questions.

The Sustainability Solutions Initiative

Through a five-year, $20 million grant from the National Science Foundation's Experimental Program to Stimulate Competitive Research (EPSCoR), SSI is focused on sustainability science, a growing field of research that supports long-term ecological and socio-cultural functioning (Kates, 2011). Sustainability science emphasizes the co-production of usable knowledge (Cash, Borck, and Patt, 2006; Lindenfeld et al., 2012; McNie, 2007; Pielke, 2007) that is interdisciplinary (Matson, 2011), integrates local perspectives (Clark and Dickson, 2003), and avoids traditional trickle-down models (Van Kerkhoff and Lebel, 2006). Within SSI, university researchers representing twelve Maine higher education institutions and twenty disciplines (e.g., communication, economics, environmental science, and engineering) work with the initiative's highly varied stakeholders, including nongovernmental organizations, communities, policy organizations, tribal communities, and governmental leaders. SSI's mission is:

> To connect knowledge with action in ways that promote strong economics, vibrant communities, and healthy ecosystems in and beyond Maine (www.umaine.edu/ sustainabilitysolutions) ... SSI's strategy for advancing the field of sustainability science and helping to solve sustainability-related problems requires the active participation of integrated interdisciplinary research teams, fundamental understanding of the dynamics of Maine's coupled social-ecological systems, and strong stakeholder-university partnerships (www.umaine.edu/sustainability solutions).

Prior to SSI, many faculty in Maine focused on sustainability but did so using their disciplinary tools with little integration. SSI works to bridge these disciplinary and community–university divides, and thus takes on many of the challenges that have thwarted past attempts to move universities toward engaged, interdisciplinary research.

In the remainder of this chapter, we use examples to show how SSI teams are tackling the issues of higher education using its resources in engaged, interdisciplinary ways. We begin with an extended example in order to illustrate the interlinked nature of the issues and then describe in briefer fashion other projects that highlight key issues in sustainability research.

SSI strategies for building engaged research on sustainability: the importance of place

A role that university researchers often play is that of forecasting trends that have yet to have their full impact but are on the horizon. The sustainability of Maine's forests is an important focus of such forecasts. As a result of a changing climate and migration patterns, invasive pests such as the highly destructive emerald ash borer, not previously seen in Maine's cold climate, are expected to impact Maine's ash trees. How such emergent infestations are being tackled illustrates SSI's community-engaged, interdisciplinary, solution-focused approach (Ranco et al., 2012).

As the SSI team notes, the story about what to study is complex. Emerald ash borer infestations have greatly damaged brown ash tree populations throughout other parts of North America. Thus, with Maine's economy being heavily forestry dependent and with Maine being the most forested state in the USA, focusing on such an infestation would seem to be an obvious choice. Yet, as it turns out, Maine's commercial forest industry sees the brown ash tree species as relatively unimportant because brown ash makes up only a small percentage of the arboreal volume and has limited commercial value. It turns out, though, that those same brown ash trees and their imperiled future is of enormous importance to the Native Americans in Maine, with the craft of ash basketry making central to the Wabanaki Nation's culture and economy (Ranco et al., 2012).

SSI faculty who study forest infestations were originally not intending to focus their attention on the emerald ash borer. The researchers had plans for studying other issues related to the sustainability of Maine's forests. Yet, the researchers report that before they became overly committed to their own direction and preferences, they sat down with leaders of the Wabanaki Nation, including the Wabanaki Basketmakers Association, and began conversations to understand which issues *were* of concern to the community. These discussions resulted in a partnership that jointly formulated a plan for identifying research priorities, calling attention to the disciplines whose areas of expertise were needed, visiting other states to see how they had addressed the infestation problem, and then developing a program of research aimed at identifying possible scenarios for tackling the impending problem (Ranco et al., 2012).

This turning to engaged research approaches among SSI researchers is by no means limited to anticipating possible future problems. This engaged approach has become a hallmark of much of the SSI work, often fostering shared learning across teams. Among those studying forests is the SSI team from Unity College, a team that is well versed in studying the hemlock woolly adelgid problem and has been engaged in long-term basic studies on hemlock infestations at study sites in its college forest. In contrast to the brown ash, the eastern hemlock is very important to the overall character of Maine's forests. As the team notes in Ranco et al. (2012):

> Most Maine citizens can readily envision a forest dominated by eastern Hemlock. Such forests are known for their tall tree boles carrying densely foliated branches that cast dim, dappled light on a sparsely populated understory. The effect is a cool, serene park-like atmosphere. Such forests mark a late-successional end point to the forest communities of this region and as such serve as critical habitat for white-tailed deer and numerous bird species, including ruffed grouse and a variety of warblers. For our neighbors in the southeastern part of the country, however, hemlock forests may invoke very different images: skeletonized canopies, well-lit understory environments, and warming trout streams. (p. 77)

The past work of Unity has been disciplinarily driven and researcher-guided with only sporadic input from the adjacent communities and impacted small woodlot owners, who would likely be the ones to use whatever information came out of the research. The Unity researchers are now exploring more inclusive ways of involving stakeholders in Maine. Additional disciplines are being drawn in and cross-conversations between researchers and stakeholders are becoming routine. The result is a program of research that gathers information in ways that, while not neglecting basic research questions, are highly attuned to the decisional issues that stakeholders face. The research agenda and research process are being transformed (Ranco et al., 2012).

One of the key lessons of this work is the centrality that local and place-based approaches play in sustainability. It cannot be assumed that each place is like every other and that what is found in one state applies to all others. Unlike forested states in the western USA, for example, where the forest lands are under federal jurisdiction or have relatively few landowners who retain control over large acreages, Maine has a significant proportion of forested lands in the hands of small woodlot owners, with varying land stewardship responsibilities typically owning but a few acres (Quartuch and Beckley, 2012). Any attempt to move sustainable practices forward in places like Maine needs to recognize the pre-eminence of the small woodlot owner. In working with this community, university researchers have encountered the challenge that this 'community' does not regard itself as a community in any traditional sense (such as sharing common views, communicating together, or having a shared history). Throughout other SSI forestry research projects, a central concern is to understand better the networks of owners, their decision constraints, and their strategies for solving their problems. This information is being used to engage owners in ways that work for them.

Attending to stakeholder knowledge

Like forests, water is a fundamental sustainability concern in Maine, and stakeholder knowledge is a central resource. As SSI researchers Peckenham, Hart, Smith, Jain, and King (2012) note:

> It is difficult to imagine the state of Maine without also envisioning its waters. Unlike some other regions across the globe, Maine is rich in rivers, lakes, streams, and wetlands. These water resources not only help to define the state's character, but also fill many valuable roles for the people of Maine. Water gives us sustenance, slakes our thirst, powers our homes and industries, and instills a sense of tranquility. (p. 47)

In Maine, concerns are growing about how to maintain the pristine water quality of lakes and streams in the face of urbanization and other emerging threats. SSI has devoted much attention to water as a sustainability issue, and many water researchers across the various campuses have become involved (Fleming and Love, 2012; Lichter and Ames, 2012; Peckenham et al., 2012). In the past, these researchers worked largely within their own 'silos': by discipline, by campus, and by water body. And much of the work – creating models, measures, and techniques – took place with little engagement of stakeholders. SSI has directed itself to changing this through faculty from different disciplines coming together and engaging with stakeholders.

The result has been important new perspectives. A key insight is greater recognition of the depth of place-based knowledge that stakeholders bring to identifying changes in Maine's lakes and streams. History faculty such as those on the Colby History and Sense of Place team are central to moving forward this work (Fleming anad Love, 2012). The Colby team (Fleming and Love, 2012) notes that sense of place reaches across generations and thus a team would do well to learn to make use of and share a usable past. The Colby team is looking at a growing problem like phosphorus pollution resulting from development and other human activities:

> Our techniques ... include textual, archival, and oral history; targeted questionnaires; and community conversations about sense of place that build identity and resiliency in the face of mounting local, regional, and global economic and environmental challenges. These various modes of concept exploration, data collection, and presentation allow people to reflect on their own experiences and share them. (Fleming and Love, 2012, p. 91)

Historians have stimulated the conversation about what lake families, whose ownership of lakeside summer cottages goes back for generations, have experienced in the way of changes. What kind of family documents might they possess that extend knowledge of lakes well beyond the shorter-term data collections now underway as a part of research? What understandings might these longer vistas provide? Equally important, how does the bringing together and making public of this information motivate and engage people to protect the waters that have been important to their families for generations? SSI faculty, like others around the country (cf. River's Calendar, 2012), are discovering that bringing together stakeholder knowledge and researcher information transforms and mobilizes. Gaps are identified and overcome. As Lichter and Ames (2012) remind us, this kind of 'history can tell us what was lost over the centuries, but perhaps more importantly, it can also help us understand how to recover what is recoverable in our once bountiful natural resources' (p. 99–100).

Attending to stakeholder–researcher partnerships

In addition to stakeholder knowledge, partnerships are crucial. We see this with marine-focused water issues. Marine issues are prominent in Maine given that the state is on the Atlantic Ocean and has a coast that is longer than that of all the other Eastern Seaboard states north of Florida combined. Many SSI partners are focusing their sustainability efforts on marine issues, including SSI partners at the University of New England (UNE). UNE faculty are engaging a broad range of stakeholders to address marine estuary issues on southern Maine's Saco River estuary, which is under broad environmental assault because of growing residential populations, rapid increases in tourist uses of the estuary, and shifts in industries. UNE SSI faculty are asking questions about how the estuary can be studied in ways that will have policy relevance for different levels of decision-makers (from individual landowners on the estuary, who need to decide whether they will fertilize their lawns that are adjacent to estuary waters, to land policy committees in the local towns along the river, and to state officials who promulgate mitigation and remediation policies). The goal is to produce research that does much more than simply appeal to academics. Creative efforts have been the hallmark of this work. SSI teams are identifying and testing innovative new ways of facilitating the conversations between researchers and stakeholders so that co-production of knowledge can occur. The UNE SSI team sponsors boat trips with the apt title 'We Are All in the Same Boat' that bring together stakeholders and researchers to build a common understanding of the problems in the estuary and their possible solution. The end result is co-development of strategies for how science can contribute to addressing the sustainability issues.

Attending to unexpected views

One may not know which sustainability issues concern a community. As SSI is finding, the importance of engaging stakeholders and their knowledge is not to be underestimated. SSI's Coastal Adaptation Project includes a focus on climate change and the impact on Maine's coastal communities. In the absence of stakeholder input, researchers had simply assumed that stakeholders' primary concern would be with the impact of rising sea levels. This turned out not to be the case. The most pressing concern to community leaders is one that has important interdisciplinary implications. It is about the likelihood that, with climate change, communities will be hit with devastating storms producing torrential amounts of rain that overwhelm infrastructure including sewers, culverts, and roads. Maine's communities are already seeing the effect of frequent, so-called 'once in a hundred years' storms that are occurring several times a decade. This is the climate change concern that Maine's coastal communities see as most pressing. By emphasizing co-identification of problems, researchers and policy leaders in communities can pursue research that focuses on those problems of greatest concern.

Attending to the importance of place: recognizing that sustainability efforts cannot be generic

Each of the above SSI examples demonstrates that successful sustainability efforts cannot be generic. Efforts must be placed-based. This theme of place is particularly well illustrated in the Maine Tidal Power Initiative (Johnson and Zydlewski, 2012). Cobscook Bay in Maine is the site of some of the most powerful tidal surges in North America. These dramatic daily tidal changes offer an important place-based opportunity for the development of renewable power in Maine – a state that remains highly dependent on fossil fuels. But Cobscook Bay's great energy possibilities are also located in highly productive marine fisheries grounds. Human–natural coupled systems again come to the foreground in the question of whether energy production and maintenance of a fishing resource can co-exist. Can renewable energy be pursued without degrading the fisheries? The sustainability problems here are deeply interdisciplinary. Any findings from research – such as impacts on the fisheries – will count for little if they are not found to be credible by stakeholders (e.g., fishers, community residents, and regulators). This situation calls for working together, and, as a part of SSI and related work, this is occurring.

But there are many attendant challenges. Maine is a large state and Cobscook Bay is far from the university where the researchers are located. In addition, past efforts to tap the tidal energy potential in Cobscook Bay came with great promises but disappointing results. Thus, the researchers are approaching co-production of knowledge in ways carefully attuned to the policies and practices in the area as well as to the science related to energy tidal power and fish migrations. The result is an integrated approach designed to foster economic development around tidal renewable energy going hand in hand with fisheries preservation. Ensuring that mechanical engineering faculty work with the fish biologists and marine anthropologists who work with the diverse local community has shifted approaches from the abstract to the concrete. Local knowledge has been central:

Armed with the knowledge of what community members wanted to know and how they wanted to receive information, we decided to tailor our research on the impacts to the bay-wide fish communities ... to involve community members, particularly fishermen, more directly. Because we want to better understand the fish community in Cobscook Bay, a logical start to the study was to use local knowledge. We discussed our knowledge gap and needs with local fishermen and identified a place-based approach to achieving our goal of engaging with the fishing community in a two-way exchange of information about the fishes of Cobscook Bay. (Johnson and Zydlewski, 2012, p. 63)

All of this is making a difference, and others are learning from co-production of knowledge models that SSI researchers are developing. As SSI researchers note:

Following SSI's approach, we are working with federal and state regulatory agencies, tidal-power developers, and community stakeholders to better link our research to their needs. By engaging the users of the information we are being asked to provide, we are improving the chances that our research will be more relevant to the decision-making processes that our stakeholders face, whether the stakeholders are developers interested to know if they should develop in a location or regulators who need to make decisions about these projects on behalf of the public. Better information conveyed to the general public, especially to local community members, is key to allowing productive dialogue and decision-making about the risks and benefits of tidal power. (Johnston and Cardenas, 2012, p. 63)

Finally, to be place-based includes looking for comparable places having the same opportunities and struggles and where the information gathered in Maine could be helpful. The SSI Tidal Power Team was recently invited to Japan, where there are similar tidal opportunities, to share its approach to the co-production of knowledge.

Attending to importance of place and recognizing links to the economy

Uppermost in SSI's commitments is finding new ways to address place-based issues in engaged ways. In Aroostook County in northernmost Maine – well away from Maine's highly visible coast and home to one of the coldest climates in the continental USA – families are spending an inordinate proportion of their incomes on fossil-fuel-based energy (Johnston and Cardenas, 2012). The economy in this remote part of Maine is also facing challenging times. The question is whether these two problems can be addressed together through SSI. As a part of SSI, faculty are carrying out research to understand fuel costs and assess the viability and acceptability of biomass energy options. As the SSI team notes (Johnston and Cardenas, 2012), the research is stakeholder-driven and focused on solutions that will work for this region:

When the research team at University of Maine Presque Isle (UMPI) began to consider options for an SSI project, energy was clearly the most pressing concern to the Aroostook River watershed in terms of ecological, sociological, and economic importance ... This project typifies both the challenges and opportunities that SSI is attempting to address. The challenges concern how to collect and create knowledge

that will be useful to local stakeholders. We have embraced the opportunity to transform academic research from its typical outlet in peer-reviewed journals to 'boots
on the ground' research, stakeholder engagement, and the recommendations that
actually are implemented. (Johnston and Cardenas, 2012, p. 69)

In the very northern tip of Maine at the University of Maine Fort Kent, an interdisciplinary team of faculty including biologists, psychologists, and environmental sociologists (Johnston and Cardenas, 2012) is using a place-based research
approach to study whether heating costs can be reduced and economic opportunities increased through biomass production.

> The focus of University of Maine Fort Kent's research is geographically narrower
> and more applied, looking specifically at the impact on the Fort Kent commu-
> nity of implementing both wood and grass biomass as a supplementary heating
> source .... Can landowners produce enough biomass to fuel a community and
> could any additional biomass product be sold elsewhere? Are the owners interested
> in producing biomass? What are the risks for farmers and woodlot owners? Are
> residents and businesses alike interested in supplementing or replacing their primary
> heating source with biomass? (Johnston and Cardenas, 2012, p. 71)

Throughout this work in northern Maine, the continued focus is on developing
place-based solutions that provide opportunities to create examples that other
areas can learn from but without making short shrift of what will be valuable for
Aroostook County:

> By engaging stakeholders at all levels without a prescriptive message of what should
> be done, we hope to avoid the mistakes of others who have recommended large-
> scale land-use changes for the County. The memory of one such environmental and
> economic disaster – Fred Vahlsing's encouragement of sugar beets ... –is still part of
> the local culture. By engaging citizens, municipal officials, policy-makers, businesses,
> farmers, and foresters, we hope to do the kind of work a university should be well
> positioned to perform. Through our analysis of economic, ecological, and societal
> costs and benefits of energy alternatives, we hope to spur planning not just about
> local energy strategy, but about optimal land-use practices. (Waring, 2012, p. 74)

The search for new tools to support collaboration and co-production of knowledge

Throughout SSI work, the concern is also on creating new tools that will advance
the co-production of knowledge. The development of the tools – such as agent-
based modelling and scenario modelling – focuses on bringing together complex
information in ways that help policy-makers to address 'wicked problems'. As
Waring (2012) notes, wicked problems are 'urgent, high stakes socio-economic-
environmental challenges that often involve ideological conflict and have no 'best
solutions' (p. 30). Sustainability problems are quintessentially wicked problems
and, as Waring notes, finding solutions to such problems calls for 'wicked tools'
that include well-constructed models to address policy-relevant issues with input
from stakeholders, and which integrate social, economic, and environmental
factors:

Carefully constructed, tested, and calibrated scientific models are powerful tools for management and planning. Such models provide the best possible meeting ground for diverse and competing interests in the quest to solve society's wicked problems. Fundamentally, scientific models are valuable because they provide objective and transparent tools for planning, predicting, and understanding the hardest challenges Maine will face in the coming decades. (Waring, 2012, p. 38)

The work by SSI's Alternative Futures Team, the Sustainable Urban Regions Team, and the Portland Watersource Sebago Lake Team all emphasizes co-production to create useful scientific tools. Unlike most model building, which occurs in isolation from ultimate users of the model, these aim to build on shared knowledge to create wicked tools. As Waring notes, in the three SSI teams, the models are

being used to unite divergent interests around a way to envision, and plan for, a common future. These SSI projects employ different types of models to different challenges in a similar way. Four characteristics that these projects share transform traditional, narrow scientific models into wicked tools. They are (1) a focus on a policy-relevant issue (2) inclusion of stakeholders and multiple interests in the design and calibration (3) the integration of social, economics, and environmental dynamics, and (4) robust and reliable scientific design, testing, validation, and calibration. (Waring, 2012, pp. 38–39)

The Alternative Futures Team, for example, is creating a statistical model on land use scenarios that combines spatial, biophysical, and economic data with knowledge from farmers, foresters, mill owners, and developers. As the team notes, its central challenge is to ensure that the divergent groups are thinking about each other's needs. The team is meeting this challenge by creating land-use suitability maps that are valuable to foresters, farmers, *and* developers and can be used to pinpoint areas of conflict and trade-off. This engaged approach has moved research forward while ultimately bringing the data into broader arenas and focusing on how complex, frequently overwhelming amounts of information can be integrated to address Maine's sustainability issues.

General lessons, implications, and next steps

We began this chapter by outlining some of the reasons why research too often fails to generate useful solutions to complex problems. We noted many reasons: university research is too specialized, it is too disciplinarily specific, and it is too focused on the problems that match a discipline's tools rather than problems that are most urgently in need of solution. In addition, study is layered upon study with little in the way of stopping rules that indicate when enough is known. Stakeholders are not involved in the formulation of the research, the research is not designed to contribute to policy, and the communication outlets for the findings remain inaccessible to most users. In large part, these problems are a result of inadequate engagement at every step in the research process: the research often does not start with problems that matter to the broader community, nor is the research developed and communicated in ways that contribute to solving those problems. With some issues this might not matter, but it is of great consequence for complex, urgent problems such as sustainability. The examples in this chapter illustrate the ways these shortfalls can be tackled in a large scale, multi-campus initiative.

There is much that can be learned from this natural experiment, and SSI has additional teams – the Knowledge-to-Action and Organizational Innovation Teams – devoted to extracting the generalizable lessons about different elements of the approach. Disciplines struggle to work together, but McCoy and Gardner (2012) are aggregating lessons learned about disciplines working together and overcoming long-standing obstacles. Faculty struggle with the notion of working with stakeholders to co-produce research, but we are learning lessons about overcoming the obstacles (Hall, Silka, and Lindenfeld, 2012). Faculty struggle with the actionable part of this approach, but again we have begun to identify strategies for strengthening such efforts (Lindenfeld et al., 2012). Campuses are challenged in working with one another (Budzinski, Lindenfeld, and Silka, 2011), but we are beginning to identify strategies for overcoming common barriers. And these SSI teams are extracting important lessons for how universities can better prepare future academic leaders to carry out engaged research through changing graduate education (Gardner, 2013).

Across all of this SSI work, an increasingly important focus is the challenge of scale-up. In other words, how do we take individual projects –often built around local face-to-face activities – and apply lessons to larger contexts and settings? How can we can take what has been learned about co-production in one small locality and expand it so that it is effective statewide or even on the national scale? Such scale-up issues are challenging. If scale-up is not done with skill, it can undermine the place-based approach to engagement crucial to sustainability.

Full answers are not yet at hand but we are exploring different models, with some of the most apt being in educational arenas. In education, concerns about scale-up are beginning to dominate discussions regarding why local educational innovations so often fail to translate to the larger scale. Deborah Meier, an educational innovator known for her successes at turning individual schools around, has elaborated on the ways in which scaling-up efforts at the district, state, or national level remain challenging. The National Science Foundation's Education Directorate has also focused on problems with scale-up, and its concern is with the many innovative science education programs that it has funded that have been highly successful at the small-scale demonstration stage, but which, as evaluations show, often fail to scale up in larger contexts. The directorate is increasingly requiring its grant seekers to explain how they will scale up their programs as they move beyond the demonstration phase.

Questions about scale-up are important for sustainability. As we attempt to scale up successful interventions, we will need to ask which variables should be considered. Similarities in research approach? In community arrangements? Something else? Should attention be paid to who has regulatory control: localities, counties, states? In short, how do we find ways to generalize the lessons to all of the different settings and contexts where change is needed?

Conclusion

As captured throughout this chapter, SSI's overarching message to higher education is that we need to focus our efforts on finding innovative ways to forge linkages and break down the barriers between and among scientists and stakeholders if we are to tackle increasingly coupled problems. Perhaps no SSI project ultimately highlights the pressing need to move to new approaches that build interconnections among areas of expertise, places, problems, and strategies better than the SSI Alewives Project (Lichter and Ames, 2012). This project takes as its starting point the central fact that alewives (also known as river herring) were once a predominant forage species supporting Maine's lobster and ground fish populations. In recent times alewife numbers have been greatly reduced, and this central component of Maine's ecology has been decimated. Fishermen are helping SSI scientists to focus on linkages in order to tackle this problem of coupled human and natural systems:

> Historical information suggests that river herring populations were a vital resource for nearshore cod populations, and without a substantial recovery of river herring, coastal fisheries will remain depleted. This insight is profound, because in addition to overfishing groundfish populations in the Gulf of Maine, human activities have undermined the marine food web to the extent that once bountiful coastal fishing grounds no longer produce any fish. (Lichter and Ames, 2012, p. 99)

Attending to linkages at many different levels – linkages not just in problem content but in the process by which the problems are solved – exemplifies what higher education must do to strengthen engaged research. We need to combine knowledge from many types of expertise, look for links among what might appear to be unrelated problems, and look for linkages in possible solutions. One needs to look no further than to fields such as ecology to be reminded of the centrality of links; what we now need is for universities to take on problems such as sustainability with same attention to linkages. Whitmer et al. (2010), in their recommendations to the Ecological Society of America in 'The Engaged University: Providing a Platform for Research that Transforms Society', point to just such a need as we move the agenda forward for universities to contribute to sustainability research in useful, constructive ways.

Acknowledgement

This research was supported by National Science Foundation award #EPS-0904155 to Maine EPSCoR at the University of Maine.

References

Bok, D. (1982). *Beyond the Ivory Tower: Social Responsibilities of the Modern University*. Cambridge, MA: Harvard University Press.
Budzinski, C., Lindenfeld, L., and Silka, L. (2011). Technical Report: Maine EPSCoR Sustainability Solutions Initiative Sustainability Solutions Partners Survey. March.

Campbell, H. (2012). Lots of Words ... But Do Any of Them Matter? The Challenge of Engaged Scholarship. *Planning, Theory & Practice* 133: 349–353.

Cash, D. W., Borck, J. C., and Patt, A. G. (2006). Countering the Loading-Dock Approach to Linking Science and Decision-Making. *Science, Technology, and Human Values* 31 (4): 465–494.

Clark, W. C. and Dickson, N. M. (2003). Sustainability Science: The Emerging Research Program. *Proceedings of the National Academy of Sciences* 100 (14): 8059–8061.

Fischer, F. (2000). *Citizens, Experts, and the Environment: The Politics of Local Knowledge.* Durham, NC: Duke University Press.

Fleming, J. R., and Love, E. A. (2012). Healthy Lakes and Vibrant Economies: Linking History, Sense of Place, and Watershed Protection in the Belgrade Lakes Region. *Maine Policy Review* 21 (1): 90–94. http://digitalcommons.library.umaine.edu/mpr/vol21/iss1/13 (last accessed 29 January 2014).

Gardner, S. K. (2013). Paradigmatic Differences of Faculty Involved in an Interdisciplinary Research Collaboration. *Sustainability Science* 8: 241–252.

Hall, D. M., Silka, L., and Lindenfeld, L. (2012). Advancing Science and Improving Quality of Place: Linking Knowledge with Action in Maine's Sustainability Solutions Initiative. *Maine Policy Review,* 21 (1): 22–29. http://digitalcommons.library.umaine.edu/mpr/vol21/iss1/6 (last accessed 29 January 2014).

Johnson, T. and Zydlewski, G. B. (2012). Research for the Sustainable Development of Tidal Power in Maine. *Maine Policy Review* 21 (1): 58–65. http://digitalcommons.library.umaine.edu/mpr/vol21/iss1/10 (last accessed 29 January 2014).

Johnston, J., and Cardenas, S. (2012). Place-Based Approaches to Alternative Energy: The Potential for Forest and Grass Biomass for Aroostook County. *Maine Policy Review* 21 (1), 66–75. http://digitalcommons.library.umaine.edu/mpr/vol21/iss1/11 (last accessed 29 January 2014).

Kates, R. W. (2011). What Kind of a Science is Sustainability Science? *Proceedings of the National Academy of Sciences* 108 (49): 19449–19450.

Kreuter, M. W., DeRosa, C., Howze, E. H., and Baldwin, T. (2004). Understanding Wicked Problems: A Key to Advancing Environmental Health Problems. *Health Education & Behavior* 31 (4): 441–454.

Lichter, J., and Ames, T. (2012). Reaching into the Past for Future Resilience: Recovery Efforts in Maine Rivers and Coastal Waters. *Maine Policy Review* 21 (1): 96–102. http://digitalcommons.library.umaine.edu/mpr/vol21/iss1/14 (last accessed 29 January 2014).

Lindenfeld, L. A., Hall, D. M., McGreavy, B., Silka, L., and Hart, D. (2012). Creating a Place for Environmental Communication Research in Sustainability Science. *Environmental Communication* 6 (1): 23–43.

Matson, P. (2009). The Sustainability Transition. *Issues in Science and Technology* 25 (4): 39–42.

Matson, P. (ed.) (2011). *Seeds of Sustainability: Lessons from the Birthplace of the Green Revolution in Agriculture.* Washington, DC: Island Press.

McCoy, S. K., and Gardner, S. K, (2012). Interdisciplinary Collaboration on Campus: Five Questions. *Change: The Magazine of Higher Education* 44 (6): 44–49,

McNie, E. C. (2007). Reconciling the Supply of Scientific Information with User Demands: An Analysis of the Problem and Review of the Literature. *Environmental Science & Policy* 10 (1): 17–38.

Mitchell, G. J. (2012). Sustainability: The Challenges and the Promise. *Maine Policy Review* 21 (1): 8–9. http://digitalcommons.library.umaine.edu/mpr/vol21/iss1/4 (last accessed 29 January 2014).

Peckenham, J., Hart, D., Smith, S., Jain, S., and King, W. (2012). The Path to Sustainable Water Resources Solutions. *Maine Policy Review* 21 (1) 46–57. http://digitalcommons. library.umaine.edu/mpr/vol21/iss1/9 (last accessed 29 January 2014).

Pielke, R. A. (2007). *The Honest Broker: Making Sense of Science in Policy and Politics.* New York: Cambridge University Press.

Quartuch, M. R., and Beckley, T. M. (2012). Landowners Perceptions of their Moral and Ethical Stewardship Responsibilities in New Brunswick, Canada, and Maine, USA. *Small-Scale Forestry.* doi: 10.1007/s11842–01209222–2 (last accessed 29 January 2014).

Ranco, D., Arnett, A., Latty, E., Remsburg, A., Dunckel, K., Quigley, E., Lillieholm, R., Daigle, J., Livingston, B., Neptune, J., and Secord, T. (2012). Two Maine Forest Pests: A Comparison of Approaches to Understanding Threats to Hemlock and Ash Trees in Maine. *Maine Policy Review* 21 (1): 76–89. http://digitalcommons.library.umaine.edu/ mpr/vol21/iss1/12 (last accessed 29 January 2014).

Rittel, H. W. J., and Webber, M. M. (1973). Dilemmas in a General Theory of Planning. *Policy Sciences* 4 (2): 155–169.

River's Calendar (2012). http://riverscalendar.drupalgardens.com/ (last accessed 29 January 2014).

Shanley, P., and Lopez, C. (2009). Out of the Loop: Why Research Rarely Reaches Policy Makers and the Public and What Can Be Done. *Biotropica* 41 (5): 535–544.

Silka, L. (2010). Community Research in Other Contexts: Learning from Sustainability Science. *Journal of Empirical Research on Human Research Ethics* 5 (4): 3–11.

Trickett, E., and Ryerson Espino, S. L. (2004). Collaboration and Social Inquiry: Multiple Meanings of a Construct and its Role in Creating Useful and Valid Knowledge. *American Journal of Community Psychology* 34 (1–2): 1–69.

Van Kerkhoff, L., and Lebel, L. (2006). Linking Knowledge and Action for Sustainability Development. *Annual Review of Environment and Resources* 31: 445–477.

Viederman, S. (2006). Can Universities Contribute to Sustainable Development? In R. Forrant and L. Silka (eds), *Inside and Out: Universities and Education for Sustainable Development*, pp. 17–28. Amityville, NY: Baywood Publishing.

Waring, T. (2012). Wicked Tools: The Value of Scientific Models for Solving Maine's Wicked Problems. *Maine Policy Review* 21 (1): 30–39. http://digitalcommons.library.umaine. edu/mpr/vol21/iss1/7 (last accessed 29 January 2014).

Watkins, B. X., Shepard, P. M., and Corbin-Mark, C. D. (2009). Completing the Circle: A Model for Effective Community Review of Environmental Health Research. *American Journal of Public Health* 99 (Supplement 3): 5567–5577.

Whitmer, A., Ogden, L., Lawton, J., Stumer, P., Groffman, P. M., Schneider, L., Hart, D., Halpem, B., Schlesinger, W., Raciti, S., Bettez, N., Ortega, S., Rustad, L., Pickett, S., and Killilea, M. (2010). The Engaged University: Providing a Platform for Research that Transforms Society. *Frontiers in Ecology and the Environment* 8 (6): 314–321.

10

University–community outreach: case study of the Illinois Institute for Rural Affairs

Norman Walzer and Christopher D. Merrett

Rural areas in the USA have lagged behind metro areas in population, income, and employment growth for several reasons. Increased mechanization and productivity have reduced employment in agriculture, a mainstay of rural areas. This population decline, coupled with transportation improvements, spurred the consolidation of retail and public services such as education and health in smaller cities and towns (Walzer, 2003). The outcome is that many rural (non-metro) counties reached their highest populations in the early 1900s and have steadily declined since.

The Midwestern USA suffered more from these transitions than many other areas because of a heavy reliance on agriculture, which underwent major mechanization and consolidation of farms. Likewise, competition for routine manufacturing jobs from off-shore locations reduced employment opportunities (Walzer, 2003). The outcomes of these trends raised concerns among elected officials and leaders in small communities about the future viability of rural places, prompting many to ask what could be done to revitalize them.

The farm crisis of the 1980s brought increased farm failures and consolidations, further reducing the number of residents linked to rural towns. Businesses in these communities could no longer survive, driving a downward spiral of economic stagnation and rural outmigration. This outmigration, in turn, decreased the demand for public services such as schools which eliminated public employment opportunities.

State governments followed several models in responding to rural crises. For instance, the North Carolina Rural Economic Development Center, Inc. (NCRDC), started in 1987, is an independent non-profit agency that works with state agencies and local community groups to administer programs designed to revitalize rural areas in the state (NCRDC, 2014).

The Center for Rural Pennsylvania (CRP), launched in 1987, is 'a bipartisan, bicameral legislative agency that serves as a resource for rural policy within the Pennsylvania General Assembly' (CRP, 2014). The CRP commissions research with faculty and staff at state universities in Pennsylvania on topics selected by the CRP board. It also is a clearinghouse on rural issues in Pennsylvania and works with state agencies to find solutions.

Illinois adopted a different approach. The State of Illinois (2010 pop. 12,830,632) launched a 'Rural Initiative' in 1986 to coordinate state agencies and create a university-based outreach agency to conduct applied research on innovative practices and work with state agencies and community leaders to implement them.

This chapter examines the creation of the Illinois Institute for Rural Affairs (IIRA), how it developed into a significant outreach program during the past quarter-century, and its programs and activities. Because it not only survived but expanded during changes in both state government and university administrations, the lessons learned can help other governments and universities to design similar outreach efforts. Specifically, this chapter addresses several issues:

- Building long-term support for programs both within state government and the university;
- Objectively recording and documenting inputs and products in a comprehensive and consistent way;
- Maintaining an ongoing dialog with clients and incorporating this input into program development; and
- Implementing a management system that bases decisions about future directions on data.

The scenario in which IIRA started

Illinois Governor James R. Thompson created a Task Force on the Future of Rural Illinois (TFFRI). The task force, with twenty-six members representing a broad base of interests including agriculture, education, business, and public agencies, was chaired and coordinated by the Lt. Governor. Staff representatives from twelve state agencies responsible for rural programs were assigned to work with the TFFRI and participated in the twenty-two hearings held in rural areas during a six-month period. During the process, the Lt. Governor and staff visited 119 rural communities to take the pulse of rural conditions across the state. Faculty from four Illinois universities researched and analyzed policy options for the TFFRI. They ultimately made recommendations regarding programs related to agriculture and agri-business, economic development, education, health, transportation, local government capacity, and social issues.

The public hearings served two purposes. First, they demonstrated that state agencies were interested in rural issues and informed state agency personnel about potential ways to address them. Second, the hearings built a sense of commitment by agency personnel to rural issues and created a rural 'community' that continued long after the hearings were completed.

The task force's report filed in March 1987 included multiple recommendations that resulted in two executive orders (EOs) by the Illinois governor (GRAC Report, 1987). These two EOs started processes within state government that have continued for more than twenty-five years through several administration changes. EO 6 created a Rural Fair Share Initiative, and EO 7 created the Governor's Rural Affairs Council (GRAC).

The GRAC, chaired by the Lt. Governor with a small staff of professionals, is charged with monitoring rural conditions and recommending legislation or administrative actions to address rural issues. Being in the Office of the Governor, the GRAC has a broad scope of authority and can directly engage statutorily authorized agencies under the governor's supervision since they are council members. The GRAC is a place where remedies for rural issues that cross state agency boundaries can be promoted with an emphasis on concerns that might otherwise 'fall through the cracks' between the main agency responsibilities.

The task force also recommended creation of an applied-research-focused university-based agency to work with the GRAC to identify innovative practices, help design policy responses, and work with local agencies to implement programs. This agency was also mandated to work with the GRAC on an annual report to the governor and the Illinois General Assembly describing rural conditions and recommending policies or administrative actions.

In fall 1989, the IIRA located at Western Illinois University (WIU) was launched as a partnership between the GRAC, a state agency, and WIU. The IIRA was designed as a state agency operating within a university. The GRAC, with IIRA support, prepared House Joint Resolution 89 of the Illinois General Assembly expressing support for the rural thrust in Illinois. This step reflected support by two branches of state government – the Governor's Office and both Houses of the General Assembly – for a 'rural revitalization initiative'.

The Illinois General Assembly, through the Illinois Board of Higher Education, provided $250,000 as a continuing revenue source for IIRA operations in the annual WIU budget. In addition, the IIRA could apply for an annual $250,000 grant from the GRAC subject to an agreed-upon specific work program that changed each year. WIU provided matching funds of approximately 25.0 percent, mainly reassignment of staff time, for the original allocation. The understanding was that if WIU decided not to support this mission at some future time, the IIRA could be relocated to another interested university.

Another mandate was that the IIRA had to be academic and university-wide in scope rather than located within one academic department or college. Thus, it reports to the provost and academic vice-president and operates with the same regulations as other academic departments or colleges. It also has authority to grant tenure status for faculty.

The original scope of responsibility for IIRA was 74 non-metropolitan Illinois counties and/or cities of 25,000 residents or fewer. These cities usually did not have professional management expertise and thus needed assistance on issues with which IIRA staff could help or find expertise. The number of non-metro designated counties in Illinois has since decreased to sixty-six with changes in definition by the Bureau of the Census. However, small towns within metro counties rarely change significantly even though the metropolitan designation changes, so they still need technical assistance.

Lesson learned

Building credibility and broad-based support for rural issues throughout state government was key to the longevity of the GRAC and programs. Placing GRAC under the governor's authority prevented competition and resistance to collaboration among state agencies.

Mission and vision of IIRA

After inventorying existing programs in Illinois, the initial IIRA staff (four persons) decided to focus research and programmatic efforts on economic development, transportation, health care, public management and finance, and education issues. Every effort was made to concentrate on issues not currently addressed by other agencies. At the outset, the greatest potential duplication would have involved production agriculture, where the University of Illinois Extension Service had significant expertise. Thus, the IIRA did not offer a program on production agriculture issues but, instead, referred enquiries to the Cooperative Extension Service. However, the IIRA worked with the State Department of Agriculture on value-added agriculture development to boost the rural development potential of many communities.

Within the IIRA, a program manager was hired for each topic area to build and supervise activities. Housing and technology were added as topic areas later, along with a stronger focus on value-added possibilities in agriculture and renewable energy including wind and ethanol.

The IIRA's stated mission is 'to improve the quality of rural Illinois by partnering with public and private agencies on local development and enhancement issues.' While the exact wording in the mission statement evolved slightly during the quarter-century of operations, the substance has not changed and continues to direct the programs and services provided to rural clients.

The vision of the IIRA is 'to be nationally-recognized for an integrated delivery system that provides knowledge, information, and innovative strategies to help rural residents improve policy decisions, overcome rural disparities, and achieve a high quality of life with strong rural communities'. This vision has been pursued aggressively over the years and is still relevant, as shown by the number of awards received, the growth in number of projects and staff, and the outputs and outcomes generated.

Lesson learned

A clear mission and vision accepted by IIRA staff early in the agency's history were vital to providing long-term programmatic direction and keeping a comprehensive rural focus.

Management philosophy and approaches

The IIRA incorporated industry standards and applications such as the *Principles of Good Practice* promoted by the Community Development Society (CDS). From its inception, the IIRA focused on accountability and transparency, with significant effort spent documenting products and results. These metrics were compiled in an annual report documenting activities and accomplishments that was distributed throughout the university and to external clients with special attention to successes with clients.

Throughout its operations, IIRA implemented management practices used by private agencies and recognized that a motivated staff equipped with up-to-date resources was the most important asset. The internal management philosophy within IIRA, especially in the early years, is perhaps best summarized by Champy (2000):

> One of the great things an organisation can do is to help people give voice to their dreams and provide the means by which people come together to create something greater than themselves. It is the gift of leaders to release the aspirations of others.

This philosophy and mindset continue in IIRA operations and in working with external groups to build local capacity.

Internal IIRA management practices and operations have been consistently guided by six core values contained in the Strategic Plan launched in 1999:

1. Community Development encompasses more than job creation; it also includes health, education, public transportation, public management, housing, and telecommunications. IIRA addresses these issues using a holistic approach.
2. The most successful solutions to local problems come from local initiatives. IIRA strives to empower residents and community leaders to make informed decisions rather than just recommending specific alternatives.
3. Rural issues are broader than agriculture even though agriculture must be included in efforts to strengthen the local economic base. IIRA programs address a multitude of community concerns to enhance the quality and ensure the vitality of community life.
4. Long-term solutions to rural issues must recognize the sustainability of the region and not deplete existing resources. IIRA explicitly recognizes environmental issues in helping community leaders find solutions for local concerns.
5. Communities in rural areas do not exist in isolation; they depend on economic prosperity at the metro, state, and national levels. IIRA understands these interrelationships and encourages partnerships among groups within and between communities.
6. Successful community development enriches the lives of all residents regardless of race, creed, age, or economic status, including disadvantaged regions and underserved population segments. IIRA believes that broad-based participation in local decisions ultimately leads to a higher quality of life for all residents.

While strategic planning efforts started in its early years, a major boost occurred when IIRA participated in the Lincoln Foundation for Business Excellence (LFBE) process in 1999. The LFBE applies Malcolm Baldrige criteria for performance excellence to management practices in private and public organizations. Applicant organizations are evaluated and rated in seven areas: leadership, strategic planning, customer and market focus, human resources, process management, and business results, with the greatest weights assigned to the latter section. The importance of the LFBE exercise was that it sharpened the focus on strategic management processes and practices within the IIRA, leading to more sophisticated management and accountability approaches.

Lesson learned
Working with a credible and recognized external organization (LFBE) raised the importance of strategic planning and management practices throughout the operations. It helped to prevent units from becoming 'silos' in their thinking and brought a more coordinated thrust within the organization. However, successfully implementing this process required strong commitment from leaders within IIRA.

Effective management requires assuring that each unit focuses on the products it is expected to deliver. However, continuous improvement requires regular learning and organizational adjustments to changing conditions. Thus, the IIRA organized staff into both vertical and horizontal teams. Vertical teams followed traditional program lines. Horizontally, staff members were grouped into administration, research, and outreach teams spanning units within IIRA. Thus, each staff member participated in vertical team activities as well as horizontal efforts designed to foster communication and learning from successful innovations in other units.

Teams at both levels identified continuous improvement goals for six-month intervals. This approach was difficult to maintain at all three horizontal levels, and some team efforts were later discontinued because of time commitments. The administrative team was most successful in generating useful outcomes and was later transformed to an executive management group.

Organizational goals

Early in its operations, the IIRA adopted the following four goals:

1. Promote sound statewide rural policies and programs;
2. Advance the state of knowledge about rural issues;
3. Provide high quality training and technical assistance to rural leaders; and
4. Use continuous improvement techniques to achieve effective and efficient operations.

These goals addressed the main components of the overall mission and specific strategies including policy development, research, and training-technical assistance activities. They were pursued within the traditional university missions to create, disseminate, and apply knowledge to a diverse clientele. IIRA faculty and staff research innovative solutions to rural issues identified by community leaders and public officials, teach classes on campus, provide training programs for professional organizations and groups, and then apply the information generated by working with groups to find remedies or solutions to local issues.

Faculty and staff also maintain an active scholarly publishing record and regularly participate in academic and professional societies. Active participation in these activities plus an organized tenure process helped to maintain credibility and respect by colleagues in other university academic and professional departments. Important to note is that funding was not seen as a primary goal within IIRA. While funds are needed to conduct activities and meet the stated goals, the focus was on outputs produced and outcomes.

Lesson learned
A clear statement of highly visible goals helps with effective management of an organization and directs efforts of staff, especially in seeing how their specific unit or division contributes to overall effectiveness. A process is used to follow up on services delivered so that insights into impacts from outputs delivered can be obtained.

Approaches to financing

Two broad approaches to financing were possible. One was to pursue specific *projects* designed to help communities or agencies address local issues. A second approach was to pursue ongoing *programs* funded by the federal or state government or philanthropic associations.

Choosing the latter direction allowed staff to gain more expertise and make a deeper commitment to specific issues. In the first year, the IIRA financed several outreach programs with state and/or federal grants for economic development and transportation. It applied to the US Economic Development Administration (EDA) to be a Rural Economic Technical Assistance Center (RETAC) serving rural Illinois. To meet its statewide responsibilities, it subcontracted with three other universities to collaboratively deliver a range of specialized services across the state. This approach supported the intent to partner with other agencies to improve quality of life in rural Illinois.

The RETAC began in 1990 and continued to 2006, when the University Center program changed direction and focused on specific problems in a region rather than on statewide efforts. More information about programmatic efforts by RETAC and its links with other IIRA operations is provided later.

Also in 1990, the IIRA collaborated with the Illinois Department of Transportation to create a Rural Transit Assistance Center (RTAC) funded by the US Department of Transportation (USDOT). The RTAC works with local transportation agencies also funded by the USDOT and provides research, educational programs, and technical assistance. The RTAC, within IIRA, continues after nearly twenty-four years and regularly adjusts services to reflect changing needs.

Lesson learned
Building on the talent and expertise in other universities and pursuing long-term programs provided more depth of expertise in IIRA and created a solid base for continuing rural programs. At the same time, however, building and maintaining collaborative efforts can be difficult because of competing interests among universities.

Organizational structure

The organizational structure (Figure 10.1) reflects programmatic activities and operations. In some instances, the specific structure was imposed by funding sources seeking a clearly identified contact point for their clients. As shown, the IIRA has eight operating units, each with a manager who reports to the director plus an executive management team including three assistant directors.

Outreach activities are provided in several ways. First, rural leaders can contact IIRA for services directly by using an 800 number and/or visiting the website and e-mailing a request (IIRA, 2014a). This delivery approach is especially useful to obtain research services and data analyses. A second way to obtain services is through a community outreach program, Management and Planning Programs Involving Non-metro Groups (MAPPING), created with funds from EDA and the Governor's Rural Affairs Council in 1991. It works with small communities across the state to formulate a vision for the future, goals for the community, and an action plan to achieve identified goals.

After completing the initial vision-setting and action-plan exercises, communities often need assistance with implementation. Several agencies in IIRA are positioned to assist with these programs and often are contacted to provide specific services such as Geographic Information Systems (GIS), transportation, health, housing, development, or other activities (see Figure 10.1).

In addition, small communities with limited expertise in development issues or other topics can sponsor a Peace Corps Fellow (PCF) in Community Development from the IIRA (IIRA, 2014b). These graduate students have completed required classwork for a master's degree in one of several disciplines and work in communities for a designated period, usually eleven months, implementing an action plan.

In addition to the MAPPING and PCF programs, the IIRA also hosts other units. The Value-Added Sustainable Development Center (VASDC) focuses on renewable energy, value-added agriculture, local foods, and cooperative development. The RTAC, mentioned previously, provides rural transit driver training and strategic visioning for rural transit planning. The Data and Technical Assistance (DATA) Center includes the aforementioned RETAC unit, a GIS specialist, and survey and research design staff.

The Small Business Development Center (SBDC) helps fledging entrepreneurs with services such as preparing business plans and securing financing for their operations. The Procurement Technical Assistance Center (PTAC) helps business sell goods and services to state and federal government offices. Finally, the Health

Director

Management team

- MAPPING strategic visioning
- VASDC sustainable development
- Health and housing
- RTAC rural transit
- DATA center
- SBDC small business
- PTAC procurement
- Peace Corps Fellows
- Faculty

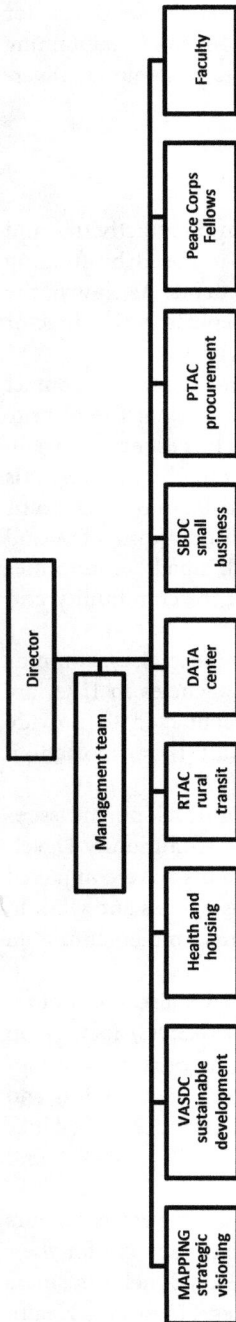

IIRA OUTREACH AND ENGAGEMENT PROCESS

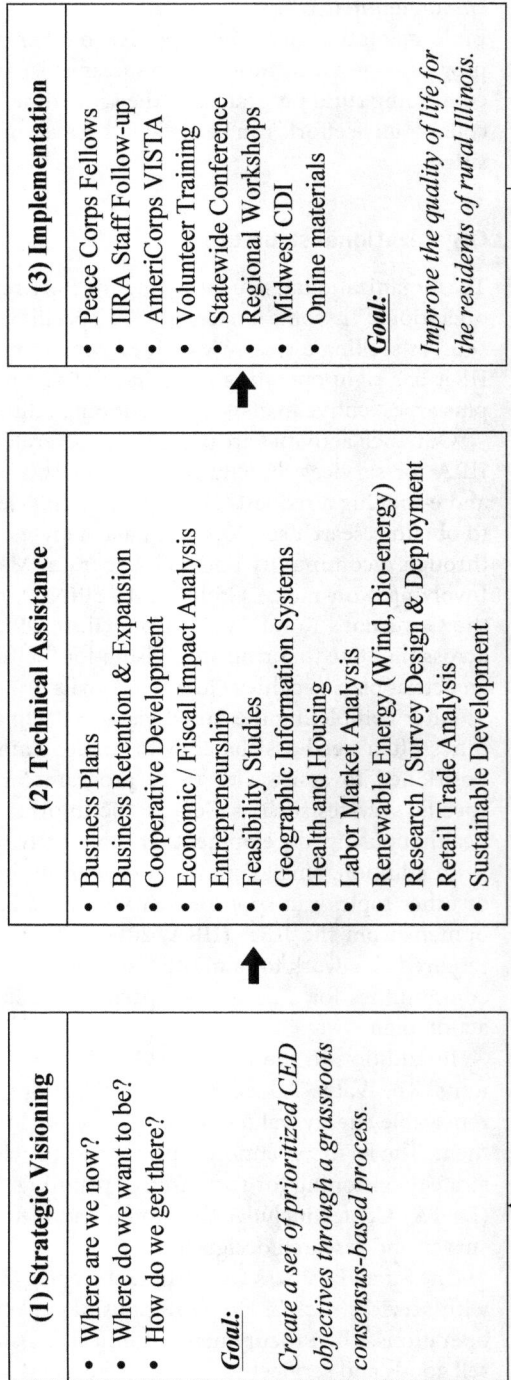

(1) Strategic Visioning

- Where are we now?
- Where do we want to be?
- How do we get there?

Goal:

Create a set of prioritized CED objectives through a grassroots consensus-based process.

(2) Technical Assistance

- Business Plans
- Business Retention & Expansion
- Cooperative Development
- Economic / Fiscal Impact Analysis
- Entrepreneurship
- Feasibility Studies
- Geographic Information Systems
- Health and Housing
- Labor Market Analysis
- Renewable Energy (Wind, Bio-energy)
- Research / Survey Design & Deployment
- Retail Trade Analysis
- Sustainable Development

(3) Implementation

- Peace Corps Fellows
- IIRA Staff Follow-up
- AmeriCorps VISTA
- Volunteer Training
- Statewide Conference
- Regional Workshops
- Midwest CDI
- Online materials

Goal:

Improve the quality of life for the residents of rural Illinois.

and Housing Unit helps communities to plan affordable housing for low-income families and senior citizens. Three tenured faculty conduct research and deliver training and technical assistance.

Lesson learned

The transition from strategic planning to technical assistance and/or research has proved to be an organized and highly effective way to deliver services to small communities. It provides continuity to clients but also builds capacity within IIRA because several related programs can coordinate efforts.

Documenting and disseminating results

Early in its history, the IIRA designed and implemented a Management Information System (MIS) to monitor operations and progress on programmatic areas. The MIS is grounded in the private sector management literature including the importance of high quality management information on an as-needed basis throughout the organization (Gates, 1999). The importance of this system was further reinforced in discussions with the LFBE.

An online data collection and retrieval system allows personnel to record activities in their cost-reimbursement requests, scheduling car activities, and other daily operations. In turn, the MIS organizes the information to make it useful in managing budgets and monitoring the effectiveness of operations. For instance, program managers use the information in compiling project completion reports for clients. Likewise, the MIS was used in monitoring the relative balance between research and technical assistance activities. The MIS is an integral part of the overall management system within IIRA because it provides real-time information for a variety of management decisions.

The IIRA incorporated a system similar to the LOGIC model advanced by the W. K. Kellogg Foundation in 2001 (W. K. Kellogg Foundation, 2001). Specifically, the IIRA's efforts are categorized into inputs, activities, products, outcomes, and impacts. While not as extensive as the W. K. Kellogg approach, the MIS allows program managers and staff to monitor and trace their efforts by type of service and location. Because efforts are coded by location where delivered, managers and staff can relatively easily compile and/or tabulate services provided and inputs used for customized regions by city, county, or zip code. This information can then be provided to legislators or state agencies interested in specific types of services. The MIS also supports internal IIRA decisions about overlooked or underserved areas within the state. Thus, the information serves internal management decisions, marketing efforts, and budget re-allocations when needed. A more complete discussion of the metrics used follows.

Inputs

The most important use of the data is to monitor efforts and outcomes over time. In the first year (1990) the IIRA had nine full-time employees (inputs), and by 2012 it had grown to thirty-eight full-time staff. Likewise, the *annual* appropriated funds budget went from an initial allocation of $250,000 to $1,606,000 by 2010, before dropping to $1,479,000 in 2012, reflecting across-the-board cuts by the state to WIU's appropriated funds. Annual funds received from grants and contracts increased from $479,600 to $2,196,000. In total, annual financial resources available to provide services through the IIRA increased more than five-fold, and collectively IIRA has raised $32.6 million during this period.

Other inputs monitored in managing IIRA operations are miles traveled to provide services, hits and/or downloads on the web page, and calls to the 800 number for assistance. The mileage travelled increased more than six-fold from 31,300 in 1990 to nearly 217,300 in 2012. Since the number of miles traveled is merely one indicator of inputs used to deliver services rather than a product or outcome, it is included only to show changes in activity. Using webinars or other technology-based delivery services that reduce number of miles traveled is an advantage.

In 1996, the 800 number received 4,164 calls in addition to individual calls to faculty and staff. A deliberate effort was made to deliver data and services in more innovative ways and reduce staff time spent responding to simple data requests. Taking advantage of increased access to the Internet, the IIRA was able to dramatically shift enquiries away from the 800 number, which represents a higher cost, to a web page delivery system that provides more detailed information using less faculty and staff time. Questions handled by IIRA staff directly now have more value-added potential.

Activities

Technically, activities are the ways in which the inputs are deployed, but because confusion sometimes existed between activities and outputs, it made sense to differentiate them. Comparing ratios of activities to inputs among IIRA agencies helped in allocating resources among IIRA delivery approaches.

The growth in activities performed has been substantial. For instance, IIRA personnel made 712 conference presentations between 1990 and 2012, which is one indicator of the exposure to persons interested in community economic development. Likewise, more than 635,000 mailings of reports, conference announcements, and other informational or educational materials plus 1,575 training programs were presented to rural constituents.

Products

Especially important in assessing the contributions of an organization is to analyze what it produces. Defining and/or evaluating products in an organization that generates, distributes, and applies knowledge in real world situations is difficult. Four indices to monitor products were selected. For instance, between 1990 and 2012, IIRA faculty and staff produced over 900 publications, including 17 scholarly or professional books and 396 book chapters, which are seen as an indicator of advancing scholarly knowledge about rural issues. The IIRA also produces a Rural Research Report series on promising or innovative practices that address rural issues. These reports are distributed to policy-makers, community leaders, rural practitioners, and libraries as well as on various web pages. Between 1990 and 2012, IIRA produced 200 Rural Research Reports with a distribution of more than 150,000 copies to local officials and practitioners.

Outcomes
Measuring outcomes and impacts for an organization with diverse products is difficult because the effects from technical assistance or training depend on many local factors and sometimes take a long time to mature. Nevertheless, the IIRA monitors several output measures that can support outcomes. The IIRA recently started a tracking system that follows projects over several years. Between FY 2009 and FY 2010, the Small Business Development Center spent 3,400 hours (input) helping 700 clients resulting in thirty-five new businesses and twenty-three business expansions (outputs), which created 252 jobs (impact). Additional examples of these metrics are available (IIRA, 2011).

The IIRA hosts an annual community and economic development conference that attracts 300 participants or more, so that nationally recognized speakers can discuss the latest development issues and promising practices. The IIRA sponsors other training events which, in total, provided training to 100,521 participants, although this is not an unduplicated count. Nevertheless, rural leaders certainly had many opportunities to learn new ideas and see new opportunities through these training efforts. The IIRA is especially sensitive to its statewide mission and therefore monitors locations where services are delivered. The locations are tracked and analyzed to identify overlooked regions.

Lesson learned
Tracking and documenting operations are important in managing an agency effectively. Faculty and staff need access to objective performance metrics to make informed decisions. The data must be collected as part of regular operations so as not to increase reporting burdens and discourage participation. Likewise, the information generated from the data must be useful in daily management decisions. An effective system can not only build pride internally but can also market the organization.

Measures of quality: recognition by peers

While measuring success is difficult, one indicator is recognition by peer agencies and colleagues for products and/or faculty and staff efforts. Between 1990 and 2012, IIRA faculty, staff, and students earned seventy national, state, and local awards for products or activities on behalf of community development.

Another indicator of success used in monitoring performance is the percentage of grant applications that were funded. During the 1990–2012 period, the success rate in applying for grants averaged 92.0 percent, with only a few years below 90.0 percent. This level of success indicates that the quality of work is respected but also means that IIRA is managing its resources efficiently because grant applications can be costly to prepare.

Replicating and extending the IIRA model

The institute has retained a clear and consistent vision, mission, and practices. It benchmarks its activities internally and with scrutiny from external evaluators; it secures feedback from clients, adjusts course of action when necessary, and has built a record of service recognized across the state. As in any social science experiment, however, the question is whether an innovative idea can be replicated with a certain level of confidence.

Members of the IIRA recently tested the transferability and replicability of their model. In 2006, the institute partnered with the WIU School of Agriculture and two universities in Mexico to secure a $300,000 four-year grant from the US Agency for International Development (USAID). The grant was designed to 'build capacity' for rural development in Chiapas, the most southern, rural, and underdeveloped state in Mexico.

Chiapas has a high proportion of indigenous peoples, who are culturally linked to the ancient Mayans. These residents had long felt marginalized, first by the Spanish colonizers and then by the Mexican government. With the implementation of the North American Free Trade Agreement (NAFTA) in 1994, a group of over 3,000 indigenous people called the Zapatistas rose up against the Mexican government. They saw NAFTA as yet another example of external actors oppressing the region. The Mexican army stormed the region to quell the revolt but was not able to capture the Zapatistas, who retreated into the mountains.

As a condition of agreeing to a ceasefire and truce, the Zapatistas insisted that the Mexican government invest in Chiapas to develop the infrastructure (e.g., all-weather roads), access to health care, and education. The Mexican government agreed and in 1997 opened the Universidad Tecnológica de la Selva (UTS).

Located in Ocosingo, Chiapas, UTS was the focus for the USAID project. The grant included many components including student exchanges, faculty exchanges and sabbaticals, workshops delivered on the UTS campus on a range of topics related to community economic development (e.g., cooperative development, value-added agriculture, and marketing), and the creation of a rural development center modeled after the IIRA.

In order to establish the rural development center at UTS, IIRA faculty and staff used many of the principles articulated above. The first point was to acknowledge that while UTS was located in a rural region, it operated in a landscape very different from rural Illinois. It was also important to recognize that higher education is perceived differently in Mexico and Latin America than in the USA or Canada. In Latin America, universities are perceived as more elitist. But the USAID grant had as a core goal the democratization of knowledge so that people would see the university as a resource for everyone, not just a select few.

So the founding principles of the IIRA were used, including adopting a holistic approach to community development. The first step was to guide the faculty and staff at UTS through a strategic visioning effort with an Appreciative Inquiry process (Cooperrider and Whitney, 2005) to help them to identify and rank the most pressing rural development issues in Chiapas. The main point was that the UTS faculty prioritized the goals rather than researchers from an American university.

UTS faculty identified livestock production, dairy and cheese production, coffee cultivation and marketing, and ecotourism as key sectors to address. By going through the visioning process, UTS faculty learned the 'bottom-up' and 'asset-based' community development outreach strategies employed in the IIRA. Once the sectors had been identified, the UTS faculty worked with each producer group, taking it through a strategic visioning process to identify a prioritized set of goals to pursue. Again, the notion was that the UTS faculty would allow the local producers the flexibility to choose what was best for the producers and rural communities rather than just what the UTS faculty thought were the best choices.

As part of the grant, UTS administrators including the rector (equivalent to a university president) traveled to WIU to see how the IIRA functioned and to learn about its organizational structure and how it operated within the context of a university. This activity mirrored the lessons learned in the IIRA, namely that it is important to develop support for the outreach center at the very highest levels of the university.

In order to incorporate practices to help sustain the rural development efforts, the UTS faculty and administrators were urged to communicate regularly with communities and producers in the region through surveys, host workshops, and build an Internet presence in order to inform residents that the rural development center is a resource for promoting community economic development in the region.

After six years, the producer groups continue to work together and with the UTS rural development center, or Centro Desarrollo Rural as it is known in Spanish. The center has a website (Centro Desarrollo Rural, 2014) that includes the mission, vision, organizational structure, and services including strategic visioning, business planning, and other outreach activities offered by the center.

Lesson learned
Basic community development principles and practices used in creating the IIRA were successful in the case of Chiapas. These approaches include asset-based development, building on solid and proven techniques, and recognizing the uniqueness of local situations. While this is only one example, the differences between rural Illinois and Chiapas Mexico are sufficient to at least suggest transferability to other areas as well.

Essential elements in university–community outreach

After more than twenty years of conducting community outreach programs within a regional university-based environment, what have we learned? Several major elements have been integral to the success of the IIRA.

Be mission-driven
Throughout its history, the IIRA remained on course with its mission and built a solid reputation among clients. While programs were adjusted to meet changing needs, the IIRA continues to promote a higher quality of life by partnering with public and private agencies on development and enhancement projects.

Be integrated within the university scope of activities
Forging relationships with academic departments and engaging faculty with specific talents was instrumental in earning and retaining a university support base. Likewise, being professionally active built support among peer departments and colleges and gained respect for outreach activities. This internal support at the highest levels was key to maintaining IIRA credibility and sustained support during the recent tough economic times for work that might not be maintained.

Furthermore, the IIRA sought external, third-party validation for the civic engagement efforts of the university. In 2012, the IIRA applied on behalf of WIU for a Carnegie Foundation Community Engagement designation. This process enabled the IIRA to showcase its outreach partnership efforts both off campus and on campus, and to have the efforts validated by a respected external academic evaluator. In some ways, it paralleled the LFBE process that earlier had secured external validation for the work done by the IIRA.

Remain non-partisan and credible in state government
IIRA's efforts have been supported by both Democrat and Republican administrations in state government. Its focus on rural issues and application of tested approaches to current problems allowed both political parties to not only support existing efforts but also to expand its operations.

Maintain regular contact and communication with clients
The combination of Rural Research Reports, an annual conference, outreach programs, and other activities gained a widespread recognition for IIRA for quality work and availability of services. This support and reputation led to additional opportunities.

Stay current on issues and incorporate them into programming.
The needs of rural areas changed during the past quarter-century, and it was important to redesign programs in ways that kept services current. The additions of renewable energy, technology, and housing were ways in which IIRA recognized these changes and built programs to address them. The flexibility to change directions as needed was instrumental in the IIRA successes.

Celebrate successes
Using the web page and social media to celebrate clients' successes is important to reward excellent efforts but also to gain recognition and support for outreach activities. The IIRA maintains a Facebook page and regularly celebrates successes by clients.

Concluding observations

Regional state universities are positioned well to deliver services such as technical assistance to local governments, development agencies, and other groups even on a statewide basis. While they do not have as many resources or often the depth in subject matter as larger land grant universities, they have the capacity to work more closely with focused clientele. They also are more likely to have a greater awareness of both local issues that need help and also innovative approaches used by community leaders.

The IIRA is one example of an outreach agency in a regional university that has built a solid reputation over nearly a quarter-century in working on rural issues in Illinois. What it has gained from these experiences can help universities in other states and countries to build strong viable outreach programs, and there is at least some evidence that this type of approach or model can be replicated, with adjustments, in other environments.

References

Ayres, J., Cole, R., Hein, C., Hunnington, S., Kobberdahl, W., Leonard, W., and Zetocha, D. (1990). *Take Charge: Economic Development in Small Communities*. Ames, IA: North Central Regional Center for Rural Development.

Buckingham, M. and Coffman, C. (1999). *FIRST, Break All the Rules*. New York: Simon and Schuster.

Center for Rural Pennsylvania (CRP) (2014). www.ruralpa.org/ (last accessed 8 February 2014).

Centro Desarrollo Rural (2014). www.utselva.edu.mx/incubador/ (last accessed 8 February 2014).

Champy, J. (2000). Seven Ways to Elevate Ambition. *Leader to Leader* 17, Summer.

Community Development Society (2014). *Principles of Good Practice*. www.comm-dev.org/index.php/about-cds (last accessed 28 January 2014).

Cooperrider, D. L., and Whitney, D. (2005). *Appreciative Inquiry: A Positive Revolution in Change*. San Fransisco, CA: Berrett-Koehler Publishers, Inc.

Epstein, P. D., Coates, P. M., Wray, L. D., and Swain, D. (2006). *Results that Matter: Improving Communities by Engaging Citizens, Measuring Performance, and Getting Things Done*. San Francisco, CA: John D. Wiley & Sons, Inc.

Gates, B. (1999). *Business @ the Speed of Thought: Using a Digital Nervous System*. New York: Warner Books, Inc.

Governor's Rural Affairs Council (1987). *Report to the Governor and General Assembly*. Springfield, IL: Governor's Rural Affairs Council.

Green, G. P., Borich, T. O., Cole, R. D., Darling, D. L., Hancock, C., Huntington, S. H., Leuci, M. S., McMaster, B., Patton, D. B., Schmidt, F., Silvis, A. H., Sternberg, R., Teel, D., Wade, J., Walzer, N., and Stewart, J. (2001). *Vision to Action: Take Charge Too*. Ames, IA: North Central Regional Center for Rural Development.

Greenberg Quinlan Rosner Research (2002). *Perceptions of Rural America*. Commissioned by the W. K. Kellogg Foundation. http://frameworksinstitute.org/toolkits/htri/docs/memo.pdf (last accessed 28 January 2014).

Illinois Institute for Rural Affairs (IIRA) (2011). Western Illinois University Economic Development Success Stories. Macomb, IL. Unpublished.

Illinois Institute for Rural Affairs (IIRA) (2014a). www.iira.org (last accessed 8 February 2014).

Illinois Institute for Rural Affairs (IIRA) (2014b). Peace Corps Fellows Program in Community Development. www.peacecorpsfellows-wiu.org/index.html (last accessed 8 February 2014).

Lasley, P., and Hanson, M. (2003). The Changing Population of the Midwest: A Reflection on Opportunities. In N. Walzer (ed.), *The American Midwest: Managing Change in Rural Transition*, pp. 16–41. Armonk, NY: M. E. Sharpe Inc.

North Carolina Rural Economic Development Center, Inc. (NCRDC) (2014). www.ncrural-center.org (last accessed 8 February 2014).

Walzer, N. (ed.) (2003). *The American Midwest: Managing Change in Rural Transition*. Armonk, NY: M. E. Sharpe Inc.

W. K. Kellogg Foundation (2001). *Logic Model Development Guide*. Battle Creek, MI: W. K. Kellogg Foundation.

11

Initiating ecological restoration and community relationships at a satellite campus

Roberta Lammers

Loyola University of Chicago purchased the former St. Joseph's Seminary, located in rural Woodstock, Illinois, near the village of Bull Valley, in May 2010 for the purpose of developing a retreat and ecology campus. I have worked on the ecological aspect of the retreat centre, especially the ecological restoration, since its inception. In the process I have interacted with many people in the community, most of whom I had not known before and most of whom had previous experience with the property. Agencies and individuals had been connected to the site for many reasons. The degree to which many of them seemed to have acquired emotional – almost spiritual – ties to the site was surprising to me. It instills a 'love of place' and draws people back repeatedly. I will describe some of the institutional and personal relationships that developed during the course of ecological restoration there, but these emotional or spiritual ties will underlie much of the story in an undefinable way.

The first time I visited what would become the Loyola University Retreat and Ecology Campus (LUREC), I had been invited to view the property with other members of the biology faculty to evaluate its potential as a field station. Previously, we had visited an unsuitable property that had been donated to the university, and so it was with great excitement that we toured this highly desirable site with its large seminary building containing more than 100 separate living and community spaces, and its 98 snow-covered acres of wetlands and woodland. On that visit in February 2010, I developed my own emotional tie to the site, looking for excuses to return. I found many.

From the outset the university was committed to making LUREC ecologically sustainable. The commitment has been due especially to the vision of Dr. Nancy Tuchman, the founding director of Loyola's new Institute for Environmental Sustainability (IES), and to the encouragement of Fr. Michael Garanzini SJ, Loyola's president, whose commitment to sustainability was enhanced when the Society of Jesus adopted the environment as a major social justice issue. The institute is being designed to offer environmental curricula in food, business, environmental policy, and restoration and conservation, as well as guiding Loyola to become one of the most energy-efficient campuses in the country. LUREC is the field station for IES, housing a student-run farm and a significant ecological restoration in addition to classrooms, living quarters, and dining facilities.

141

Dr. Tuchman described her vision of the new campus to neighbors and the Bull Valley Board on 22 July 2010 during the Bull Valley Village Board meeting (held at the Farm Bureau building, 1101 McConnell Road, Woodstock, Illinois 60098) and again on 22 October 2010 at a reception hosted by neighbor D. Staley in her home. Dr. Tuchman assured the audience that Loyola's ecological ethic was similar to that of the Boone Creek Watershed Alliance (BCWA) and McHenry County Conservation District, both of which are conservation leaders. Our hope was to construct a campus with the smallest environmental footprint possible, producing much of our own food, generating minimal waste and recycling most of that, and even trying to get off the electrical grid with geothermal heating and other energy-conserving measures. With sustainability the goal for the LUREC campus, it was a given that we would work to improve our degraded natural areas. The only question was how.

I was interested in learning more about the property. I had been working on a wetland restoration on McHenry County Conservation District (MCCD) land for fourteen years, and this very interesting site seemed to be a place where I could continue restoration work. My role has expanded from being an interested (non-tenure-track) faculty member to being the halftime Director of the LUREC Restoration Project. This chapter is my attempt to describe the community relationships that developed during the first two and a half years of Loyola's ownership as we proceeded with plans for the ecological restoration of the natural areas on the property. I will discuss these relationships under the following themes:

- Neighbors previously worried about the potential development of a retirement facility;
- People connected to the property through their Catholic religious commitments;
- Professional conservationists in the county;
- Neighbors who have devoted their own lives and property to sustainability and ecological restoration;
- The wetland ecology course as an example of how all of these community factors have worked together in developing the restoration plan.

These themes overlap. All of them, however, include people who have a profound love of, or concern for, the property and who are willing to go to great lengths to guarantee a successful restoration. These efforts and sentiments did not originate with Loyola's acquisition of the property. In fact most of what we are doing relates back to efforts begun years ago; thus our current effort is an attempt to integrate many pre-existing elements.

The site

LUREC is located atop the Woodstock Moraine in McHenry County in northeastern Illinois. McHenry County is a center of biodiversity in Illinois because of its varied habitats, many of which did not lend themselves easily to agriculture, and because of the foresight of the county in conservation. Ecological restoration of the LUREC property is congruent with the county's efforts to maintain both oak woodland ecosystems and wetland ecosystems. For both ecosystems LUREC is part of a larger landscape.

When European settlers arrived, an estimated one-third of the county (about 140,000 acres) was covered with oak savanna and denser oak woodland. The oak timbered lands were decimated in the 150 years following European settlement. Oak timbered acreage in McHenry County has declined to an estimated 18,000 acres, much of it existing now in small, isolated parcels. LUREC occupies part of a 60–acre block of oaks, which is one of the larger remaining parcels. Woodlands throughout the county are choked with invasive shrubs except where private and public restoration efforts have brought them under control.

In low-lying areas among the oak timbered lands, the settlers found wetlands fed by springs and seeps in the moraines and insulated from underground drainage by impermeable layers of blue clay. Peat had accumulated in the basins, and sedge meadows and calcium-rich fens – an ecosystem that is globally rare – were found near the springs and in their drainage basins. European settlement decimated wetlands as well as woodlands. Whereas 90 percent of the wetlands throughout Illinois were drained (Illinois Department of Natural Resources, 2001, p. 22), according to E. Collins, in a personal conversation with the author on 25 April 2010, only 70 percent were destroyed in McHenry County. These areas are also full of invasive shrubs. The LUREC wetland is a 20–acre parcel in a larger basin that is more than 200 acres. Prior to human manipulation, the wetland was probably mainly fen. An Illinois Nature Preserve, the Julia M. and Royce L. Parker Fen, is part of the basin, and we abut it directly.

LUREC is in the watershed of Boone Creek, a 13–mile-long, pristine, cold-water stream. It is near the top of the watershed of Powers Creek, the only named tributary to Boone Creek. A portion of its oak woodland is in a Class III watershed, which means it is highly protected because its water impacts Parker Fen. Many resources have been expended to conserve the entire watershed. In the Boone Creek watershed, as of 2009, there were twenty-seven permanently protected sites – twenty-one private and six public agency lands – covering 1,444 acres. What we do on LUREC's land matters to our community, and there has been much community interest in and encouragement of our restoration efforts.

Political ecological history of the site

We have speculated about, and attempted to document, the ecological history of the LUREC property so that we will have a better idea of how to restore it. Many people have shared their reminiscences, shown us county records and aerial photos, and imparted their impressions based on observations of similar sites. One of our most important resources is a series of aerial photographs obtained from the McHenry County Conservation District (MCCD). The earliest aerial photograph, taken in 1939, shows agricultural fields on the upper areas of the moraine; the presence of fields implies that some areas of oak savanna had been cut and plowed. The hillsides show scattered oaks, but the surrounding buildings would have been reason to suppress wild fire, and subtle changes would have occurred in the understory vegetation as a result. Aldo Leopold, working on oak timbered lands not far north of us in Wisconsin, maintained that as soon as European settlers came and the fires stopped, oak regeneration stopped as well. The youngest oaks in our restoration area are about 150 years old, supporting his observation.

The wetland has no sign of structural damage in the 1939 map, but a photo taken in 1954 shows ditching. In McHenry County and elsewhere in the Midwest, farmers dug ditches to drain wetlands and make them serviceable for agriculture. The striations on the 1954 map look like the result of mowing. It was common in McHenry County to use drained wetlands for summer forage. Because of a constant input from nearby springs, the area probably did not dry sufficiently to be plowed and cultivated or even to have cattle graze on it, but mowing in later summer was probably feasible.

Tiles were also used to drain wetlands. Trenches up to six feet deep were dug along a downslope gradient, and tiles of 3.5 to 6 inches or more in diameter – either terracotta clay or, later, plastic – were laid end to end to allow water to drain more efficiently toward a stream that would carry it 'away'. Tiles were place in the LUREC wetland, but they were removed, and only one existing tile line has been found still present. It was identified for me by James Miner of the Illlinois State Geologic Survey when he visited on 23 February 2012. The tile line cuts across a small piece of the southeast corner of the fen. The tile line has 'blown out', meaning that the tiles have broken and the water they normally would have carried has eroded a ditch where the former tiles ran. At its head there is a sudden opening in the ground about two feet deep, and large shards of terracotta clay are visible in the ditch. It carries a significant quantity of water away from the wetland. The land immediately south of us appears to be tiled as well.

A 1967 aerial photo taken after St. Joseph's Seminary had been dedicated in 1960 by the Resurrectionist order shows a 3.5 acre pond had been dredged, and three smaller ponds had been dug upstream from the larger pond in what appear to have been peat mounds. The purpose of the smaller ponds may have been two-fold: to provide ponds that could be stocked with trout for the fishermen among the priests and to divert additional water into the pond basin. A priest named Father Grabowski drowned in the pond in the mid-1960s when he walked out on thin ice to rescue his dog Thunder, who had fallen into the water. The dog survived. Visitors continue to walk on the pond ice, which is always unstable because of the water at 55 degrees Fahrenheit that feeds the pond.

The building first functioned as a seminary, and when a seminary could no longer be supported, the Resurrection fathers established a retreat center which served Catholic youth and adults throughout the Chicago area for several years. The center was affectionately called 'the Rez'. A fifty-bed addition was built between 2004 and 2005, expanding the center to 110 rooms. Initially the property location was designated unincorporated McHenry County and had a Woodstock address.

In the meantime the village of Bull Valley developed nearby. According to the *Encyclopedia of Chicago* website, 'local residents voted to incorporate in 1977 to protect their estate-style development, tucked into hilly, wooded terrain'. Bull

Valley became an exclusive address. Current Bull Valley zoning prohibits lots that are less than five acres in size. Additional land can be annexed to Bull Valley only if it is adjacent to other Bull Valley property, and the village grew in an irregular pattern, expanding to include land adjacent to the Resurrection Center.

Meanwhile, the retreat center proved financially unsuccessful for the Resurrectionists. The situation probably became more difficult when the nun who directed retreats left and the director of the center was seriously injured and lost his sight. The retreat center closed in September 2008. The citizens of Bull Valley would not be happy with what the Resurrection fathers proposed next.

The concerned neighbors: Resurrection Village and Loyola University Chicago

After closing the retreat center, the Resurrectionists decided to build a retirement center. The main building would be adapted to serve dependent elderly, and a few, small, freestanding homes would be built for the more independent elderly. Neighbors began a legal fight against the planned 'Resurrection Village', which they argued would lower their property values. In their legal search for ammunition, they had discovered that the Resurrectionists had not applied for the proper zoning change when they shifted the function of the building from a seminary to a retreat center (many of these details were related to the Loyola faculty and staff who met with the concerned neighbors on 22 July 2010, prior to the Bull Valley board meeting). The neighbors obtained an injunction with which they threatened the Resurrectionists. Extensive and expensive engineering work was done, and environmental plans developed to meet the demands of the community. On 19 May 2009, the McHenry County Board voted to issue a conditional use permit to allow construction to begin, but by then the Resurrectionists had run out of money, and they put the property up for sale. Patricia Carty, manager of the property, and her husband Tom tended the empty building until Loyola and its president, Fr. Michael Garanzini SJ, came calling.

Loyola purchased the property in May 2010, just three months after the biology faculty had come to view it. Our neighbors appeared to be delighted, but within two months some of them approached us about being annexed to Bull Valley. They called for a meeting at the center early on the same evening (22 July 2010) when members of the Loyola administration were scheduled to introduce themselves at the public meeting of the Bull Valley Village Board. The neighbors who came to the meeting insisted we pursue annexation. Their argument was that, on the basis of their recent experience with the Resurrectionists, they feared that Loyola might change its mind about what we wanted to do there and build something else. They thought their best interests would be served if Loyola became answerable to Bull Valley for any change of use or construction rather than to McHenry County officials, whom they characterized as 'rubber stamps'. Loyola's counter-argument was that we were much more amenable to interactions with the neighbors than our predecessors had been, as the current meeting demonstrated, that for Loyola to attempt to use the property differently was as likely as the university closing its doors, and finally that, because the Bull Valley board was notoriously obstructionist to any kind of development, we would probably never get any further construction approved if we did become part of the village.

The meeting itself was an interesting series of contradictions. The neighbor who shares our property line to the northwest brought a bottle of wine to welcome us, and words of welcome were delivered throughout the meeting. But at the same time, all the neighbors were adamant that, unless annexation arrangements were begun immediately, the pending lawsuit regarding lack of zoning for retreats would be invoked, and the university retreats scheduled for the next month – August – would *not* take place. One of the most vehement spokespeople for the neighbors was a local realtor and our neighbor to the southeast. Wayne Magdziarz, Loyola's senior vice president, remained remarkably composed considering that he had not been aware of the injunction previously. Some of the neighbors suggested it had been Patti Carty's responsibility to inform Loyola of the injunction, but having been neither an owner nor their legal representative, she had not been present at any of the negotiations. Underlying the interactions at the meeting was the unspoken knowledge that the annexation of LUREC to Bull Valley would make some of the participants' properties eligible for annexation because they would then be adjacent to the village, and a Bull Valley address would increase the value of their properties.

As a result of the meeting, Loyola agreed to proceed with annexation and became part of Bull Valley shortly thereafter. Retreats were initiated prior to the 2010 fall semester as scheduled.

The neighbors' motives had no doubt been mixed. The fact that some of them were interested in becoming part of Bull Valley was confirmed by the fact that eight newly eligible properties were annexed to Bull Valley at the same time as LUREC. Some residents feared a repeat of the experience with Resurrection Center and were concerned with the consequences for their own property but also about the development of another piece of the oak-hickory woodland.

Loyola's interaction with the community regarding annexation was determined by the neighbors' experiences with previous owners of the property and probably had very little to do with Loyola itself. The adjacent neighbors seemed pleased that we proceeded with annexation, but some of those a little farther away wondered why we gave in so easily to the pressure.

Regardless of how individuals felt about annexation, people have expressed only pleasure that Loyola is the new landowner. I believe that view is based on the assumption that Loyola will work responsibly to carry out its professed aim of making the campus sustainable, restoring its ecosystems, and being a good neighbor.

The Catholic connection

Patricia Carty came to Resurrection Center in 1979, first as a volunteer and eventually as the paid manager. She was a member of the Resurrection congregation, which was part of the center at that time, and had volunteered to help prepare the orders of service for Sunday mornings. Patti still works at the center, now as manager of the retreat side. She has proved to be an invaluable asset, introducing me to former staff and current neighbors and helping keep straight the history of what has happened there in the last thirty years.

Between 1999 and 2007 Colette Fahrner, a Sister of the Living Word (SLW), served at the center, organizing retreats and restoring the landscape. She organized an advisory committee which included representatives from the MCCD, The Land Conservancy (TLC) of McHenry County, McHenry County Soil and Water Conservation (SWC) District, the Bull Valley Board, the Illinois Nature Preserves Commission (INPC), and the owner of Parker Fen. Her advisors would recommend a plan of action, Sr. Colette would carry it out, and then she would schedule another meeting. Together they planned the mechanical clearing of invasives from the fen in 2004. The prairie was established during Sr. Colette's tenure. A parishioner who had the resources to construct it turned the soil, planted prairie plants, and left it to Sr. Colette to manage, which she did enthusiastically. Sr. Colette returns periodically to join Patti in the office and to see how we are doing with the restoration.

Kevin Ivers, the son of the previous retreat director at the center, worked with Sr. Colette. Kevin would later become President of the Board of Trustees of the MCCD. The MCCD raised money from local conservation agencies as well as neighbors to clear the fen in 2004. Ed Weskerna of the SWC District told me he had never seen such large buckthorns. Buckthorns, trees originally planted as fencing for animals, have become invasive. Some large native trees were left standing to provide bird habitat. Some herbiciding and subsequent seeding were done, but the center did not have adequate human resources for the necessary maintenance to prevent buckthorn from resprouting and creating the dense, impenetrable shrubland that was present when Loyola purchased the property six years later. It was not even able to sow all the seed that had been given to it by MCCD.

Dr. Patricia Inman and her husband Guy are owners of part of the wetland basin. Pat was one of the first people to come to the LUREC office, volunteering to help us in whatever way she could. Her interests are mainly on the agricultural side of our activities, but she knows many of the neighbors and has helped us make contact with them, as well as helped us figure out how to do so. Pat is a member of Resurrection Church (which is now separate from the center) and has a long history of connection to our land. She views it as a holy place and hopes Loyola is successful both in creating a sustainable campus and in assuming its place in the community.

Loyola alumni, many of whom are Catholic, have also helped us establish community connections. Our alumni office invited alumni in McHenry County to our Harvest Festival in 2011, and as a result we met close neighbors, people who have participated in our monthly restoration workdays, and one alumna who was on the McHenry County Board and is now a state legislative representative from the area.

The conservation professionals in McHenry County

Our relationship to local conservation agencies – especially the MCCD – has been critical to our work. Our ability to work with local conservation agencies was facilitated by previous work that some of us had done in the county and by our working relationship with Ed Collins, who is now the Natural Resource Manager for MCCD. I first met Ed in 1996 when I started a fourteen-year project evaluating the return of vegetation to a restored calcareous fen at Glacial Park, the site of the district's headquarters. In addition, Martin Berg in Loyola's biology department had graduate students who surveyed aquatic insects in streams at Glacial Park. I also had students who spent significant time working with MCCD field crews as part of their requirements for my Restoration Ecology service learning course.

I contacted Ed Collins soon after we visited the property. Ed had been part of Sr. Colette Fahrner's advisory committee and was familiar with her effort to clear the fen. MCCD had recently conducted a survey of remaining McHenry County oak timbered lands, which was published as 'The Oaks of McHenry County'. It recognized the center was part of one of the larger parcels. He recommended that Loyola purchase the property. He would have recommended the county purchase it had it been larger. On 10 April 2010, I walked the property with Ed, Bree Sines, a biology instructor who would co-teach both plant biology and wetland ecology at LUREC, and Robert Morgan, an ornithologist who would teach a bird unit for winter ecology. Ed commented that the property was 'beaten up but recoverable', and showed us many signs of recovery including skunk cabbage – the sign of calcareous seeps throughout the county. Soon I started exploring the property, finding many other signs of potential recovery.

Ed Collins has been indispensable to our progress. He gave me the contact infor-mation for Sr. Colette's former advisory committee and suggested I reorganize it. On 20 September 2010, he gathered his staff to discuss the LUREC property with several Loyola faculty and staff. The owner of Parker Fen also attended. We were introduced to the plat map and series of aerial photographs mentioned earlier that have become so important to our understanding of and teaching about the history of the property. We were given invaluable advice about prioritizing our work: 'Figure out exactly what you have. You don't want to lose what you can't replace, and so start with your best piece.' We were also encouraged to start our restora-tion work in the woodland, where results would be apparent much more quickly.

Ed spoke to my classes and consulted with me individually. He recommended we consider hiring Randy Stowe to work on the wetland restoration. He encour-aged me to seek a 'buffer to an Illinois Nature Preserve' status. And he suggested that Loyola consider a Memorandum of Understanding with MCCD to facilitate our potential work together. When Ed and the rest of the reconstituted advisory committee met with me and my supervisor, Nancy Tuchman, on 6 June 2011, we discussed the pond and its failing berm. The advisory committee made it perfectly clear that trying to restore the berm would be very expensive and diffi-cult to have permitted, and would leave us with a pond and structure that would probably present ongoing problems. That discussion, combined with the growing realization of the pond's liabilities, resulted in a consensus of Loyola officials to decommission it.

Lisa Haderline, the executive director of TLC of McHenry County, had also been a member of Sr. Colette's advisory committee. We met Lisa on 11 October 2010, when a local expert on green infrastructure and a member of the BCWA took me and Gina Lettiere, a Loyola staff person, on a tour of the watershed. TLC facilitates conservation easements in the county. It has also organized 'Project *Quercus*', which seeks to preserve and maintain oak timbered lands. Lisa helped define our priorities when she said that healthy oak woodlands are less common in the county than healthy wetlands, thus encouraging us to start on the woodland restoration, as Ed Collins had also advised. She spent a significant amount of time trying to put us in contact with neighbors to the north through whose property one of our drainage ditches flows.

Lisa had worked with Sr. Colette in clearing brush from the wetland and hoped to do a prescribed burn in the oak woodland. The LUREC property had been, and still is, included on her annual burn permit. She facilitated the mechanics of a burn for us on 12 November 2010, providing many volunteers, who came with their firefighting gear. She also put me in touch with the local wildlands fire team through the Woodstock Fire Department and Matt Schultz, who planned the burn for us. Fire trucks, volunteers, and students converged on the center, prepared to burn. Meanwhile I had not yet been able to obtain official permission from Loyola to carry it out. People waited, and we fed them (starting a tradition of feeding our volunteers). Finally, Senior Vice President Wayne Magdziarz came to our rescue and gave the necessary permission. Unfortunately, the fire was unsuccessful because the litter was too wet. This is a common problem when honeysuckle and buckthorn get very thick.

Other professional conservationists who had been part of Sr. Colette's advisory group and who became part of ours include Ed Weskerna and Dave Brandt. Ed works for McHenry SWC, and Dave is now retired from US Department of Agriculture's Natural Resource Conservation Service. Dave visited LUREC on 23 October 2011, soil corer in hand, and helped us figure out where our water had flowed historically and how the pond had been dug. Ed had been instrumental in securing funding for Sr. Colette to clear the wetland of woody brush. He shared his 'Resurrection' file with us, providing many details of the original restoration. He also helped us interpret aerial photos of our property at the SWC office.

We met many other conservationists when a prominent member of the Bull Valley community invited representatives from every major environmental organization and agency in the county to a 'meet and greet' reception and series of presentations at her home in October 2010. This meeting made it very clear that both the neighbors and the county had great interest in what we were going to do.

Neighborhood conservationists

McHenry County, in general, and Bull Valley, in particular, have many private citizens who are concerned about environmental restoration and who work to restore their own property. Many of them also work professionally on environmental issues through engineering, legal advocacy, and so on. I will describe our relationship with one of them in particular.

Ed Ellinghausen is a member of the Bull Valley Village Board, the Board of Directors of the Environmental Defenders of McHenry County, and the Boone Creek Watershed Alliance. He is a licensed professional engineer with a degree in civil engineering, and he is semi-retired. Ed has been concerned about the buildup of salt in local wetlands, and since 2003 he has been sampling the increasing chloride concentration of the water flowing into Boone Creek. One of his sites has been the LUREC property.

We first encountered Ed at our meeting with the Bull Valley Village Board soon after Loyola purchased the property, and we met him again at the 'meet and greet' in October, when I discovered his interest in hydrology. I asked him to participate in the wetland ecology class the following spring. Ed visited the property several times and was very helpful in interpreting its hydrology. He has been instrumental to two significant projects. One is the berm, whose deterioration he was the first to point out, and he warned us to take at least temporary measures to halt the erosion so that it did not 'blow out'. He also made us aware that our water softener brine could be recovered, and that McHenry County Department of Transportation (McDOT) would be willing to recycle it on the roads in winter. After meeting with McDOT, interested faculty are in the process of setting up a recovery system with Ed's help. Currently much of the brine flushes down the back hill with runoff from the roof and possibly into the wetland. The rest of it goes to the septic system located south and east of the building and thence down to the water table.

The case of the wetland ecology course

We have developed many different types of relationships within the community. Those relationships having to do with ecological restoration have been driven by particular purposes – understanding what happened previously on LUREC and the neighbors' properties, needing help and cooperation in carrying out some particular activities like prescribed burns, seeking expertise on some type of restoration work. I will use the case of the wetland ecology course which I co-taught during the spring semester 2011 as a way to describe the interrelationships. The class was assigned a group project: develop a plan for restoring the LUREC wetland, including working with the neighbors. The work included the elements of planning, research, building relationships with the adjacent neighbors, and building broader relationships in the community. We made several weekend field trips to the site.

Planning
Wetland restoration projects by their very nature – and because they require permits from several agencies – may take years to plan but only days to construct. The first thing the class had to understand was the hydrology of the site – where the water comes from, where it resides, and where it goes when it leaves the site.

There were two intensive preliminary planning activities. The first was a session at MCCD, where Ed Collins gave a presentation on forensic ecology focusing on the LUREC property. He also informed the students of many county resources and records that they could use for historical research.

Secondly, the class met on a Saturday with a consultant and two neighbors. At that time the restoration work was contracted to JJR, a large company which oversees work on other Loyola properties. The person in charge was Mark O'Leary. Mark spent Saturday afternoon discussing the potential restoration with the class. Before Mark joined JJR, he had lived and worked in the surrounding area. Ed Ellinghausen developed some ideas about dealing with our berm. We discussed not only the ecology of the site, but also how we would approach our neighbors. Pat Inman, herself a neighbor, was especially helpful with that aspect of the planning.

Research

The students then carried out various types of research. They made a general inventory of the wetland and mapped where the invasives were, even though it was winter and only a limited number of plants could be recognized. In the process they discovered an area of sedge meadow that proved very useful in our subsequent work, as well as an extensive area of the fen indicator, skunk cabbage. They measured water chemistry. Some of them went to MCCD offices to look at historic maps and ownership records, while others gathered information on who our wetland neighbors were and how to contact them.

Our adjacent neighbors

Awareness of how you may impact your neighbors is an important element of wetland work, especially when the wetland – like ours – is part of a larger basin shared with other landowners. The class decided to hold a wine and cheese 'meet and greet', inviting our adjacent neighbors to come, get to know us, and see what we were thinking about doing. They organized a formal reception, catered by LUREC's excellent chef and his crew. Although only one of the adjacent wetland owners came, it turned out to be a significant neighbor.

One neighbor had violated many wetland regulations earlier in the year (in January 2011) and been fined heavily for attempting to dig his own pond immediately north of us without permits. The Army Corps of Engineers (ACE) was alerted. It shut him down, promising not to leave until he 'put it back together again'. Neither I nor the class knew what to expect when his wife responded positively to our invitation. We were relieved to find that both our neighbor and his wife were very friendly and outgoing. They had come to the reception with another couple who were not adjacent neighbors but who knew us quite well. Our neighbor was self-critical about his *faux pas*. He invited us to come on to his land and said that students could work there. It was the beginning of a very positive and continuing relationship, as he has restored his fen and given us help restoring ours.

The larger community

The class decided it would be helpful to let the broader community know what we hoped to do, and so we agreed to present their class project to a larger community group. They invited both neighbors and alumni in the county. About 75 people came for the presentation, lunch, and tour of the site. We were especially delighted that Sr. Colette Fahrner came, as well as a larger number of adjacent neighbors who had attended the wine and cheese event.

Two of the neighbors who attended were owners of nearby properties that had been designated as Illinois Nature Preserves. An additional aspect of trying to engage students and faculty in a restoration like ours is to learn from both professional and non-professional conservationists and restorationists how they carry out their work and to accept their advice with the utmost respect. The two owners are non-professionals with a great deal of experience. The owner of Gladstone Fen Nature Preserve is a very active member of the community. Although Gladstone Fen is not in our wetland basin, it has a pond similar to ours which the class had visited. The owner is happy to have people visit her restoration, even when she is not there. She invited us to participate in her annual workday, and a couple of people did so. This led to the hiring of one of our students to do restoration work at Gladstone Fen. It has been a wonderful relationship from our perspective. Our former student learns a great deal working on the fen and then brings the knowledge back to LUREC on our volunteer workdays. She also volunteers setting up our herbarium and will be employed to help us train restoration interns in the summer. We have received seed worth probably a few hundred dollars harvested from the Gladstone Fen Nature Preserve. Our former student and I were allowed to use their facilities to process seed which we had collected at LUREC.

The owner of Parker Fen Nature Preserve is of an older generation and quite a different personality. Although many people had suggested she would be a challenge to work with, Patti Carty suggested early on that I phone her and ask to visit her fen. Parker Fen is of great interest to us, because it is adjacent to LUREC and because it is an Illinois Nature Preserve. Patti made a preliminary call, and I was pleased to find the owner quite cordial and, to the surprise of many, willing to show me her fen. Her property is not managed with the same intensity as Gladstone Fen, and I did not feel comfortable asking to bring students during the wetland ecology class. The owner was invited to but did not attend the 'meet and greet' reception, but she did attend the students' class presentation, and we talk periodically.

Conclusion

As I have thought back through the past two and a half years of ecological restoration at LUREC, I have come to view my role as like that of an orchestra conductor. Many different instruments are working together to produce the restoration. Most of the score was written by others having much more experience than I. Most of the instruments were already present, many having been put in place by others who worked on this property previously, but some also by me and my colleagues in our previous work in McHenry County. My contribution has been to recognize the potential of the many different players, pull them together to produce the music, and contribute additional elements to enhance the performance.

References

Annexation data from the Village of Bull Valley, on file in the Village office, 1909 Cherry Valley Road, Bull Valley, Illinois 60098.

BioTechnical Erosion Control Ltd. (2013). Loyola University Retreat and Ecology Campus Fen Restoration Preliminary Alternatives Analysis, p. 2. Unpublished report.

Illinois Department of Natural Resources (2001). Office of Realty and Environmental Planning. Critical Trends in Illinois Ecosystems, Report 8M/PRT 320114, February.

Encyclopedia of Chicago (2013), p. 7. www.encyclopedia.chicagohistory.org/pages/183.html (last accessed January 2013).

Leopold, A. (1986). *Sand County Almanac.* New York: Ballantine Books.

McHenry County Conservation District (2014). The Oaks of McHenry County, p. 13. www.mccdistrict.org/web/assets/publications/brochures/OaksofMcHenryspreads_WC.pdf (last accessed 31 January 2014).

Northwest Herald (2009). www.nwherald.com/2009/05/19/resurrection-center-okd/a4b2r 55/ (last accessed 20 May 2009).

Watershed Protection Strategy for Boone Creek (2013). 23 May. www.boonecreekwatershed.org/downloads/BCWAplan.pdf, p. 43 (last accessed 4 February 2014).

Conclusion

This book opened with the call for courageous action in light of the many environmental challenges our world faces. Not only must our institutions be courageous, but they must also be willing to address ecological complexity. This is especially true for institutions of higher education known more for an education supporting a status quo of unlimited consumption than for their innovative plans for austerity.

How do our institutions turn the 'knowledge economy' into the 'knowledge society' embracing an ethical wisdom for a sustainable future? Osborne, Duke, and Wilson (2013) identify the role of universities in sustainable development as that of promoting education and public awareness. This includes identifying issues raised by regional stakeholders. While issues are local, many regions throughout the world are facing similar challenges. 'The university is perhaps best equipped in its locality to place the possible solutions in their wider context and in so doing persuade local and regional partners the need to begin implementing a transition to a sustainable society' (Osborne, Duke, and Wilson, 2013, p. 67). The roles of 'listener' and 'convener' are often new to institutions that are more inclined to present themselves as 'experts'.

The need to integrate a vision of environmental sustainability into infrastructure, administration, policy, and curriculum was also discussed. Creation of an operationalized governance structure supporting interdisciplinary studies needed to address the wickedly complex issues presented by environmental challenges is easier said than done. It is necessary to 'to go one step further-beyond declarations, and not only give commitments but also create mechanisms by which internal and external communities can hold universities to account (Osborne, Duke, and Wilson, 2013, p. 68). Universities need to go one step further and do something which is not in the comfort zone of 'expert' institutions – collaborate. Inter-institutional collaborations would honor what each has developed as their 'niche'. The institution providing guidance in regional policy offers the environmental agenda every bit as much as those providing state-of-the-art research in water quality. We must eliminate duplication when possible for efficiency as much as ease and clarity of collaboration.

Finally, the need for innovative tools that focus on complexity and relationship is suggested in this publication. These methodologies are very different from expert-driven consultation that has played a prominent role in university–community relationships of the past. These convivial tools are based on diverse stakeholder representation, community definition of issues, and asset-based focus. The following three methodologies focus on listening to and honoring community and environmental voices and offer useful tools for universities to use in fostering sustainable economic development. As a button distributed at Earth Day festivities stated, 'The earth has a voice, too.'

Asset-based community or regional development

Building on the skills of local residents, the power of local associations, and the supportive functions of local institutions, asset-based community development draws upon existing community strengths to build stronger, more sustainable communities for the future. For more information see the website of the Asset-Based Community Development Institute (2014). In a larger context this same approach works for regions. Regions can build upon existing resources and often substitute for what they lack. Regional resilience becomes the art of the possible as opposed to a diagnosis of need. *Cities and the Wealth of Nations*, Jane Jacobs (1984) makes the point that economies are 'place-centered' and not abstract markets. Import substitution, when possible, is discussed as one of the greatest tools to sustainability.

The primary effect of import substitution is to minimize the flow of dollars outside the region. But the substitution of imports has substantially greater impact. 'Cities that replace imports significantly replace not only finished goods but, concurrently, many, many items of producers' goods and services. For example, first comes the local processing of fruit preserves that were formerly imported, then the production of jars or wrappings formerly imported for which there was no local market of producers until the first step had been taken. Regions can do this only when they know what resources exist and how to best take advantage of them.

Fourth Generation Evaluation

It takes a holistic, systemic, and multidisciplinary approach to organize and develop a sustainable community. Creating a viable network that supports this complex system proves a challenge. Fourth Generation Evaluation is a means to include 'the myriad human, political, social, cultural and contextual elements that are involved' (Guba and Lincoln, 1989). This methodology is unique in that it combines both qualitative and quantitative research. In order to reflect the complexity of systems, this process frames the research in qualitative narrative but validates or invalidates stories that emerge through the use of quantitative data. This is quite the opposite of the more frequently used quantitative research process that uses narrative as 'thick description' supporting data selected to be reviewed by the researcher. As policy decisions are often based on stakeholder perceptions, this process allows us to look at perceptions of those within a system and determine whether these are grounded in data. For more information see Guba and Lincoln (1989).

Open Space technology

Open Space technology is one way to enable all kinds of people, in any kind of organization, to create inspired meetings and events. Over the last twenty years, it also has become clear that opening space, as an intentional leadership practice, can create inspired organizations where ordinary people work together to create extraordinary results with regularity. In Open Space meetings, events, and organizations, participants create and manage their own agenda of parallel working sessions around a central theme of strategic importance. For more information, see the website of Open Space (2014).

Preparing for tomorrow

The students of today are tomorrow's change agents and practitioners of sustainability. Our universities face the twin challenges of preparing students for green jobs and careers that do not currently exist and of providing learners with new perspectives and frames of reference to engage effectively in the development of resilient communities.

With respect to the former challenge, six opportunities to shape constructive activity around green careers were identified in the Pascal University Regional Engagement initiative. These offer a promising foundation on which to build curriculum to prepare a green workforce and include:

- Green skill identification – what new intellectual and technical skills are required for green occupations and industries and to what extent might they be internationalized?
- Regional needs analysis – what is the role of higher education in convening, conducting, supporting, and implementing this work?
- Green-focused learning regions – what practices are proving the most effective in using environmental protection and sustainability to support the development of learning regions?
- Green entrepreneurship – How can higher education play an instrumental role in supporting green entrepreneurship?
- Sustainable regeneration practices – hw can institutions of higher education mitigate the impact of development on the natural environment?
- Greening higher education – what is the role of higher education in connecting and responding to the green agenda? (Osborne, Duke, and Wilson, 2013, pp. 76–77).

The later challenge, as the Global University Network for Innovation (GUNi) has written, will require a much stronger commitment to institutional change in culture and design by our institutions of higher education. As laid out in the introduction to this book and underscored by each of the contributing authors, this will require embracing a vision of sustainable development, promoting interdisciplinary work, engaging community, owning and participating in sustainability initiatives, and offering a green curriculum. While the tools of collaboration discussed above can play a part in each of these endeavors, leadership and investment from all higher education stakeholders will be needed. Many are illuminating our path forward.

References

Asset-Based Community Development Institute. School of Education and Social Policy, Northwestern University. www.abcdinstitute.org (last accessed 1 February 2014).

Guba, E., and Lincoln, Y. (1989). *Fourth Generation Evaluaton*. Newberry Park, CA: SAGE Publications.

Jacobs, J. (1984). *Cities and the Wealth of Nations*. New York: Vintage Books.

Open Space. www.openspaceworld.org (last accessed 1 February 2014).

Osborne, M., Duke, C., and Wilson, B. (2013). *The New Imperative: Regions and Higher Education in Difficult Times*. Manchester and New York: Manchester University Press.

Index

De Soto, Hernando 28
development 25, 29, 30, 31, 32
D'kar 5, 100–108
D'kar Reformed Church Farm 100
D'kar Trust 101
Drucker, Peter 26
Durkheim, Emile 29

ecological footprint 53
Ecological Society of America 121
ecoversity 15
Ellinghausen, Ed 150
employment 28, 31
entrepreneurs 31
    entrepreneurial 31
    entrepreneurship 31, 32
Environmental Defenders of McHenry
    County 150
environmental engineering 62

Fahrner, Sr. Colette, SLW 147, 152
    advisory committee 148
fertilizers 90, 93
Food and Agriculture Organization
    (FAO) 12
Fourth Generation Evaluation 155
Fukuyama, Francis 26

Gandhi, Mahatma 28
Garanzini, Fr. Michael SJ 141, 145
Garry oak meadow 4, 48, 54, 55, 58
Garry Oak Meadow Preservation
    Society 52
Garry oak ecosystem 48
Gay-Lussac, Joseph Louis 47
Gintis, Herbert 27
Global University Network for Innova-
    tion 2, 61, 156
governable 26, 27, 29
    ungovernable 31
Governor's Rural Affairs Council
    (GRAC) 125
Grabowski, Fr. (first name unknown)
    144
Grace Communications Foundation
    77
Gramsci, Antonio 23
Grandview-Woodland Community 53
green 23, 24, 25, 26, 27, 29, 32

guerrilla geographers 4, 48, 55, 57
GUNi Knowledge Community 63

Haderline, Lisa 149
honeysuckle 149
Hopper, Catherine 30
human exceptionalism 13
human transformation 3, 9
Huntington, Samuel 23

Illinois Institute for Rural Affairs 125
Illinois Nature Preserves
    Commission (INPC) 147
    Gladstone Fen 152
    Julia M. and Royce L. Parker Fen
        142, 147, 148, 152
Implementing the Third Mission of
    Universities in Africa 96
indigenous knowledge 3, 35, 36, 43
Inman, Guy 147
Inman, Patricia, Ph.D. 147
Institute for Environmental Sustain-
    ability (IES) 141
Institute for the Humanities 53
institutions 24, 25, 27, 28, 31
    institutional 26
interdisciplinary collaborative work-
    ing 69
International Conference on Adult
    Education 94
'The Islands of the Salish Sea' 57
Ivers, Kevin 147

JJR 151
Johnson Jr., Henry 31

Kellogg Foundation 101, 102, 107,
    133
knowledge economy 154
Knowledge-to-Action Team 120
knowledge transfer 57, 61, 74
Korten, David 26

labour 26, 27, 28, 31
Lake Superior Good Food Network
    Region 83
Land Conservancy (TLC) of McHenry
    County (The) 147
    Project *Quercus* 149

EU authorised representative for GPSR:
Easy Access System Europe, Mustamäe tee 50,
10621 Tallinn, Estonia
gpsr.requests@easproject.com

www.ingramcontent.com/pod-product-compliance
Lightning Source LLC
Chambersburg PA
CBHW070845300326
41935CB00039B/1490